Latina/os and the Media

Media and Minorities
Kent A. Ono & Vincent N. Pham, *Asian Americans and the Media*
Catherine R. Squires, *African Americans and the Media*
Angharad N. Valdivia, *Latina/os and the Media*

Latina/os and the Media

Angharad N. Valdivia

polity

First published in 2010 by Polity Press

Polity Press
65 Bridge Street
Cambridge CB2 1UR, UK

Polity Press
350 Main Street
Malden, MA 02148, USA

ISBN-13: 978-0-7456-4007-5
ISBN-13: 978-0-7456-4008-2 (paperback)

A catalogue record for this book is available from the British Library.

Typeset in 10.5 on 13 pt Swift
by Servis Filmsetting Ltd, Stockport, Cheshire
Printed and bound by Maple Vail, USA

The publisher has used its best endeavours to ensure that the URLs for external websites referred to in this book are correct and active at the time of going to press. However, the publisher has no responsibility for the websites and can make no guarantee that a site will remain live or that the content is or will remain appropriate.

Every effort has been made to trace all copyright holders, but if any have been inadvertently overlooked the publishers will be pleased to include any necessary credits in any subsequent reprint or edition.

For further information on Polity, visit our website: www.politybooks.com

Contents

Introduction

IN the film *Barbershop* (2002), a scene has a bunch of African American men in a barbershop discussing the value of a woman's booty. That booty is valued is not at issue, but rather the size and shape of that booty is the matter at hand. After much banter, all men agree that Jennifer Lopez has a most desirable booty and body. Simultaneously, states ranging from Tennessee, Arizona, Pennsylvania, Michigan, Kansas and Iowa to Oklahoma have had some form of measure or major political officer, such as a governor, running on an English-only platform. "English-only" is a misnomer for these measures are really anti-Spanish, as Ruben Rumbaut from the University of California at Irvine reminds us. Back to Hollywood film, *Milk* (2008), a film about the legendary San Francisco political figure Harvey Milk, earned three nominations for a 2009 Oscar: Best Picture, Best Actor, and Best Supporting Actor. However, nobody mentions that the most uni-dimensional comic relief character, in a movie providing a welcome respite from heteronormative representations of US history, is the only Latino in the movie, Jack Lira, played by Diego Luna, whose hysterical, silly, and maniacal ways elicit uniform scorn from Harvey's friends and end in a suicide by hanging. This is the contemporary terrain of Latina/os in mainstream media.

How do we make sense of the hotness of Latina/os such as Jennifer Lopez, Eva Longoria, Salma Hayek, Eva Mendez, and America Ferrera against the backdrop of the immense backlash against immigration and the Spanish language that codes and treats all Latina/os as actual or potential illegal invaders who will pollute the US national body? Why is *Ugly Betty* popular at the same time as there is widespread support for criminalizing immigration? Why are Latina/os allowed to join the armed forces yet not allowed to vote? How do we explain the love–hate relationship the US mainstream media have with Latina/os? How is it that, although Latina/os actually predate the existence of the United States as a nation, they/we are still treated as the eternal foreigners and have to continually assert their/our belonging and citizenship? What is the difference between noticing how Latina/os appear in media and the way audiences interpret these images and the effects that patterns of representation might have in the short and long term on our culture? These are all issues that can be, have been, and continue to be fruitfully explored by Latina/o Media scholars.

Latina/os and the Media is written so as to be used by scholars and general-interest readers, as a first port of call for anyone wanting to know about the relationship between Latino/as and the media, whether that be as part of a survey course on minorities and the media, of a more focused undergraduate or graduate course on Latina/os, by those researching in the field of Latina/o Media Studies, or by a member of the public seeking information on this important component of the US ethnic population. The impetus for this book lies in the fact that, although there is a solid core of communication scholars working on issues of *Latinidad*, the process of being and/or becoming Latina/o, there is still not a single book that synthesizes this scholarship in one coherent and accessible volume. Much as Charles Ramirez-Berg's *Latino Images in Film* (2002) brought together research that had appeared over decades in a large variety of publications, this book aims to provide an overview of research and approaches to the study of Latina/os and/in the media in an integrated and cumulative way and to suggest the many areas for further research in a field that still contains huge gaps. Furthermore, given that Latina/os, as of the 2000 US Census, have been acknowledged to be the largest single minority group in the USA and that their/our numbers continue to increase, documenting the experiences of, and understanding, this demographic category is absolutely essential. As an indication of the impetus to understand this category and the efforts of students and community activists who have labored to include Latina/os and the study of Latinidad within the academy, long-standing Chicano Studies and Puerto Rican Studies programs are now being joined by centers, programs, and departments of Latina/o Studies throughout US universities. As well the category "Latina/o" and its previous incarnation as "Hispanics" are now almost always included in Ethnic Studies programs and departments as a result of student demand for Latina/o-focused learning material, and industry and government needs to understand, serve, and control this segment of the population. This book addresses these heterogeneous demands.

While there is heterogeneity of Latina/o media, from the mainstream in English to Spanish-language media and a whole range of alternative and community media, this book focuses on the English-language mainstream. In other words, exploring what is widely available to general markets, which is in turn circulated globally, is enough to fill one introductory volume such as this one. However, we need to acknowledge that in some markets in states such as California, Texas,

Ugly Betty crosses the Atlantic into Spain. Arrives on June 11. Photos all over Madrid metro. Author's own image.

and Florida, and in cities such as Los Angeles, El Paso, and Miami, the mainstream is likely to be shared by a plurality of mainstream groups. In these locations the majority–minority, center–margin distinction historically demarcated by whiteness and otherness no longer holds. These markets have more than one dominant force and, given the endurance of Spanish media produced by and targeted at Latina/os, these markets have mainstream Spanish components. The very presence of these markets signals the changing face of mainstream media due to demographic developments, which are followed by changing marketing approaches when the lure of profit is large enough. In relation to mainstream media, there is also a whole range of dynamic and creative alternative and grassroots media. However, these are beyond the scope of this book, although, whenever possible, alternative media will be mentioned in relation to the mainstream. For the study of alternative media, one needs additional theoretical and methodological tools that exceed the focus of this book.

Theoretically this book combines and integrates two interdisciplinary areas of study, Latina/o Studies and Media Studies. Latina/o Studies is the latest in a number of more nation-specific academic pursuits to be discussed at length later in this chapter. Media Studies, while overlapping with related areas such as Film and Cinema Studies, Popular Music Studies, and Cultural Studies, includes humanistic and social scientific elements. Latina/o Media Studies combines these two heterogeneous areas in a constructive and synthetic manner. In this book, their integration is deployed to study Latina/os in/and mainstream media.

Latina/os and the national imaginary

Latina/os and the media is not a new subject. Latina/os are not a new population. The fact that we are now studying Latina/os does not mean that they/we recently began to exist. Rather it indicates that a number of interrelated forces have come together so that there is institutional, representational, and everyday attention paid to issues of Latina/os in general, and Latina/os and the media in particular. Indeed, Latina/os predate the arrival of the Anglo and the African populations in the Americas, prior to the creation of the United States as a nation. Thus, as Greenberg et al. concluded in the 1980s – a conclusion that is just as applicable in the first decade of the twenty-first century – "Their length of family residence in the U.S. ranges from centuries to hours" (1983, p. 7). However, in the overlapping fields of Communication and Media Studies, the study of Latina/os is rather new. Prior to the latest Latina/o boom, in the late 1990s, which coincided with the death of crossover Tejana Selena in 1995 and the rise to popularity of both Ricky Martin and Jennifer Lopez (Paredez, 2002; Fiol Matta, 1999/2002; D. R. Vargas, 2002), there was scant attention paid to Latina/os in the mass media, and relatively little research on Latina/os and the media in Communication and Media Studies. Until then, and still in some locations, the conception of the United States was that of a binary composition – black and white. Yet as media scholars who have conducted historical research can attest, the late nineties were but the latest Latina/o boom in popular culture. Previous booms in the 1920s and the late 1940s to early 1950s coincided with immigration and "new media"[1] technologies, only to subside with the backlash of anti-immigration sentiment that seems to be a regular component of US politics (Beltrán, 2002; Garcia, 2001). Booms and busts in the economy ripple through culture and have ramifications in terms of popular sentiment about the meaning of our nations, and the meaning of groups within the nation-space, such as natives and immigrants.

As a way to account for and categorize this newly acknowledged segment of the population, US government administrations have sought to label this group of people at least since the 1960s. The Nixon Administration (1969–74) deployed the term "Hispanic" to refer to the population of Latin American and Peninsular descent. This definition means that, until the present, many government, education, and business organizations count the Spanish and Portuguese as part of the "Hispanic" category. This means that funds carved out to support "Hispanic" people can and do get allocated to white Spanish and Portuguese immigrants. When Penélope Cruz and Antonio Banderas are referred to as "Hispanic," the reference is correct according to US government categories. One can see that this Nixon-era definition of the category referred to geographical origin – which loosely was supposed to overlap with a particular light-brown skin-color ethnicity – rather than to an explicit race or language.

The "Decade of the Hispanic" in the 1980s was part of the advent of niche marketing and coincided with the expanded use of the term "Hispanic" especially within government and marketing circles. The move from mass to target audiences opened up a space for ethnic groups identified as having the disposable income to sustain commercially supported media. The late 1990s Latina/o boom shifted terms from "Hispanic" as in the "Hispanic decade" to "Latino" as in the "Latino boom." By the 2000 Census the federal government differentiated between race and Hispanic origin. The tension between these two terms was played out in the margins as the mainstream represented the long-standing racial binary.

The national imaginary, in the sense of how most institutions and organizations perceived the national populace and culture, which included the field of Media Studies, remained firmly entrenched within a binary black-and-white conception of self. That is – government officials and institutions, the popular press, entertainment culture, and the academic field of Media Studies continued to talk, write, and act as if there were only two types of race and ethnicity in the country, and these were black and white. The black-and-white binary still holds in many locations. To be sure, there were already a few dedicated scholars who had assiduously – sometimes with less than warm reception to their work – been documenting issues of Latina/os and the media, such as Latina/o media scholars Félix Gutiérrez and Federico Subervi-Vélez and Latina/o film scholars Charles Ramirez-Berg, Chon Noriega, and Rosa Linda Fregoso. However, as a field of study, Latina/os and the media had yet to rise to their current level of saliency within the academy.

In 2009 the growing Latina/o population, both in absolute terms and in relation to their proportion of the US population; acknowledgment by government, industry, and educational institutions (the fact that they are even treated as a category); perceived economic power, which in a capitalist economy means economic citizenship (not to be confused with cultural or political citizenship); and undeniable influence, at least on presidential candidates in the 2008 campaign politics – all mean that Latina/os have begun to be included in the national

imaginary. This inclusion is composed of both willing and unwilling elements, but it is an inclusion nonetheless. Latina/o inclusion,
as shown by recent efforts to reach out to this segment by presidential candidates in 2008[2] and backlashes such as Proposition 187[3] in
California, is implicitly political as it challenges established power
arrangements. Latina/o inclusion unsettles both dominant culture
and the careful balance within minority politics. The assertion,
acknowledgment, and documented presence of difference challenges
racial arrangements predicated on unfair advantage and therefore
discrimination and racism. The mainstream media help to naturalize
the superiority of white people and justify a system of racial inequali-
ties while denying that racism exists (Larson, 2006; Mukherjee, 2006),
mostly through implicit and "common sense" strategies that will be
documented and explored in this book.

Acknowledgment by the private sector means that Latina/os exist
in numbers and disposable income large enough to matter in terms
of marketing products and expanding audiences. This in turn leads
to commodification of Latina/o cultures, from which resulting profit
might not necessarily be going to Latina/o hands. Latina/o solidarity
and community formation promise to assert a presence and generate
attention and services from government as well as intervene in media
genres, paradigms, and practices. Latina/os possess value and strength
in their culture. If and when they manage to deploy this value and
strength and exploit it for their own means, they can achieve progressive change. However, not all Latina/os are the same, nor do they share
goals and politics. There is both solidarity and tension among Latina/
os. Del Río (2006) sums it up succinctly and appropriately: "the solidarity of 'Latinismo' is a politics without guarantees" (p. 396). All of
these complexities have implications for the production, circulation,
consumption, and effects of media, both within the United States'
national boundaries and globally, given the transnational reach of
much of US-produced commercial media.

"Latina/os" is a US-created category. In contrast to the previously
mentioned and government-generated "Hispanic" category from the
Nixon era, the Latina/o category is most often linked to populations of
Latin American origin living in the United States.[4] While the tributary
roots are multiple, most scholars in the USA see Latina/os' national
location as singular, in the United States. Previous social movements
and academic formulations were nation of origin specific or regionally specific. Slowly the terrain included in Latina/o Studies has
expanded to cover the entire USA. Some scholars have extended their
studies to include Latina/os' eventual resettlement and relocation to
Canada as well.

Contemporarily, the terms "Hispanic" and "Latino" both continue to be widely used. Within the academy the latter has more currency within Latina/o circles, though not necessarily in other departments. There are debates about the usage of either term, with the former being seen as more connected to Spain and the latter to Latin America. Furthermore, those are not the only terms used. Regional differences remain, with the Southwest, for example, continuing to widely use "Chicano." This book uses "Latina/o" as the default term, though throughout there will be instances of the other terms as both are part of the names of organizations and categories still in use. For example, the National Council of La Raza (NCLR) claims to be the "largest national Latino civil rights and advocacy organization in the United States, NCLR works to improve opportunities for Hispanic Americans" (NCLR website). Likewise the Pew Foundation sponsors the Pew Hispanic Center, whose subtitle is "Chronicling Latinos' diverse experiences in a changing America." Thus Pew manages to use both terms in its title. Nonetheless, nearly all of the many reports released by this center use the term "Latino" in the title, such as "The National Survey of Latinos." Both of these major organizations, the NCLR and Pew, illustrate the usage of both terms, one more generally and the second more academically. Admittedly, there are political and semantic differences between these two terms, and naming, as discussed below in relation to the term "Chicana/o," is an intensely political act. In this book, as it is an intellectual project, the term "Latina/o" will be favored. However, the term "Hispanic" continues to be used, even within some sectors of the academy, and I will use the term whenever referring to research that uses it.

The usage of either term is not meant to suggest that all specificity and difference between the contributory groups to Latinidad are erased, but rather that it makes sense to study the affinities and commonalities as well as the differences and fault lines among and between the different Latina/o populations (Aparicio, 2003). While mainstream media often, though not always, flatten difference between Latina/o groups, Latina/o Studies scholars continue to investigate the differences within Latinidad. For instance, Rinderle (2005) provides a useful categorization and differentiation among the labels used to refer to peoples of Mexican origin:

> Although more extensive explanations follow, briefly the five groups can be defined as such: (a) Mexican refers to Mexican nationals, and those born in Mexico despite their current country of residence; (b) a Mexican American is a U.S. American of Mexican descent, born and living in the United States (assimilationist); (c) a Chicano/a is a person of Mexican descent, born and residing in the United States, who possesses a political consciousness of himself or herself as a member of a historically and structurally oppressed group (dis-assimilationist);

(d) Hispanic denotes a person with origins or ancestry from Spanish-speaking countries (not necessarily Mexico), residing in the United States; and (e) Latino refers to a person residing in the United States of Latin American national origin or descent regardless of race, language, or culture. (p. 296)

To be sure, there is much overlap within these categories. At any given time an individual or a group might choose to identify with different ones. This dissection of some of the nuances between people of Mexican origin should alert us to the many possibilities of affiliation and identification among that umbrella group we now refer to as "Latina/os." Mayer (2001) adds yet another wrinkle to this differentiation. Speaking of Latina/os and Latina/o media in San Antonio, Texas, she notes that, while most Latina/os there are Mexican American, "this is not to say that this population . . . shares a common experience as people with Mexican ancestry. Indeed, each wave of immigration, as well as naturalized Mexican Americans had their own experiences and social backgrounds that were specific to each group" (p. 292). This type of careful specificity is the work of Latina/o Media scholars who must negotiate between the pan-ethnic and pan-national construct of Latinidad, with attention to the particularities of the components of that general category, and the specificity even within particular national origins – neither all Mexicans nor Mexican Americans are alike. In a study of border youth, Bejarano (2005) highlighted the differences between cosmopolitan Mexican immigrants from Mexico City and rural immigrants, whose national commonality had to be constructed in the USA given that, in Mexico and in terms of many of their cultural proclivities in the United States, they had little in common, other than being discriminated as inferior Mexicans by the school system and the dominant-culture white kids in their new school system. Similarly, Gonzalez's (2007, 2008) careful research maps out some of the differences between border Mexican youth whose cultural orientation is toward the US and in rejection of internal Mexico.

Latina/o roots

The field of Latina/o Studies is bursting with books and studies on social, political, educational, psychological, historical, literary, philosophical, economic, religious, and communication studies research into this particular segment of the population. While the application of this name to the field is rather recent, the study of Latina/o populations is less so. Within the United States the group of people we now call Latina/os have previously been studied under more specific national categories: Mexican Americans, Puerto Ricans, and Cuban Americans. People of Mexican origin have been studied both as "Mexican American" and as the more politicized category of "Chicanos and Chicanas." Naming is an intensely political act, of presence and power, and as such the name chosen for people of recent or previous Mexican origin remains a subject of debate. Choosing one's name in relation or opposition to a dominant culture's categories is an assertion of resistance. Remember Rinderle's differentiation between assimilationist and dis-assimilationist labels. Colonized peoples are usually named by the colonizers. Thus, regaining the power to name oneself is extremely important as a group seeks to assert agency. The fact that a large chunk of US territory today once belonged to Mexico makes it more complicated since 1848 as some Mexican American people lived in their home country and were crossed by the border rather than moving themselves.[5] All of a sudden, people who were Mexicans and lived at home became foreigners to be feared and demonized, who had to demonstrate both allegiance and belonging. Mexican Americans continue to be the most numerous component within the Latina/o category, composing 64.1 percent of the total Latina/o population (Pew Hispanic Center, www.pewhispanic.org, retrieved May 30, 2008). Within the academy, the study of Mexican Americans and/or Chicana/os has largely resided in the Southwest, especially, but not exclusively, in the states of California and Texas. However, there are Mexican Americans all over the United States and in other nations.

The study of Puerto Ricans also predates contemporary formations of Latina/o Studies. Puerto Ricans occupy an interstitial space within Latinidad, as they are considered Latina/os even though Puerto Rico is a commonwealth and has been a US territory since 1917. Puerto Rico is not a state and therefore its citizens do not have the same rights as other citizens of the USA do – they cannot vote in US elections – yet they have US statutory citizenship which means they can be drafted. Due to their large migration to the New York area, the term "Nuyorricans" has been coined to refer to the population that migrated from the island to more or less permanency in New York. The study of Puerto Ricans within mainland US territory has also been called "Boricua Studies," a term related to Puerto Rican heritage. Whereas Mexican Americans have had the border cross them or have crossed land and the Rio Grande into the USA, Puerto Ricans have to cross the Atlantic from the Caribbean. Puerto Ricans compose 9 percent of the US Latina/o population. That Puerto Ricans arrive from a tropical location becomes quite relevant in terms of how they are construed within the national imaginary in relation and difference to the more land-grounded Mexican American population. Notions of what "island cultures" and "tropical peoples" mean in our nation are often projected onto the cultures and bodies of Puerto Ricans. As well, given their original migration in large numbers to the East Coast, Puerto Rican Studies centers have largely existed in that geographic area.

The third group whose history and experience composed an area of study prior to Latina/o Studies is the Cuban American population. Cuban Americans compose 3.4 percent of the total US Latina/o population. Only 90 miles from US territory, in terms of the Monroe Doctrine, Cuba has been in the USA's backyard politics for quite some time. Although migration of large numbers of Cubans can be dated back to 1959 and the Cuban Revolution, prior to that Cuba was an important trade partner as well as being the location for one of the offshore playgrounds of the USA. Gambling, prostitution, drugs, beaches, and large club entertainment beckoned to tourists within close range of the USA. Since 1959 large numbers of the Cuban population, in relation to the total population within the island, have immigrated to Miami.[6] While the number of Cuban Americans has been much smaller than those of Mexican Americans and Puerto Ricans, their influence vis-à-vis politics and mass media has been quite large. Prior to the Cuban Revolution, large media monopolies resided in Cuba. Following the Revolution, these migrated to Miami. As a consequence, Miami still occupies a gatekeeping position in terms of Latin American talent crossing over into the United States. As well, scholars attest to the preferential status of Cuban Americans within the USA. Within minorities in the USA, Asian Americans function as the "model minority." That means they are treated as the least offensive and as more likely to assimilate, but nonetheless as a minority. Within Latina/os in the USA, until the Elián González spectacle in 1993 in which the custody of a Cuban child was challenged by his Miami relatives (Molina Guzmán, 2005, 2008), Cuban Americans were treated as the "model Latina/os." Part of this was due to their special immigrant status as political, rather than economic, refugees, who were granted asylum and therefore legality. The Cuban Revolution increased the US resolve to keep communism from spreading, domino-like, over the Americas, and the special status granted to Cuban political refugees was remarkably different from the near criminalization with which other refugees from the Americas were treated. Another part of this special status is that, at least at first, many of the Cubans who migrated were from a particular socioeconomic class that brought wealth, or at least resources, and their demographic characteristics included the prominence of whiteness. Recent scholarship on Cuban Americans, especially after the Elián González spectacle, suggests that, after successive boatlifts, the special status of Cuban Americans has been at least tarnished, if not altogether diminished (Molina Guzmán, 2005, 2007b, 2008). The influence of the Cuban American lobby in relation to their proportion within Latina/os in the United States was significant. Furthermore, the Cuban American influence in city of Miami and Dade County politics is undeniable.

All three of the above groups are now included within Latina/o Studies, though in many places Chicana/o Studies, Boricua Studies, and Cuban Studies still remain as specific centers of research. Because of their coastal location – West, East, and Southeast – this tendency within Latina/o Studies has been called "coastal." Those focusing on other regions have dubbed their focus "within the coasts." In fact the fastest growth in the Latina/o population is now occurring in the South and the Midwest, neither of them original regions of focus for Latina/o Studies. Also, doubtless, other countries, in fact all other countries in the Americas, contribute migrants to the USA. However, their numbers are not as large as those of the three groups above. Nonetheless, it must be noted that great influxes of people from the Dominican Republic have migrated to the East Coast just as large numbers of Nicaraguans and Colombians now reside in Miami, and Los Angeles is the second largest city of the world, in terms of population, for both Hondurans and Salvadoreans. Moreover, the large Midwest metropolis of Chicago includes at least a century-old history of coexistence, and sometimes solidarity, between Mexican American and Puerto Rican populations, sometimes working in concert with African American groups. The heterogeneity of Latina/os has inspired scholars to seek a pan-ethnic and pan-national understanding, but that does not preclude the importance of and attention to specificity in research – that is, the importance of focusing on nation- and/or ethnically specific groups and their separate histories and experiences. This is obviously and absolutely important, and we hope that, as more research is conducted in Latina/o Media Studies, both the differences among nation-specific groups and their common history and experience as racialized members of the US body politic will continue to be studied in a nuanced approach that does not flatten difference yet simultaneously makes connections.

The state or experience of being Latina/o or the assignment of Latina/o traits to people, culture, and habits is called Latinidad. Notice that Latinidad does not have to be produced by Latina/os, inhabited by Latina/os, or even consumed by Latina/os. The aura or feel of that which is understood as Latina/o can be embedded into cultural programming, food products, clothing, etc., with their consumption being carried out by Latina/os or anyone else. For example, Dora the Explorer products sell quite well in Greece where awareness of Latina/os is nearly totally absent. Yet that component of Latinidad is globally marketable. For the average Greek kid wearing a Dora backpack, their consumption of the little brown Latina is not only not linked to Latina/os but outside of any nation-specific knowledge, unlike that made by some members of the US audience who demand to know exactly where the island that Dora inhabits is located (Harewood and Valdivia 2005). Similarly, many who consume Taco Bell products may not be Latina/o or even understand that they are consuming a product that is marketed through discourses of Latinidad. The use of tropical music as a background to commercials, movies, and public festivals can be adopted within and without Latinidad. Salsa is now the no. 1 condiment in the USA, selling more than the quintessentially US ketchup, yet we certainly cannot say that it is being either produced or consumed only by Latina/os. Yet adding salsa instead of ketchup to a casserole or hamburger gives it that "Latina/o" touch. This does not mean negating that some Latina/os cook with salsa, but rather that it becomes an element that resignifies or recodes foods, occasions, or styles. These examples are useful in understanding that Latinidad can be produced and consumed from within and without Latina/o cultures, and cannot be controlled by either those belonging to or those outside of the Latina/o community.

Both the heterogeneous composition of the Latina/o population and the impossibility of controlling the deployment of Latinidad make the call for specificity all the more urgent while simultaneously more difficult to carry out. There are two related issues that make the call for specificity more complex from a methodological and demographic perspective. First, methodologically, until quite recently much of the work of Latina/os and/in the media was subsumed under the "minorities and the media" perspective (see, for example, Larson, 2006). In turn that meant two things. First, given the previously mentioned national imaginary of "black and white," the focus was primarily on African Americans. Many scholars did not or could not measure Latina/o presence. Second, even when Hispanics or Latina/os were included, there was no disaggregation between "minorities," so we are left to wonder if we can extrapolate between Latina/o population percentages and apply that to the research findings. Disaggregation would subdivide that lump sum into specific categories, according to gender, ethnicity, national origin, or whatever other significant factor of difference. Sometimes it makes sense to disaggregate. For instance, in many countries literacy rates are around 85 percent. However, if one disaggregates for gender, one could find a near 100 percent rate for men and a 60 percent rate for women. Disaggregation would help in terms of the "minority" category for Media Studies. For example, if figures state that 15 percent of journalists are from a minority background, we are left to ponder if Latina/os compose

0, 1, 7, or 14 percent of that figure. Similarly if the audience was 45 percent minority, how are we to know the Latina/o percentage? Once again, given the black-and-white imaginary, "minority" often equaled African American. However, we are left to ponder when it did, and when it included Latina/os and other ethnicities. Calls for nation-specific research would have to be made anew as many of the data do not differentiate between minorities, let alone specific segments within Latinidad. At the very least, Latina/o Studies demands disaggregation within minority groups.

From a demographic standpoint, a different set of issues arises. The assignment of ethno-specific categories to differentiate between groups of people has been fraught with difficulties since its very beginning. The five major US ethnic groups include Caucasians, African Americans, Latina/os, Asian Americans, and Native Americans. However, there is no purity within any of these categories. Moreover, there is overlap between them. In particular, how are we to code a Black Nuyorrican – as African American or Latina/o? How are we to code Cristina, from *El Show de Cristina* – as white or Latina? The US Census further added to this dilemma as it constructed "Hispanic" to include whites, since Hispanics were elsewhere excluded from whiteness as in "White, not of Hispanic origin." That meant that if you were a white Latina/o, you were prevented from filling forms according to race and you had to fill it out according to heritage. Essentially, that marked the "Hispanic" category as different from the other census categories, for it included people according to heritage rather than ethnicity. If you are of mixed race, as an increasing segment of the world population is now acknowledged to be, then how on earth do you fill these census forms? These are extremely relevant issues to Latina/o Media Studies. In studying the production of media, for example, if we pursue the question of whether the ethnicity of a producer or group of producers matters, then how do we study those with mixed ethnicity? In studying representation, how do we decide if Rosario Dawson, an Afro-Latina actress, represents African Americans or Latina/os, and to whom? In audiences, if a guiding question is issues of recognition – that is, does the viewer recognize her/himself according to, among other things, ethnic identity – how do we study those with mixed ethnicity in the audience or how audiences identify with someone like Mariah Carey, with a white Irish mother and Afro-Venezuelan father? Depending on media outlets, she is identified as white, black, or Latina. Both Katerí-Hernandez (2003) and Quiñones-Rivera (2006) note that Afro-Latina/os fall between the cracks in contemporary categorizations of race and ethnicity. Within African American populations, their Latinidad, especially if accompanied by a Spanish accent, codes them as outsiders. Within Latina/os the power of discourses of the Brown race codes their blackness as other. Moreover, mixed ethnicity refers not just to dual possibilities – that is, for instance, Asian-Latina/o – but to multiple heterogeneity, for example Cuban, Jewish, Native, Latina/o. The interaction between ethnicity and vectors of religion, nation, sexuality, etc., generates a far more diverse grid of heterogeneity than scholars had earlier anticipated and studied. Given that Latina/os are a very diverse segment of the population, one that cannot be reduced to a single ethnicity (as even the US Census recognizes), the study of Latina/os and the media promises to become far more complex even as scholars are literally just beginning to explore the presence and experience of Latina/os vis-à-vis the media.

As a group of people and cultural products, Latina/os and Latinidad clearly cannot be contained within US national boundaries. The great mobility experienced by large segments of the population in the contemporary stage of globalization includes Latina/os who travel, migrate, and move between Latin America, the United States, Europe, and, indeed, the entire world. However, even greater mobility is displayed by transnational capital, a mobility that fuels the production and consumption of media and celebrities far beyond their location of origin and/or residence. Transnational capital, embodied within media as an interconnected and globally convergent range of cultural industries, whose reach and mobility are extensive, produces and markets with a global strategy in mind. Since both US-produced and other media material circulates globally, through mainstream channels such as film distribution and television networks but also through less formal and maybe slightly less legal internet and street-vendor pirated sales, the reach of these media cannot be limited to the USA. While much of the research that informs this book is written from a US perspective, recent scholarship takes Latina/o Studies into the transnational arena. After all, in an era of global media mergers and thus global distribution and circulation, not only of media products but also of Latina/o stars and workers, the nation-bound notion of Latinidad cannot any longer be sustained.

Latina/o demographics

In the contemporary setting it becomes imperative to study Latina/os and their overlap with the mass media, especially against the context of the study of issues of race, ethnicity, nation, and gender. Demographic data about Latina/o population growth, media use, and media production further underscore the fact that Latina/os are numerous and that they/we use and appear in the mass media.

Contemporary discourses about population growth in the United States foreground the "Hispanic" component of that increase. Representative of this trend is the following:

> According to the Pew Hispanic Center's population estimates and projections, the Hispanic population increased from 8.5 million in 1966–67 to 44.7 million today. Latinos accounted for 36% of the 100 million added to the population in the last four decades, the most of any racial or ethnic group. Immigration from Latin America and relatively high fertility rates among Latinos were major factors in this increase. The white population grew from 167.2 million in 1966–67 to 201.0 million today. That represented 34% of the 100 million added since 1966–67. (Pew Hispanic Center Fact Sheet, October 10, 2006, p. 2)

Thus, in a forty-year period of population growth, the Hispanic proportion of the total population increased the most, even more than whites who began as 84 percent of the population yet represented only 34 percent of the growth. In fact 1971 was the last year in which US whites reproduced at a rate high enough to replace their absolute and proportional numbers within the US population (Campbell, 1996). Singled out as explanatory factors in the above quote, key concepts are "immigration from Latin America" and "high fertility rates." The Pew Fact Sheet adds that immigrants and their offspring accounted for 55 percent of the population growth in that forty-year period. This means that immigrants in general have higher reproduction rates than the native population. Nonetheless, while immigrants across all races and ethnicities accounted for more of that 100 million people growth than the native-born, most popular press coverage highlights the Hispanic component of this demographic trend over all others. Despite the nearly hysterical popular fears about Hispanic population growth as demonstrated in much press coverage and particular television news shows such as CNN's *Lou Dobbs Tonight*, demographers consistently project the Asian population to be growing at a faster rate in every region of the United States.[7] Indeed, the above-mentioned Fact Sheet documents the fact that the highest growth rate attributable to immigrants – 85 percent – occurred among the Asian and Pacific Islander segment of the population. The fear of Latina/o reproduction is displaced from the general – the immigrant – to the particular – the Latina/o immigrant.

In terms of the proportion of the total population composed of Latina/os, the data do not testify so much to unbridled reproduction among Latina/os as to declining birth rates among the general population and continued flows of immigrants. In data released in 2007, out of a total of 300 million people in the United States, the American Community Survey (ACS), working with US Census data, estimates that nearly 15 percent are Latina/o. That is an increase from the 12.5

percent in the 2000 Census,[8] the time when Latina/os were acknowledged to be the most numerous minority in the country, surpassing the previously most numerous minority of African Americans. The Pew Hispanic Center report "U.S. Population Projections: 2005–2050" (February 11, 2008) finds: "The Latino population, already the nation's largest minority group, will triple in size and will account for most of the nation's population growth from 2005 through 2050. Hispanics will make up 29 percent of the U.S. population in 2050, compared with 14 percent in 2005" (http://pewhispanic.org/reports/report.php?ReportID=85, retrieved May 28, 2008).

Projections take into consideration the trend that most of the population increase within the United States takes places within immigrant groups. US-born women's birth rates have leveled off after a sharp drop. The other two major variables that contribute to population growth are immigration and death rates. The former remains dynamic for Latina/os, and although the latter is lower for Hispanics than for the general population, it is not low enough to skew the population growth projections. As will be seen in future chapters, both realist and fictional media represent Latina/o demographic growth in alarmist tones. These representations, in turn, contribute to audience perceptions of a "brown tide rising" (Santa Ana, 2002) and general effects that likely influence policy formulations about issues ranging from immigrant policy to bilingual education and health care access.

Language

Front row and center among Latina/os in the USA, and therefore in Latina/o Media Studies, is the issue of language. According to many Pew surveys, Latina/os have consistently indicated that language remains a main source of discrimination. Whereas skin color marks African Americans, the Spanish language marks Latina/os. In other words, race is to African Americans as language is to Latina/os. The language in the dominant culture's construction of Latinidad is Spanish. This does not mean that all Latina/os speak Spanish, or that all Latin Americans speak Spanish, or that all Spanishes are equal. Rather, in terms of how Latina/os are envisioned in relation to the dominant-culture population, they are thought of as Spanish speakers. Language marks us as different, foreign, and unassimilable. Much of the common sense and public discourse discussion on this issue is based on assumptions that may not be supported by research and statistics. The Pew Hispanic Center's report "English Usage Among Hispanics in the United States" (November 29, 2007) finds that, by the second generation, nearly all Hispanics born of Spanish-dominant immigrants are fluent in English. This is a finding that applies generally across second-generation immigrants whose parents speak languages other than English. In the Pew study, the difference between the immigrant parents and their children is 23 percent to 88 percent, nearly quadrupling the ability to speak English. In terms of national specificities, Pew finds some differences according to region of origin: "Among the major Hispanic origin groups, Puerto Ricans and South Americans are the most likely to say they are proficient in English; Mexicans are the least likely to say so" (http://pewhispanic. org/reports/report.php?ReportID=82, retrieved May 28, 2008). This finding accords with narratives of Latinidad that will be explored in chapter 3. That is, Mexican Americans are represented as less assimilable than other segments of the Latina/o population. College education is also correlated with English proficiency, not surprisingly given that higher education is most likely to be carried out in English. Also, English is more likely to be the language at work than at home, again not surprisingly given that English is likely to be the language used in upwardly mobile settings. This latter finding might not apply to working-class or agrarian jobs such as low-skilled industrial and farm work, wherein both workers and foremen can share Spanish-language skills.

For a number of complicated reasons, many Latina/os rely on, prefer, or sample Spanish-language media and materials. To begin with, since translations are often inadequate and insensitive, many Latina/os rely on Spanish-language media and materials such as health pamphlets. As a second language speaker myself, I am continually aghast when major governmental and business organizations such as the US Postal Service, airlines, health care providers, and the like cannot seem to find a decent translator for their materials. Sometimes the poor translation actually impedes understanding and can have hazardous consequences.

As well, Spanish language remains a way to connect to heritage, whether immediate or in the historical past. While consecutive generations of immigrants may not speak Spanish well or at all, Spanish remains a signifier of identity and pride. It also remains a reason for exclusion and prejudice. The eternal foreigner status assigned to Latina/os rests partly on perceptions that we cannot speak English without an accent, despite plentiful evidence, some mentioned above, that, by the second generation, most Latina/os are fluent in English. Mainstream media continue to represent Latina/os as speaking with an accent. Charo might be one of the most caricatured celebrities, but many other contemporary popular culture characters continue to bear this element of stereotyping.[9] While the Frito Bandido controversy, caused partly by his thick accent, might be in the historical past, contemporary versions of this commercial device continue to be reproduced. The Taco Bell Chihuahua is one such contemporary example. On the pride side, Spanish-language media can be used as one way to keep whatever Spanish skills one retains, to learn the language for those who have lost it altogether, or to refuse to use a language other than Spanish for whatever reasons. Whereas it has been accepted practice for crossover artists from Latin America, such as Shakira and Salma Hayek, to learn and perform in English, we are now witnessing the crossover success of Juanes who refuses to perform in a language other than Spanish, even though he can speak English.[10] This pride position would have been unthinkable and untenable even a decade ago. Many long-term US residents try to learn the language after it has been lost in their families. Those who consume or favor Spanish-language media might also do so because it pays more attention both to US Latina/o and Latin American and global issues. The mainstream US media are highly insular – that is, they pay little attention to what goes on outside of US national borders – so that readers who wish to remain informed about other countries and global regions have to seek that information elsewhere. For instance, the quantity and quality of coverage of the immigration issue, and its regional and global dimensions, are much more and better covered in the Spanish than in the English mainstream press. The same goes for arguably less important but far more popular content such as World Cup *fútbol* (soccer) and the Olympics.

However, as indicated above, reducing Latina/os to one language is one of the ways that culture in general, and media in particular, flatten the differences between Latina/os. An important caveat to the prominence of Spanish as a language that signifies Latinidad is that not all Latin American countries speak Spanish – the major exception being the huge and populous Brazil whose people speak Portuguese. What remains a gap in the research is attention to Brazilian Americans, as the focus on Spanish as a signifier of Latinidad erases the presence of Portuguese-speaking Brazilians from the Latina/o diaspora. Moreover, Latin America contains many indigenous groups, large in number and with surviving languages. If we add the residual Spanish and Portuguese presence within Hispanidad dating back to the Nixon era, we have to account not only for Portuguese but also for the range of languages spoken in Spain, which include Castilian (in the USA known as "Spanish") but also Basque, Catalan, and Galician. Additionally Latin America includes regions of Dutch, French, and English speakers. These have survived alongside, and mixed with, a range of indigenous languages and dialects, and these too are brought to the United States. In the overwhelming construction of Latinidad with the Spanish language as dominant, these other languages literally get lost in the shuffle. One of the components of the drive for specificity in media is that language diversity be honored, especially in the case of Portuguese and the indigenous languages in danger of becoming extinct. Since all media include a language component, the prevalence of Spanish as *the Latina/o language* in the mainstream has ramifications in terms of language maintenance and survival.

Latina/o heterogeneity

The above wrinkles of Brazilian inclusion in the Latina/o diaspora and the acknowledgment of a multiplicity of languages in Latin America are but the tip of the iceberg regarding the heterogeneity of the category "Latina/o." While, inside and outside of Latinidad, some scholars and many in popular culture reduce the category "Latina/o" to the "brown" race, and indeed many of the previous generation of Chicano scholars celebrated the "Bronze" color of this segment of the population (see, for example, Rosalinda Fregoso's *The Bronze Screen*), the fact is that Latina/os come in all racial, religious, and nation-of-origin combinations, which in turn means the entire spectrum of skin colors. To be sure, the vast majority – 90 percent – of those Latina/os who participated in the 2000 Census declared themselves to be monoracial, and mostly White, but this statistical homogeneity belies the complicated mixtures borne out by those in the category, as well as recalling racial narratives in both the USA and Latin American countries that privilege whiteness and therefore make the "White" answer the preferable one. "Brown" is therefore as much a flattening of difference as "Spanish" is. That means that although most Latina/os are some shade of brown (indeed isn't all skin a shade of brown?), there are many other shades whose omission speaks to colonial and more recent histories that are important to take into account in the contemporary era and in Media Studies. The accepted "bronze" mixture of indigenous (Aztec, Inca, Aymará, Quechua, Araucano, Guaraní, Iriquois, etc.) with Spanish – implicitly alluding to a white and brown combination – forms the background for the pervasive representation of Latina/os as the brown race. However, there is a much more heterogeneous mixture within Latinidad. First, there was not a brown similarity among indigenous peoples. Some were darker and others lighter. Facial features varied and there were similarities to all of the four major racial categories as we contemporarily know them: Caucasian, Asian, African American, and Native American. For example, *altiplano* (Andean highlands) indigenous peoples found in what is now

Peru and Bolivia look much more "Asian" than Zapotec peoples in what is now Mexico.

Second, the Spanish were not the great pure origin of whiteness that some accounts would assign to them. In fact, only if we ignore the eight-century occupation of Spain by the Moors could we even begin to pretend that there were no African or Asian traces in the Spanish population. Thus, even from those two simplistic tales of racial origin in Spain and the Americas, we already have a diverse and heterogeneous Latinidad. When we add waves of slavery and colonizers, the situation gets even more hybrid. For example Chinese laborers migrated to Peru from Macao and others were brought in as coolies in the nineteenth century for the sugar and guano trades. African slaves were brought in to Brazil and along the Pacific coast of the Americas in Colombia, Ecuador, and Peru, as well as along the Atlantic coast north of Brazil from French Guyana through Suriname, Guyana, Venezuela, Colombia, Panama, Costa Rica, and Nicaragua, not to mention the Caribbean – Hispanic, British, and French and Dutch. We have Afro-American combinations that span the racial spectrum. Given the British, Dutch, and French colonies on the "East" coast, some of whose subjects also had migrated to the Americas, and the fact that the Columbus expedition was financed by the nationalist Spanish kings, one of whose policies was religious singularity – Jewish and Moorish populations from Spain also headed to the Americas. This brief account of racial, national, religious, and ethnic mixture only dates back to the Columbian era. We will not go back any further, though historians now widely suggest that Columbus was not the first European to reach American soil.

The above is not a meaningless detour into racial heterogeneity and migration flows but rather a necessary reminder that the heterogeneity of the contemporary Latina/o population dates back at least five centuries. Despite self-reports of homogeneity to the US Census takers of 2000, the hybrid mixture that most Latina/os embody cannot be contained by the contemporary categories. Indeed, if we look back to the Spanish *casta* paintings of the eighteenth century in Mexico and Peru,[11] the two most developed viceroyalties of Spain in the New World, we see that the Spanish attempted to account for the racial and socioeconomic class diversity in their colonies centuries ago. The link between skin color and socioeconomic class was explicitly made in these paintings and the fiction that the Spanish stood for purity and whiteness was constructed. As Katzew (1996) asserts, the casta paintings were meant as reminders of the hierarchy of status and privilege in the colonies, not as a celebration of the wonders of *mestizaje*. Whereas the latest US Census acknowledges the numbers of Hispanics, it is unable to speak to our heterogeneity. The mass media

and popular culture, however, somewhat invested in targeting minorities and much more invested in selling ethnicity as a commodity
(Halter, 2000; Dávila, 2002; Valdivia, 2007), have begun to purposefully represent a heterogeneous Latinidad, sometimes inadvertently.
In addition, Latina/o community demands for inclusion and representation, as well as differentiation, have contributed to building
the dynamic and difficult-to-summarize terrain of Latinidad and the
resulting media issues and cultural politics.

Class matters

As has been suggested in many instances above, socioeconomic status
largely influences language skills and other access issues. For instance,
socioeconomic status overlaps with higher education achievement
which in turn means upwardly mobile jobs, both of which require
English-language proficiency. As well, socioeconomic status overlaps
with proximity to whiteness, materially and metaphorically. For
example, college-educated Latina/os have higher levels of English
proficiency and tend to be overwhelmingly light and/or operate
within white-coded situations, which often means middle-class status
(Amaya, 2007). This often translates into a performance of whiteness being middle-class rather than an embodiment of light skin. Of
course, the racial spectrum in any given situation varies. For instance,
what might count as white or light-brown in Mexico gets coded as
dark-brown in the United States and then slips into a connotation of
working-class, less educated, non-English-speaking, etc. Below I quote
at length from Hector Amaya's autoethnography wherein he explores
the performances in which he must engage in order to be read as
white/middle-class in particular settings, and how that performance
is always temporary, as he is once more interpreted as brown when he
leaves that social setting:

> My personal appearance is not the only thing that influences the
> relational and material constitution of my self. Although my materi-
> ality casts me in a performance of race and class, the stage for this
> performance is also part of the physical (symbolic) elements around
> me (Goffman). For instance, I am keenly aware of my friendships,
> immediate social circle, the class status of the activities I carry on, and
> the protocols of class interaction among upper middle- and upper-
> class individuals. Without consciously intending to, during the last
> few years I have cultivated a group of friends outside academia, all of
> whom are respected professionals: they are lawyers, engineers, artists,
> and entrepreneurs. Almost all of them are white (although there are
> a few locally brewed Latinos) and upper middle class. This has meant
> that I regularly rub elbows with an economic class that I do not belong

to. With my assistant professor salary, I am barely able to keep up with some of my friends, but I try. What I bring to this group of people is never clear; they accept me partly because I am educated and have the same political inclinations that they have (most are leftist and politically active), but also because I have made an effort to learn to participate in activities they enjoy such as playing tennis, squash, and appreciating art. Most of these relationships began with these activities, all of which are heavily class coded and class segregated. (2007, p. 204)

Education, politics, activities such as sport and art, in a Bourdieuian sense, all contribute to a class performance and acceptance within a group of people, despite the subject's relatively brown skin color in US professional and academic circles. In fact, Amaya details how he sought higher education in an explicit effort to escape the discriminatory and prejudicial treatment he received within Anglo culture at large. This is an option that is not necessarily open to many immigrants, especially in the current conditions of prohibitively rising higher education costs, immigration-status barriers to entry, and declining financial aid.

In a related topic, Hispanics with lower levels of education and English proficiency remain largely disconnected from the internet. This has implications in relation to access to almost any type of information. For example, applying for financial aid almost assumes not only access to computers but also long time-spans online and the latest hardware and software. Jobs, banking, educational opportunities, fellowships, and loan information may all be available only or primarily online. News and entertainment sources are also online. Communication services, such as Skype™ which allows for nearly free online telephony, assume computer and internet access. The information divide has migrated to the internet and it overlaps with socioeconomic class more so than with ethnicity. Given that most of the Latina/o population is working-class, the digital divide disproportionately affects Latina/os. The prevalence and enduring pockets of Spanish speakers in the working class also contribute to the digital divide, given that English is the lingua franca on the internet. Socioeconomic class affects access in economic terms given the material cost of owning an up-to-date computer, or even through the accessibility of steady electricity. The rapidly changing standards and technologies related with computer and internet access mean that, even when a working-class family manages to pool resources to purchase a computer, they will not necessarily be able to stay updated. The digital divide disenfranchises those Latina/os and others who stand to gain the most from these potentially democratic technologies.

In a capitalist system, wherein profits and therefore the sale of products are privileged above all else, the attention to Latina/os in the mainstream has been partly fueled by the realization that, beyond mere numbers, there is a significant amount of spending power among a segment of the Latina/o population. The preferred segments are the Latina/o middle and upper middle classes who possess the disposable income to make programming commercially viable. Low-cost foods, products, and services are marketed to a working-class stratum, which partly explains the prevalence of cigarette and alcohol billboards in neighborhoods primarily populated by working-class Latina/os and African Americans. Thus, from both within and without, there is an acknowledgment of class differences within Latinidad that have ramifications in terms of political intervention. Politically, while the Latina/o vote has been assumed to be Democrat, recent elections show a growing split, partly fueled by socioeconomic class and residency and longevity status. The heterogeneous composition of the Latina/o population against the backdrop of tendencies to flatten the diversity within has huge potential consequences in terms of media access, production, representation, and audience interpretation.

Socioeconomic class is one, yet not the only, important vector of difference, in addition to race, language and nation of origin, that speaks to the heterogeneity of Latina/os. Dominant constructions of the category also assign it a religious dimension – that is, the suggestion that all Latina/os are Roman Catholic. While this is partly true – roughly 70 percent of Latina/os share that religion – there are also Protestant, Jewish, Muslim, and Buddhist Latina/os. Latina/os come from every religion, with all other religions making inroads into the Catholic component rather than the other way around. Religious proclivities have implications in terms of media. Religious channels and programming are produced for and by, and have begun to target, Latina/os in certain geographic areas. As well, religious membership has implications of class belonging and performance. While the Catholic religion might predispose Latina/os in terms of approaches to sexuality and reproduction, research shows that, like language, the conservative approaches of the Roman Catholic religion do not necessarily last as intensely beyond the first generation of immigrants. Moreover, there is a significant component of Latina/os that belongs to sexual minorities, and a more than significant component of Latina/o Studies that pursues this area of investigation. In sum, the heterogeneity of Latina/os and the still relative lack of attention paid to this growing segment of the population make it imperative that we pursue Latina/o Media Studies as vigorously as possible.

Latina/o Media Studies

Latina/os and the Media combines the intersecting interdisciplines of Media Studies and Latina/o Studies. Media Studies is an interdiscipline with a near 100-year history that has generated theories and methodologies for studying the relationship between media, culture, and society. Within Media Studies, as within other established and older disciplines, the inclusion of ethnicity was usually introduced as minority studies. Given the national-imaginary binary already mentioned, the original operationalization of "minorities" was through the inclusion of African American Studies. E. P. Johnson (2000) outlines three waves of social science that have investigated ethnicity and the media in the United States. The first phase, in the 1920s, foregrounded assimilation as a strategy for inclusion. Immigrants were supposed to give up their culture and take up US culture. The second stage, acculturation, argued for taking part in mainstream channels of the host culture even if one kept elements of one's original culture. Johnson locates this strategy in the 1960s in relation to civil rights movements. The third stage, from the 1970s, and drawing on Subervi-Vélez's (1986) germinal research, is pluralism, a process of "sustained ethnic differentiation and heterogeneity, implying practice of one culture while participating in the majority society" (p. 232). Hispanics begin to show up only in this third phase, and this is the stage on which this book focuses. Beginning from a standpoint of heterogeneity and multiplicity, "some of the most important and innovative debates about transnationalism, gender, class, hybridity, and citizenship occur in Latina/o media studies" (Del Río, 2006, p. 390). Del Río adds that Latina/o Media Studies can be divided into two approaches. The first, "the traditional," focuses on issues of stereotypes and the "quality and nature of representations" (p. 400). The second, the "Latino problematic," coheres around the following themes: nationalism; citizenship and immigration; language and culture; and race, class, and gender and the politics of representation. The previous section of this introduction has revealed to the reader the heterogeneity and tensions within Latinidad and Latina/o studies. Drawing on both approaches, and integrating them, this book brings together a broad range of scholars who pursue communications research as it overlaps with Latina/o Studies. Until recently, volumes on ethnicity, if they acknowledged Latina/os at all, included one chapter or a boxed section in a page on Latina/os. Overview volumes such as *Media & Minorities* (Larson, 2006) include sections on "Hispanics" that draw on limited and dated material.[12] Best-sellers in the communication field, such as *Gender, Race, and Class in Media* (Dines and McMahon Humez, 2002) included much more material on other ethnicities than on

Latina/os. The relative lack of attention paid to Latina/os within Media Studies is matched by the same lack of attention to Media Studies paid within Latina/o Studies. The journal *Latina/o Studies* issued a call for papers for a "special issue" on Media Studies (June, 2008) as if this were a novel area. The newly released *A Companion to Latina/o Studies* (2007) has one article about the internet but none on mainstream media. The book *Latina/o Popular Culture* (2002) includes many essays that ignore or avoid mainstream media. This despite Media Studies research over the past few decades that shows that, in the absence of personal experience, people use mainstream media to make decisions about ethnic minorities. Coupled with patterns of representation that often border on the prejudicial, the lack of attention paid to mainstream media is inadvisable, if not downright foolish. Three versions of the dismissal of Latina/o Media Studies yield the continual replay of the myth of discovery. These include: "mainstream media are beneath us and not as authentic as grassroots or folk culture"; "media are so pervasive as to make everyone a Media Scholar"; or "I must be the first person to think of this research topic so I do not need to conduct a literature review." As a result, many scholars within Latina/o and Media Studies write as if they just discovered, all on their own, that someone like Jennifer Lopez is important to study. Conducting a cursory literature review on the subject, as we are all taught to do in a basic "introduction to academic writing" course, seems to fall out of the picture. Those of us reviewing articles for journals have read, many times, the "I just discovered Jennifer Lopez" article (Valdivia, 2008). For those explorers in search of virgin academic territory, this book should help as a map to that already-existing area of Latina/o Media Studies. Nearly a decade into the new millennium, the intersection of these two fields has grown so much that it merits being called a specialty of its own. *Latina/os and the Media* illustrates this growth, and the necessity to take up these issues together and centrally.

While this book is grounded in the intersection between Latina/o Studies and Communications and Media Studies research, it includes material from related areas such as Popular Music and Cinema Studies. The above-mentioned *Companion to Latina/o Studies* in fact included two chapters on popular music and one on cinema. However, while those two areas of study can be read through Media Studies, *Latina/os and the Media Studies* seeks to fill two overlapping gaps in the literature. First, there is no other single overview book on Latina/os in Communication Studies. *Latina/o Communication Studies Today* (2008) comes the closest as an edited collection of new scholarship. Second, quite often when people in other disciplines write about communications and Latina/os, they do so in an under-theorized manner, often taking communications and media as transparent independent variables rather than as constitutive components of a communications process that is both social and cultural with a long historical tradition of research.

Since the academy is part of society and culture, it was inevitable that the study of Latina/os and the media would increase following the twin forces of the nineties Latina/o boom and the US Census announcement that, as of 2000, Latina/os were the largest component of the minority population. Other forces, such as the growth of Ethnic Studies in US universities and the demands, throughout the United States – usually stemming from undergraduate and graduate students – for courses, faculty, and programs dedicated to the study of Latina/os (Cabán, 2003), resulted in a body of work that enriched scholarship in general, not just the study of Latina/os. Random events, such as Selena's posthumous crossover (Paredez, 2002; D. Vargas, 2002), the Elián González spectacle (Banet-Weiser, 2003; Molina Guzmán, 2005, 2007b, 2008), and 9/11, further increased the attention to issues of Latina/os and immigration. In a historical context partly framed by the North American Free Trade Agreement (NAFTA) signed in 1994, increased terrorism (none of it yet linked to any Latina/o), and a general backlash against immigrants fueled by the right-wing policies of two consecutive Bush Administrations and mass-media locations for that sentiment, such as *Lou Dobbs Tonight* on CNN, Latina/os have come to occupy center stage in discussions and narratives to which they do not necessarily contribute.

In this climate, Latina/o Media scholars carve out an area of studies. We build on already-existing research in Popular Music, Cinema and Film Studies, and Literature. What Media Studies contributes to Latina/o Studies scholarship is the theoretically and methodologically rigorous – creatively so – engagement with issues of mainstream media. Media are something we all encounter daily. That makes them a deceptively easy area of life to understand. For at least a century people have had "common sense" ways of understanding the relationship between media and culture. Decades of research have taught us that how people produce, interpret, and are affected by media is indeed a very complex area of study. While in many academic and social circles there is still a tendency to dismiss media as trivial, there is an equally contagious desire to claim media expertise. Contextual variables resulting from ongoing global mobility of population and culture and the instability of political arrangements as a result of this mobility, in concert with economic fluctuations, create a dynamic situation in which the study of Latina/os and/in the media must be carried out with careful dedication.

The growth of Latina/o media is but one component of Latina/o Media Studies. In 1999, C. Rodriguez documented more than 1,000 US television outlets, some 400 Spanish-language radio stations, 14 US Spanish-language daily newspapers, and dozens of Spanish-language magazines and weekly newspapers (2001, p. 47). The incredibly useful Latino Media Project (www.latinosandmedia.org/) managed by Federico Subervi provides continuously updated materials on Latina/o media, Latina/o media research, and Latina/o media organizations. At this point in time, it takes this type of continuously updated resource to keep track of the dynamically growing forms of Latina/o media. However, Latina/o Media Studies is not just about Latina/o media, as Latina/os and Latinidad consume, appear in, and work in all forms of media. Especially within the mainstream, where messages reach the widest audiences, Latina/os appear both in Latina/o and general programming and are consumed by both. This makes the task of a Latina/o media scholar all the more exciting.

Organization of this book

This book follows an organizational model based on Denis McQuail's *Mass Communication Theory*, dating from the original version (1983) to the latest (2005). Despite changes in technology and the audience, the four major areas of study in Communications and Media Studies remain: production, content, audiences, and effects (Valdivia, 2003). Although we as individuals and members of groups, nations, and diasporas experience all four together, these need to be separated out for the purposes of research. Yet it is undeniable that they are all linked to each other. For instance, the production of media, including its structures and organizations, has to be conducted with audiences in mind. The content of the media is what audiences engage with and what sponsors pay for in a "free" system. Effects of the media result from engagement and, in turn, for different motives, those producing the media aim for a set of effects. We cannot study effects without studying content. The effect has to be in relation to (a set of) content.

Paradigms within Media Studies include the social scientific and the cultural. In the United States the social scientific remains the dominant paradigm. One development in contemporary Media Studies research is a more holistic approach, so that one study may actually overlap all four areas of research. Within the field of Communications and Media Studies, James Carey identified two approaches: the already-mentioned effects paradigm which he termed the "transmission approach," and a second one, which he favored, the ritual/cultural paradigm. The second paradigm relies primarily on qualitative methodology. This book takes a position within Media Studies that draws from its distinctive components as mutually informative. Whereas some continue to oppose the social scientific to the cultural turn, I see them as mutually informing. Treating all components of

Media Studies with respect enables us to profit from the immense and mutually informing body of research.

One cannot write a Latina/o Media Studies book ignoring the effect component. Yet as the reader will notice in the fifth chapter, research in that area remains relatively scarce, especially in relation to research on representation. Thus the chapter on effects is in essence the deployment of the dominant paradigm in the field of US Media Studies. In some regions of the world, media effects and the social scientific paradigm are dominant, while in others they are nearly absent. Thus, writing from a British location, for example, Georgiou (2007) argues that the three areas of Media Studies are content, reception, and production. She does not even mention effects. On the other hand, in the Netherlands there are entire research centers and journals devoted to media psychology. Many times content analysis is the first step in the study of effects. After all, it is necessary to know what people are watching to examine the effects. The problem is that we do not know if what we see is also what other people see, so that becomes the area of study known as "audiences."

When we watch a television show at home, in an airplane, or on the internet; read the news, a magazine, or a novel; listen to music on an i-Pod, any MP3 player (including our mobile phone), or on the old-fashioned radio; go to the movies, or rent or download a DVD (legally or not); or engage in any of the myriad experiences wherein the synergistic tendencies of contemporary media come together – such as in girl culture where clothing, books, movies, music, food, and furniture are all marketed and consumed through Bratz, American Girl, and Dora the Explorer brands – we are relating to the means of communication in a social and cultural context. That context informs the production, circulation, and consumption, and effects, of media. Most importantly for the purposes of this book, that context includes issues of race and ethnicity at an epidermal level, or surface level, to use Shohat's term (Shohat and Stam, 1994), or in an implicit sense, as in the assumed normativity of whiteness, for example. It is the experience and process of media engagement that organizes the structure of this book rather than individual media. Organizing the book around Media Studies categories such as production, representation/content, interpretation/audience, and effects rather than particular media such as newspaper, advertising, television, etc., will allow for conceptual clarity and minimal repetition.

After this introduction, the book has four Media Studies chapters: production; content and representation; audience and reception; and effects – all within Latina/o Media Studies. The conclusion will wrap up the chapters and suggest paths to pursue in future research, as well as possible uses of this material for students and activists. I warn you at the outset that research discussed in each of these chapters demonstrates the heterogeneity of Latinidad and therefore the complexity of pursuing the study of a constructed ethnic category: Latina/os. In the production chapter, one of the major issues looming over the scholarship is how to determine what is Latina/o-produced media and who is a Latina/o producer. As easy as that determination might seem to you, the chapter will explore the difficulties in determining whether a media product is in fact produced by Latina/os and what counts as Latina/o production. In the chapter on content and representation, that difficulty continues as, given the heterogeneity within Latinidad, how do we know if any individual represented in media is or isn't a Latina/o. Also, since we are asking for less stereotypical representations, how do we recognize the subtle and ambiguous forms of Latina/os and Latinidad? In the audience and effects chapters, we encounter institutional and practical barriers to studying Latina/os as audiences and how non-Latina/o audiences interpret Latina/os. The same applies to effects. How does the predominantly stereotypical representation of Latina/os in mainstream media affect Latina/os and others? Once more, given the ambiguity and subtleness of much contemporary representation, how do we compose a research project without tipping the ambiguity to our research subjects? Latina/o Media Studies is not an easy enterprise.

Each of the four Media Studies chapters will end with two case studies. First, "The Homicide Report" from the *Los Angeles Times* will serve as a case study to explore issues of production, content, audience, and effect in a particular newspaper's effort to document death in a community. The stakes in this case study are literally life or death. A second case study, on Jennifer Lopez, will follow the previous one. The latter case study shifts the focus to a celebrity who has managed to turn herself into a brand and thus can also be studied across the four Media Studies components. This case study represents the possibility of success in the mainstream. Together, these two case studies should give readers the possibility of applying Latina/o Media Studies to a realist form of media as well as to an entertainment celebrity figure/ enterprise.

This chapter aimed to introduce the reader of the book to the topic of Latina/os and the area of Latina/o Studies. It then combined this area of ethnic studies with Media Studies in order to pursue Latina/o Media Studies. The organization of the book follows that of a Media Studies approach: production, content, audience, and effects. To highlight and explore the usefulness of this approach, the two case studies, "The Homicide Report" and the one on Jennifer Lopez, illustrate some of the avenues of research. Together, all of these elements provide the tools for the continuation and development of Latina/o Media Studies.

CHAPTER

1 Production

You take some kids, perhaps your own, to see the latest version of *Spy Kids* (2001, 2002, 2003), or you go to a chick flick such as *Tortilla Soup* (2001), or you go to a hybrid detective love story such as *Out of Sight* (1998) and you walk away wondering how in the world those movies came to be produced? You listen to some reggaeton, or read *Latina* magazine, or run into a website on *quinceañeras*,[1] or watch *Ugly Betty* on prime-time television, or read about Latina/os in the news and you enjoy and/or learn from their content without thinking about what it took to produce them. Yet in the study of production, who directed and/or produced these media items and under what conditions is the focus of the research. Did the fact that *Spy Kids* was directed and written by Robert Rodriguez, a Latino, add any Latinidad to the movies? Was he influential in having Latina/o actors such as Alexa Vega, Cheech Marin, Salma Hayek, and Roberto Montalban play some of the main and supporting characters in the movies? Was the further inclusion of Spanish actor Antonio Banderas as the kids' father yet another nod toward Latinidad, albeit a Peninsular one? What about *Tortilla Soup*? What made it possible to produce and distribute a movie about Mexican food cooked by a Mexican principal character (played by Hector Helizondo) and his three beautiful daughters as well as the scheming older woman, played by recently outed Latina Raquel Welch? And does the fact that two of his daughters are played by actresses Elizabeth Peña and Constance Marie, who usually appear as the Latinas in a range of film and television shows, mean that there are very few talented Latina actresses or that mainstream media hesitates to venture into a broader talent pool? Does the production of *Tortilla Soup* signal Hollywood film is finally acknowledging Latina/o culture, the Latina/o audience, and Latina/o talent? *Out of Sight* also brings up a number of questions. Since Jennifer Lopez co-starred with George Clooney does that mean that the mainstream and Hollywood are ready to envision mixed-race couples? Granted, Jennifer Lopez does not play a Latina character, but her Latinidad is hardly a secret, so that she brings that baggage into any character that she plays.

What about *Ugly Betty*? Would that show have made it to prime-time network television without the steadfast influence of Salma Hayek and her production company Ventanarosa Productions' collaboration with more mainstream powerhouses such as Touchstone Pictures, a Disney subsidiary? Would America Ferrera ever have made it to a starring role on network television without her break-out role in *Real Women Have Curves* (2002), an art-house Latina coming-of-age story that crossed over into the mainstream? Prior to this, Ferrera had been in Disney films, but was not exactly the headliner that Lindsey Lohan was. Listening to popular music, you might have to find special "Latin" or "Hispanic" radio stations and/or programming on cable television, or you might be able to listen to and/or view Latina/o music on mainstream channels. Surfing through the web, you might be linked to a Latina/o website through Google or on the right-hand side of your g-mail, or you may have purposefully, and with some background information, searched for culture-specific material. In the newspaper realm, newspapers, when covering the 2006 immigration rallies, represented a whole new range of actors – Latina/os of all types exercising their freedom of speech in an organized and orderly manner. Who were the sources that newspaper rooms contacted in relation to these rallies? Why was radio as a medium far more helpful in organizing Latina/os than the press?

All of the questions above are about the production of the media. When people think of media, or most anything else for that reason, they seldom consider how these are produced. However, this is indeed one of the four most important questions to think about in relation to Latina/os and the media.[2] Latina/o Media Studies scholars have to consider the conditions and terms of production of media and popular culture because these determine the content that we experience as media. The way media are produced, how they are produced, and – indeed – whether they are produced at all speak to contemporary political and economic arrangements in our society that, in turn, illuminate wider issues of distribution of power and privilege. In other words, while most popular discussions about Latina/o Media Studies focus on content – that is, what we see, listen to, or read, in a television show, a movie, a song, a website, a newspaper article, etc. – in the study of production we ask how and why were that television show, movie, and newspaper article produced. Implicitly, we also question why more of them or something else was not produced. Often this second question yields more information than the first, especially in periods or cases of relative Latina/o absence from the media.

We need to study both Latina/os in media industries and Latina/o media industries and to remember that these two do not necessarily go together. We cannot assume that Latina/os work in Latina/o media industries, nor can we assume that Latina/o media industries are populated by Latina/o workers or owned and controlled by Latina/os. Considering the global circulation of talent and material, we need to take up a central component of contemporary Latina/o Studies – issues of the authenticity of the US-based Latina/o vs. Latin American talent, whether in front of or behind the camera (Dávila, 2001). While this is an incredibly difficult issue to explore – some would even say impossible – scholars and activists implicitly and explicitly ask if Latina/os will produce more Latina/o media. Of course, what is considered a Latina/o producer on Latina/o media ranges widely, as does the answer to that question. Nonetheless, from a Latina/o Media Studies perspective, this question needs to at least be discussed. Does Latina/o input into production make any difference in the Latinidad of the resulting media product? What counts as Latinidad in a media product – Latina/os in the production or inclusion of Latina/o themes or appeals to a Latina/o audience?

Given the definition of that which is Latina/o as descending from populations and cultures of Latin American origin, issues of production must include transnational talent flow, especially a discussion of the feeder role that Latin America continues to play in US Latina/o media. For instance, in Latin America, US Latina/os are not necessarily considered "authentic" in language, style, or mores. Within the USA, Latina/os sometimes seek to differentiate themselves from Latin Americans, and other times they try to make alliances and stress solidarity. If US Latina/o media production is made mostly by Latin American personnel, does this count as Latina/o media? Conversely, does the broadcasting of Latin American telenovelas on Telemundo and Univisión count as US Latina/o media?[3] From an outsider's perspective, one that flattens the difference between Latina/o and Latin American, these questions appear diversionary. Yet from within Latinidad these questions go to the core of belonging and borders – and indeed the assertion of identity and presence – between Latina/os and Latin Americans, and date back to a complex and difficult history of inclusion and exclusion in areas such as art, literature, popular music, and film.

To make matters a little more complex, the study of the production of Latina/o media includes English, Spanish, and bilingual media, both mainstream and alternative. Latina/o-market media, as a result, include at least five components. First there are media produced within the USA, destined to be circulated first in the USA, and later globally. Global expansion and distribution is a crucial component of contemporary mainstream media production. A successful media product is most likely envisioned to have global potential. An example would be *Dora the Explorer*, a program that was originally created to increase the bilingual skills of US mainstream children and now is distributed globally. Just because a product is distributed globally does not mean that it will achieve the same goals as when it was originally marketed to the national audience. In Israel, Dora teaches Hebrew-speaking children English and in Chile she teaches Spanish speakers English, for instance.[4] Similarly, US-produced *Ugly Betty*, first produced in Colombia, was then marketed globally. A second type of production, and one that is increasingly the norm, is that of a transnationally produced and marketed form of media. Here you have the United States, which previously produced media inhouse – that is, with US talent and capital – now partnering with transnational capital, other countries, and individual actors and/or investors. An example of this type of production would be *Guerrilla* (2008), a Steven Sodenbergh film, starring Benicio del Toro as Che Guevara, which was filmed with US and Spanish funds partly in Spain and the USA yet circulates globally as a representation of US Latina/o talent and Latin American history. Granted, Che Guevara is a historical and mythical figure with global resonance, and thus the marketing of such a movie draws on a widespread knowledge of the mythical main character. A third type of Latina/o-market media is made up primarily of Latin American and Peninsular (mostly Spanish, sometimes Portuguese) productions that may be aimed at a broader Spanish, Peninsular, American, and/or global audience, with the US audience being just part of a more generalized distribution strategy. Many Brazilian, Mexican, Spanish, and Venezuelan telenovelas would be part of this type of production. Because of linguistic, historical, and cultural proximity and resonance to some of the Latina/o audience, these media target the Latina/os' market. The paradigmatic telenovela, *Simplemente María*, arguably the "most popular Latin American telenovela of all time" (Singhal, Obregon, and Rogers, 1995), originally Peruvian, but later remade by nearly every Spanish-speaking country, as well as by Brazil in Portuguese, would be an example of something that was also distributed in the United States to Latina/o audiences with great success. Fourth, there are Latina/o media that target the Latina/o market. As we will read later in this chapter, there is no guarantee that Latina/o media are owned by Latina/os or employ mostly Latina/os. Television examples would be Univisión and Telemundo. Fifth, mainstream media also try to target the Latina/o market by inclusion of subtle signifiers of Latinidad. Neither *Dora* nor *Ugly Betty* is subtle in this sense. Here we have something like *Dragon Tales*, a children's television show whose Latinidad almost takes an informed native to discern, or a range of advertisements whose ambiguous representation could be read as white or Latina/o, thus not alienating any segment of the audience yet potentially addressing a range of ethnicities. These five options suggest that, inevitably, synergy and convergence forces will take effect between all successful – in market terms – media, including English- and Spanish-language media forms, mainstream and Latina/o-targeted, and funded by national and transnational capital. This takes us into at least partial transnational ownership and control of Latina/o media production. Thus, whatever the debates about the location of Latinidad in US Latina/o Studies, the study of production inexorably takes us into a global and transnational arena, and the very difficult tasks of even being able to identify the origin of production of, and composition of the media workforce that produces, Latina/o media.

One fruitful point to begin to consider is the history of Latina/o media. Different types of media have differing histories. Latina/o print media date back to the 1880s, radio to the 1920s, and television to the 1960s. While television in the United States can be dated back to the 1950s, in Latin America its deployment came nearly a decade later and not necessarily in the commercial realm. In most countries, television began as a government-sponsored and/or -controlled medium. It is not until Latin American television crossed over into commercial production that it began to export its tremendously successful genres. This history is important to note because, at first, most television targeted at US Latina/os came from Latin America. Given television's exponentially higher costs than radio and its demands for highly skilled and expensive labor, US Latina/o television had to slowly accumulate enough resources and had to demonstrate economic viability in a commercial system that was, for a long time, the global power within the medium. Thus, Latina/o television is a rather recent development. Originally, print media, in particular newspapers, were much more likely to be in Spanish due to their beginnings shortly after the US expansion over formerly Mexican territory. Radio, an interesting and often forgotten technology in Media Studies that remains the most globally available form of media, originally allowed for greater local and democratic, albeit marginal, opportunities. Radio and newspapers, if locally produced, can serve community needs quite directly. Television, with its nearly prohibitive costs – except for the most resourceful and wealthy countries – and its centralized form of production, comes into its own in terms of reaching out to diasporic audiences through transnational capital. Slick and professional television production is a minimum standard given the widespread availability of network television in the USA. Thus the history of US Latina/o television differs much from radio, though they are both forms of broadcasting. Recent developments in local cable, and video, and digital technology open up a space for production and distribution that was not there at the outset of television. Contemporary internet development and deployment also opens up a space for production, although much of the internet, as with previous telecommunications technologies, is not only being commercialized but also becoming part and parcel of established media industries – think of NBC radio, NBC television, and NBC.com as an example. We need to remember, as briefly discussed in the introductory chapter, that issues of access are paramount to consider when speaking of digital technology. Digital technology access assumes, at the very least, electricity and constantly updated computer technology. Other forms of media and popular culture such as movies and popular music also include moments and chunks of Latina/o media production and ownership. Cinema scholars date the participation of Latina/o actors in the film industry to the beginnings of Hollywood film. Definitive histories of popular music and Latina/os have yet to be written, though the work of scholars such as Juan Flores and Raquel Rivera has begun to illuminate Latina/o popular music production from "bomba to hip hop" (J. Flores, 2000; R. Rivera, 2003). In the case of hip hop, both of these Latina/o Studies scholars document the presence of Latina/os within that form of popular music since the 1970s, despite their virtual erasure in more popularly circulated histories of that musical genre. As you can see, Latina/os have been historically present in mainstream media production.

The study of production from a Latina/o Media Studies perspective has to ask whether the diversity of ethnicity on the part of workers makes a difference. Are Latina/o-produced media more attentive to issues about Latina/os, and under what conditions do Latina/os in the workforce make a difference? Given the acknowledgment by official institutions, such as the US Census, a US government component, and all sorts of other non-governmental institutions such as universities and the medical community, as well as the panoply of commercial enterprises – including mainstream mass media – that Latina/os not only are here to stay but compose a growing majority of the minority population nationally and are the majority population in some regional areas, it is indeed relevant to ask whether Latina/os are included in the production of media that circulate the beliefs, myths, and common sense understandings of a culture within the USA, and by extension, since US media are globally available, throughout the world. An additionally relevant detail is that, in the United States, some of the media are protected by the First Amendment. Freedom of speech entails the freedom from prior censorship from the government and, as such, that protection comes with some degree of responsibility for fairness and diversity. Within this realm of responsibility, under-represented groups in the USA can make claims upon media industries for more employment as well as better representation.

Consequently, one of the major reasons that it is relevant to pursue research into the production of media is that it illuminates matters of the workforce and the degree of influence that individuals or groups may have in the production of the messages that circulate in our culture. Is employment in media something that is open to Latina/os? Is it a career path we should be encouraging youth to pursue? Are different types of people producing the media that we consume? If employed in media industries, what role do Latina/os have in the production of the media? Does it make a difference if and whether Latina/os participate in the production of media? If so, at what level of participation can a Latina/o make a difference? Beyond the level of the ethnicity of a particular worker, are the rules, written and unwritten, that guide the production of media somehow compatible with the goals and cultural proclivities of Latina/os or not? If so, what are these? And is there a difference between the goals and products of media produced by Latina/os, and mainstream media that are largely not produced with a significant proportion of Latina/os? Some of these questions have begun to be answered. Others are begging for research. Still others are nearly impossible to answer as the data required are not available or not yet gathered; yet we can make informed speculations on the latter. Still other questions, such as intent, are nearly impossible to pursue – how can we trust individual mass communicators when they say they "intended" for this and that to happen? This book does not take up the issue of intent as it has not proven to be a productive pursuit in Media Studies.

Levels of analysis

One way to pursue some of the above questions is to study production via a sociological approach that includes the individual, organizational, and institutional levels of analysis – that is, we study how these layers interact in the workplace in order to get the media to us. Although, when we experience media, all three levels come together for us in one product or set of products, such as a television show or series, it is useful to separate these for the purposes of understanding different layers as they affect production. The institutional level of analysis refers to the norms and values that guide production at a societal level. At the organizational level, we study the rules, written and unwritten, enforced at the site of production. The organization has to abide by institutional norms and values and is composed of individual communicators. At the individual level of analysis, we study those who actually work to produce media. These individuals work in organizations with rules but can also appeal to broader institutional values. Thus, all three of the levels impinge upon each other. Levels of analysis include issues of ethnicity and Latina/os, even though these were not original components of such research.

Media production is cut-throat, and getting media to us is quite a task. Some forms of media have to be delivered daily, such as the newspaper; others come out less regularly, such as movies; television might come daily or weekly; and some internet sites, especially "breaking news," are constantly updated. In any case, given the highly competitive nature of mainstream media industries, the huge sums of money invested in it, and the profit motive that drives most of it, production is highly complicated and has to be polished and slick. Nearly nothing that we experience as media content was accidentally produced. Even bloopers, in the modern television and cinema age, are planned, scripted, and produced. It takes a highly trained workforce, massive amounts of investment, and very expensive technology to produce seamless and slick material such as the television show *Ugly Betty*, the magazine *People en Español*, and the website Quince Girl, to name a few instances of media that are about Latina/os and may be produced partly or wholly by Latina/os. Planning and organization guide just about all media production. At the individual level of analysis, we study how workers in media production negotiate the many roles required of them – such as creative, business, and technological ones. Here we strive to understand the degrees of freedom of the individual communicator in relation to the organization, or actual workplace issues at the scene of production. How much freedom does any individual have in relation to the rules and forces of production – or what are called the organizational and institutional levels of analysis in Media Studies? In fact, the tension between structure and agency is one of the major themes in much production research, dating back at least to Marx's observation that workers within capitalism do not necessarily labor under conditions of their own making. Translated into contemporary terms for the parameters of this book, this means that Latina/os who work in media industries do not necessarily make the rules under which they work, nor do they necessarily contribute to or share in the values that guide such production.

At the individual level of analysis, we study the individual communicator. In production of media you have at least three types of individuals who contribute to production: creative, technical, and financial. Creative individuals include the advertising campaign creator/s, the script writer, the journalist, the blogger, the lyricist, etc. I have named just a few of the possibilities for creative personnel who produce media. It is also immensely helpful to remember that people seldom work individually in media production. People work in teams, and there are many layers of workers, according to status and skill. Try sitting through the credits the next time you go to a movie to get some idea of the many types of individual communicators involved in the production of that cultural form. More often than not, you probably come from a movie remembering the major actors, but their performance would not be available to you without the labor of all those others involved. Many times, the credits to a movie, as long as these might seem to you, do not include everyone who actually worked on it. In media production, as in most forms of industrialized labor, there are many who are nameless. To bring this to a concrete level, somebody as well known as Jennifer Lopez, the actress, is an individual communicator on the creative side when she gets to interpret a character – such as Karen Cisco in *Out of Sight*, Marisa Ventura in *Maid in Manhattan* (2002), Charlotte in *Monster-in-Law* (2005), Lauren in *Bordertown* (2008), etc. Gloria Estefan, formerly of the Miami Sound Machine (MSM), and now a major solo recording artist, is also a famous individual communicator. Her albums include original songs in tropical-style English and Spanish and covers of mainstream English hits. She is a crossover artist in the sense that she initially entered the spotlight in "Latin" music but has had hits in mainstream music as well. Other Latina/o individual communicators include Myreya Navarro who writes for the *New York Times*, and the "world's most popular blogger," Perez Hilton at www.perezhilton.com. All of the above are highly accomplished and successful individual communicators of the creative type. Their degrees of freedom in the workplace are arguably greater than those who are at the beginning of their media career or who have not reached such heights of accomplishment and popularity. Those who are at the beginning of their careers or who do not reach the success of those mentioned above have to closely conform to rules and the competitive climate in the workplace. Somebody like Mary, a Cuban American woman who appeared in *The Bachelor* (ABC television network) in both its fourth and sixth seasons, has much less input into her role as "herself." Dubrofsky (2006) finds that, whereas in the fourth season Mary was ethnicized as an exotic Latina other – a sexualized Cuban American who was not to be Bachelor Bob's choice – by the sixth season she was whitened and thus proved to be the ideal partner for Bachelor Byron. The choices made about Mary's dress, style, language use, behavior, screen time, etc., were not made by Mary, nor Bob nor Byron, but by the producers of *The Bachelor*. We suspect the same applies to Betty of *Ugly Betty*. America Ferrera does not choose the clothes and make-up that she performs in for that television show. The same can be said about a journalist in relation to Myreya Navarro; the former has much less choice over stories and emphases than the latter. Editors, who hold power in newspapers as a workplace, might impinge more on the stories of the former than of the latter. However, it would be very difficult for us to find out whether Ms. Navarro's stories are assigned to her by her editors or are independently pursued by her and approved by her editors. Newspaper editor ranks are not the most racially integrated in media industries, but Rick Rodriguez, for example, was not only the executive editor of the *Sacramento Bee* but also the first Latino president of the American Society for Newspaper Editors (ASNE). Rodriguez began at the *Salinas Californian*, moved to the *Fresno Bee*, and moved on to become a professor at the Cronkite School of Journalism at Arizona State University ("Top Editor . . .," 2008). As he moved up the ranks of journalism, he achieved a higher degree of influence in the newspapers with which he was associated. It would take comparative research to examine whether his Latina/o heritage influenced the types of stories pursued in the newspapers that he edited. As an interesting aside on nameless production in the media, the above news release about Rick Rodriguez, an important individual Latino communicator, does not contain a by-line; therefore we do not know who wrote the story about Rodriguez. This becomes an example of an item whose producer/s cannot be identified. You thus have a variety of individual communicators who work in a range of media whose agency, or personal ability to control what they produce in their respective workplaces, varies greatly.

Within Media Studies, we see how every "new" medium is discussed as the salvation from previous evils, one of them being racial discrimination and minority under-representation. Contemporarily, the internet is discussed as such, though historically we find that similar statements were made about the telegraph, radio, television, and cable. The internet might still stand out as a space where individual creativity is pursued with relatively high degrees of freedom, yet the workplace security in that arena remains very low (Pew & Internet American Life Project, 2001; Vuong, 2001). We do not know how many people labor on websites about or by Latina/os. We suspect there is a huge amount of creativity going on but we also fear that the internet, like previous technologies, will be at least partly subsumed by transnational capital. This might mean that we see a presence of Latina/o websites, but further research might reveal ownership and control by some of the traditional conglomerates.

Given that none of the individuals I have mentioned work alone, production of media is carried out by a range of individual creative communicators. The nature of contemporary media is such that massive numbers of people are required for this kind of professionalized production. Thus there are countless individuals who contribute to the creative side of any media product, but we do not know of them because of the way that credit is given and intellectually property assigned within the contemporary workplace and media industries. Less often an issue, but still important to mention, is the fact that profits do not necessarily go to the creators of media, sometimes because of corruption or outright theft of intellectual property. An underfinanced individual looking to break into this competitive industry might not have the resources to make sure that what s/he creates is credited to them. This nameless and relatively powerless group is likely to include many Latina/os, some of whom will eventually move up in the ranks.

As I have mentioned before, it is nearly impossible to have access to editors who will give a researcher insight into whether ethnicity had anything to do with resulting coverage of a topic, group, or culture. Yet the following case study gives nearly unheard-of insight into editor's choices. An interesting and unusual study interviewed editors in the Black Press of the new Latino South. The South has been considered as a location for Black activism and has a corresponding dynamic Black Press. Weill and Castañeda (2004) interviewed a number of editors who compose this local press and derived a finding of "empathetic rejectionism." This means that, while the editors recognized the struggles that Latina/os were encountering in the South, especially as many of these struggles resonated with African American struggles in the same area, they were reticent to cover them. Editors feared that Latina/o demands for equality would impinge negatively on the hard-won resources and representation already gained by the African American community. While the Blacks and the Browns – the words used by the authors of the study – have much in common, the continued lack of coverage in the Black Press indicates that the tensions arising out of Latina/o demographic growth are felt in other minority communities as well as in the dominant white culture. This type of study focused on Black editors as individual communicators. Their perspectives on Latina/os have an effect on the kind of coverage, if any, that Latina/os receive in the Black Press.

The second type of individual communicator is the technical one. This person might be in charge of technology at the level of editing or at the level of lugging it around (think of the people who run around with mikes and lights in the countless "reality" television shows). This person might be concerned with the durability of the equipment as well as with its possibilities and limits. People in this function sometimes overlap with those on the creative side. Who is to say, for instance, that the film editor is not making creative cuts? Other times these people conflict with the creative personnel, in terms of possibly disagreeing when it's appropriate to use technology, and how. Technology people also have to negotiate with individual communicators on the business side. Perhaps the technology required for a particular shot or story exceeds the budget. The fact remains that mass media are technology-intensive and thus this type of communicator, the individual who works with the technology and takes care of it, is totally essential to media production. Whatever the media industry we study, chances are again that there are some Latina/os involved. Here the limits and possibilities of the technology might seem to be value- and therefore race- and ethnicity-neutral. However, this is not entirely the case. For instance, photography students until quite recently were taught lighting techniques in terms of white skin. Make-up personnel as well need to be taught in terms of a range of skin-color possibilities. Hiring practices for this type of communicator ought to be "color-blind" but until recently, and still in certain categories, media workers remained primarily white and male. In other words, hiring and promotion practices include traces of ethnic and race discrimination though there is also an element of training access that might not be equally available.

The third type of individual communicator is the financial worker, the person who deals with business matters and budgets. This person needs to make sure there is enough money to fund the production and that the production is conducted so that it will not only stay within budget but also, if made for commercial media, turn a profit. Quite often this person might work at odds with both technical and creative communicators as their visions might exceed the budget. This person might very well be trained in marketing or finance, and media are just a location to deploy their financial expertise. Their relation to the audience might be almost irrelevant if funding sources alone guide their concerns. However, this type of individual communicator is arguably more powerful than the other two, as this person controls the budget and therefore the very specter of production. In this powerful producer post, we find Montecsuma Esparza who has produced such films as *Selena* (1997) and *The Milagro Beanfield War* (1988). Participating in a range of productions about Latina/os and with Latina/o talent, Esparza is one of the most influential Latina/o individual communicators in Hollywood film and mainstream television production. Because of the increased agency and control that results from engaging in the business and finance side of things, many individual communicators who began as creative talent cross over into the business side. Others, since they began with small budgets that had no room for division of labor, began by working in the creative and business sides of their media. The previously mentioned Robert Rodriguez wrote and produced the *Spy Kids* trilogy. On the other hand, Jennifer Lopez, Gloria Estefan, and Salma Hayek – to name but three contemporary prominent Latinas – have all worked as producers, with the express aim of increasing Latina/o industry representation in the creative and financial roles. Through her production company, Ventanarosa, Salma Hayek has been the executive producer both of *Ugly Betty*, the highly successful television show that propelled America Ferrera, another Latina, to fame, and of the movie *Frida* (2002), as well as of the made-for-TV movie based on Julia Alvarez's book *In the Time of the Butterflies* (2001). A production company such as Ventanarosa contributes not only to higher Latina/o employment in media industries but also to more Latina/o-themed products and the circulation of other forms of Latina/o culture, such as books turned into movies. Individual communicators who explicitly set out to produce Latina/o themes, genres, and talent – such as Esparza, Lopez, Hayek, and Gloria Estefan – make a difference in the overall production of media and the viability of Latina/o media.

While it is difficult to say how many Latina/os function as the financial type of individual communicator, as this type of data is either not kept or hard to access, the answer to the question of whether ethnicity makes a difference in this type of a position is ambiguous. Given the overriding capitalist values guiding the production of mainstream media, the profit motive would rationally appear to be race-neutral. Ethically, a company might involve minority-owned subcontractors so as to diversify the labor pool. However, this is a rather recent development in the contemporary age wherein the acknowledgment of niche markets makes the presence of ethnic audiences impossible to ignore. The still residual tendency to mainly produce for the white market really challenges the tenets of capitalist expansion. Yet individual producers with a mission, such as Hayek, prove that, in such cases, their ethnicity heavily influences their choices of both projects and workers. As both mainstream media and Latina/o-targeted production have shown, producing media with Latina/o content and/or employing Latina/o workers has generally been a successful and profitable venture. So even the often nameless, or lesser-known, Latina/os in the workforce can make a positive contribution, in terms of professionalism and furthering the profit motive. Furthermore, Latina/o media professionals can function well in both mainstream and ethnic and Latina/o-oriented media. If bilingual, they are even more marketable. This makes them a very versatile workforce.

There are at least two other arenas wherein individual communicators function: Latina/o or ethnic media and alternative media. Whereas mainstream media implicitly target a white audience and may appeal to other segments of the audience without alienating their primary target, ethnic media in general and Latina/o media in particular seek out the ethnic and/or Latina/o audience. Given the diversity within the Latina/o audience, some of these forms of media might aim for a broad pan-national, pan-ethnic audience, such as the monthly English-language-dominant, short Spanish-language transla-tion aim of *Latina* magazine. Local community newspapers might be much smaller in their focus, budget and size yet address geography-, language-, and/or class-specific segments of the Latina/o audience. While one might assume that individual communicators in both the national and community media organizations targeting Latina/os have to be somewhat, if not entirely, knowledgeable of their respec-tive Latina/o audience and draw on a history and cultural background that resonates and connects with their audience, this is not neces-sarily the case. While some individual communicators, in addition to their training as journalists, advertisers, film producers, etc., have to integrally understand some version of the contemporary condi-tion of Latinidad, the research on Latina/o radio is instructive here (Castañeda, 2001; Castañeda Paredes, 2001, 2003; C. Rodriguez, 2001). As Latina/o radio transitions, for better or worse, from single ventures in a community to components of a national or transnational conver-gence in media industries, the level of local input, connection, and knowledge decreases. C. Rodriguez (2001) warns: "Typically, Spanish language radio stations establish a relationship with Latino com-munities based exclusively on ratings and ultimately profit-making" (pp. 129–30). In other words, we cannot assume Latina/os are the ones who own Latina/o media (Subervi and Eusebio, 2005), or that Latina/o media have Latina/o interests, whatever these may be, in mind.

This was not always the case. C. Rodriguez (2001) unearthed the stories of those who were Latina/o media brokers in early radio. Through interviews with those former brokers, Rodriguez was able to flesh out the early history of Latina/o radio in the United States. "Brokers" is a term that refers to local Latina/o people who rented a time slot, usually undesirable and unprofitable for the Anglo market, from an Anglo radio station. The broker would be in total control of the rented time, from transmission through the acquisition of com-mercial spots to fund the show. Many of them told Rodriguez that they became local celebrities among the Latina/o community, and none of them engaged in brokerage for profit. In fact, all of them had a "day job." However, the autonomy these brokers had in producing their radio shows was total, especially since the Anglo station owners and managers spoke no Spanish. This meant that they had no idea about the content being broadcast over their radio stations. Thus, for instance, in a radio station that usually broadcast Top-40 songs, the broker might fill his or her time with news about the Latina/o commu-nity, Mexican music, and advertisements for local Latina/o businesses. Brokering has been largely superseded by commercial local stations, many of which have been absorbed into national radio networks, some of which might be part of a diversified transnational media conglomerate. Latina/o Media Studies scholars have yet to explore the fate of Latina/o workers as a radio slot goes from brokering to local to national to transnational.

The jury is still out on whether Latina/o media is populated by profit-oriented, not community-involved, workers, or whether mainstream media, because of enduring barriers to entry and mobility for ethnic workers, lose much talent to ethnic media. Some suggest that Latina/o journalists, especially those with bilingual skills, find that working in Latina/o media is far more rewarding and leads to greater upward mobility within the news organization than laboring in the mainstream. L. Castañeda (2001) finds that highly trained bilingual Latina/o journalists are, in fact, moving over to bilingual or Spanish-language media. In this article, Hernandez of *La Prensa* says: "In mainstream media, you spend a lot of time explaining why something is racist or discriminatory or insulting. That's not an issue here, and it's wonderful not to have that burden." Still, some broadcast journalists, especially those on television, report lower salaries and the reproduction of Eurocentric appearance for on-air reporters. You may have noticed that one of the prime-time on-air weather reporters on the weather channel is a Latina beauty called Jennifer Lopez. CNN as well has two prime-time reporters with Latina names and beautiful light brown looks.

To add another wrinkle to this area of study, A. Rodriguez (1999) suggests that highly trained Latina/o journalists who work in making Latino news, are, in fact, quite distant from the audiences they write for. Being "college educated and professionally salaried" (p. 47) is something they share with journalists working in mainstream media but not necessarily with the bulk of the Latina/o audience. This statement makes an argument for class identification being stronger than ethnic orientation. It implies both that middle-class Latina/os abide by class rather than ethnic standards and that the working-class audience does the same. From a Latina/o Media Studies approach, this opens up a number of research possibilities that would involve both production research, somehow tracking these professional Latina/os in terms of the coverage they generate – remembering always that they are not at liberty to cover whatever they want, however they want to – and audience research to determine whether working-class audiences interpret these Latina/o communicators as distant and detached from their issues.

Clearly, issues of employment are important and embattled. At the very least, a working salary means survival and possible upward mobility. At best, the inclusion of ethnic workers in general and Latina/os in particular, as mentioned previously in this chapter, potentially means even greater employment for under-represented minorities and an expansion of the themes circulated in mainstream popular culture, possibly covered or represented in ways beyond the stereotypical tried-and-true patterns that will be discussed in the next chapter on content and representation. In terms of minority employment, while over the past few decades there has been improvement, the latest data from the National Association of Hispanic Journalists (NAHJ) reveal that more journalists of color are leaving than entering newsrooms (National Association of Hispanic Journalists, 2008). Groundbreaking scholars Wilson and Gutiérrez (1985) found that, in the early 1970s, less than 2 percent of the workforce in the mainstream press was composed of minorities. One constant factor to remember is that most of the figures include all minorities; thus it is very difficult to extrapolate which percentage of that fraction is composed of Latina/os. We can guess that in the 1970s much of that minority portion was composed of African Americans. We can hope that, as the percentage of Latina/os in the general population rises, more of that minority workforce will be composed of Latina/os. But we are extrapolating here. While there have been marked increases in the employment of minorities, these gains have to be constantly monitored as they are not guaranteed to hold. In fact, in a 2008 census of the newspaper industry, the American Society of Newspaper Editors (ASNE) documents that more journalists of color left than were replaced in the nation's newsrooms in the year 2007. The figures show minority journalists accounted for 13.52% of the news workforce, 300 less than the previous year, at 7,100. Of the 2,346 Hispanics reported in the newspaper census, their job distribution was as follows: 516 (22%) supervisors; 425 (18%) copy/layout editors; 1,055 (45%) reporters; and 349 (15%) photographers. Most of those minorities, two-thirds, were employed in larger newspapers. Minority internships,[5] another measurement by the newspaper census, were also concentrated in larger newspapers. Internships are also part of the advertising industry's efforts to diversify their workforce. The American Association of Advertising Agencies (AAAA) funds the "Multicultural Advertising Intern Program" whose slogan is "diverse minds, one passion." It must be noted that since, at the entry level in advertising, most of the workforce is female, so are the interns.[6] The fact that there is an internship program must be considered a positive step in terms of future employment. Returning to the newspaper census, regionally, minority employment was higher in the West South Central (18.15%) and Pacific (17.88%) states that include Texas and California, and lower in the West North Central States (10.20%) that include the Dakotas and Minnesota (ASNE, 2008). Such figures suggest that long-term employment gains have to be constantly protected; that regional concentrations of Latina/o population correlate to their presence in newsrooms; and that the bulk of Latina/os in the newsroom are concentrated in the reporter role, though a statistically significant portion are supervisors.

In alternative media, production matters might differ markedly from the above. Quite often, given the radically smaller budgets of non-mainstream production, an individual might function at two, or all three, roles simultaneously. In fact, with bigger budgets come increasing specialization and less control by any single individual (Citron, 1988). In other words, one sacrifices individual autonomy in the workplace for greater financial funding. Indeed, if one looks, for example, at Lourdes Portillo and Frances Negrón-Muntaner, their roles in their films were at once creative, technical, and financial. For instance, in *Lourdes Portillo: The Devil Never Sleeps* (2001), Rosa Linda Fregoso documents how, for each of her documentaries, Portillo literally mortgages her house and invests all her personal wherewithal to produce the next project. In fact, Portillo is such a firm believer in the importance of the topic that she films that she made a recent production, *Señorita extraviada* (2001), freely available on the internet for all to download and participate in some form of activism regarding the issue of missing women in the Ciudad Juarez / El Paso border towns. This is in stark contrast to capitalist tendencies to sell intellectual property for profit. Another way of funding independent and alternative work is through foundations. For instance, Frances Negrón-Muntaner is the recipient of a wide range of fellowships, such as the Ford, Truman, Scripps-Howard, and Pew, that in part have funded her films, such as *AIDS in the Barrio: eso no me pasa a mí* (1989) and *Brincando el charco* (1994). Of course, recent developments in technology make it more possible for members of the general public to produce and distribute media. Facebook, YouTube, MySpace, and other similar online websites are examples of amateur yet widely distributed media. Still we must not lose sight of the digital divide – for all of these new online communities and sites of possible dissemination for grassroots production assume access to computers, with accompanying computer literacy skills, that, as previously discussed in the introductory chapter, are not evenly available, especially to working-class ethnic minorities.

Organizational level of analysis

Moving from the individual communicator to the organizational level of analysis, we study the workplace wherein the media are produced. Here we study the specific location of the radio station, newspaper, film studio, editing lab, advertising agency, etc., where particular media are produced. So we study *Latina* magazine, the *New York Times*, CNN, Telemundo, Google, etc. We find that rules and conventions, written and unwritten, guide the production of media within the mainstream. Given that there are far more trained personnel than positions available, there is great competition for jobs in media industries. This translates into rigorously enforced rules at the workplace that could possibly be deployed in racialized ways. Thus, one of the tasks of Latina/o Media Studies scholars is to assess whether rules at the organizational level serve to privilege whiteness, especially as it overlaps with middle-classness, under their cover of professionalism. For example, one of the most cherished values in mainstream news production is "objectivity," operationalized, or defined, as some form of neutrality or "balanced" situation (Tuchman, 1972). The former implies that all are treated as equals. The latter implies that there are two sides to every story, thus precluding multifaceted issues as well as ones that might only have one side. This binary, or two-sided, operationalization of objectivity tends to throw us right back into the black-and-white national imaginary. Often Latina/os fall through the cracks. Objectivity as an organizational strategy brings up many questions. How does the news organization deal with an individual communicator's objectivity if race and ethnicity are organizationally and implicitly seen to compromise this cherished ideal? Is there a suspicion, among the top level of news organizations, that Latina/o journalists cannot be objective when it comes to Latina/o issues and people? Is there a tendency to assign Latina/o journalists only to Latina/o issues and thus clip their mobility and versatility within the organization, since these are seen as a marginal pursuit in mainstream media organizations? Some of these questions, such as whether ethnic people are assigned to the ethnic beat – the answer is "usually" – are easy to study. There is more research on minorities in general and African Americans in particular, but research that includes Latina/os in a comparative perspective needs to be conducted. In an excellent review of the literature, Subervi-Vélez (1994) references Ericksen (1981), saying that "Hispanic reporters face unwarranted challenges of their latitude and credibility as professional journalists . . . considered lacking the acumen to write about issues other than ethnic problems or strife, they are also perceived as too partial for 'objective' in depth reporting about educational, economic, or the type of policy issues of importance to their community" (p. 307). Other research questions are more difficult, if not impossible, to investigate. In the USA objectivity is a central component of a professional journalism education. If trained as a journalist, Latina/os working in the mainstream newsroom have to abide by objectivity, though they could treat the "either–or" form from a white or a Latina/o viewpoint. As you can see, the result is that whiteness is steadily privileged in such coverage and a more complex multifaceted approach might be difficult to sell to editors.

Many other decisions, in terms of planning the news, that have implications for coverage of particular groups, are made at the workplace. Dating back to the women's movement in the sixties and seventies, Tuchman (1978) also found that many journalists worked during the regular working hours of 9–5 whereas many groups, especially those composed of working-class women and minorities, can only manage to hold their meetings or events after hours. This meant they either received coverage by the second ghost-string of reporters, or no coverage at all.[7] This is an issue at the organizational level of analysis in that the way work is parsed out in relation to schedules and resources impinges on coverage of particular issues and groups, beyond the overarching value of objectivity. A follow-up of this elegant study in relation to the Latina/o category seems in order. Furthermore, these are studies carried out in relation to the print newsroom. One wonders whether the digital newsroom inherits some of these tendencies or if the 24/7 pace of all news channels makes this finding obsolete. That is, given the constantly updated nature of television and online news, does this expanded clock have implications for greater coverage of Latina/o issues, especially those in which the working class engages after regular office hours? The data on other media – radio, advertising, internet, movies, and popular music – are equally important to gather.

In relation to hiring and promotion within media industries, how do Latina/o news organizations compare to mainstream news organizations in terms of Latina/o issue coverage and treatment of Latina/os in the workforce? Clearly, asking people whether they made hiring and coverage decisions based on race and ethnicity will elicit a "no" answer as this is unethical and illegal. Similarly, one would have to either design a study that artificially compares hiring and promotion (for example by having dummy applicants participate in a study, with qualifications being equal other than race or ethnicity) or conduct longitudinal research to study promotion patterns across race and ethnic categories. The latter might be more feasible now that media industries are both (a) hiring a more diverse workforce, and (b) possibly keeping data on the diversity of their personnel (see the previously reported ASNE census). Since these data were seldom, and in some cases still are not, disaggregated according to particular ethnic groups, we would find it difficult to ascertain Latina/o discrimination in hiring. At this point in history, there is greater – though barely – employment of African American than Latina/o journalists in US newsrooms. Another two problems with these figures are that only

65.87 percent of those surveyed responded, leading one to ponder as to the employment composition of that very significant 34.13 percent – more than a third of newspapers – and that, given that so much of the media workforce is piecemeal and non-union, there would be little data on that, possibly majority, portion of the workforce. Even with all of these components, gains are not guaranteed to last. In the current period of recessionary economics, we suspect that people of color, including Latina/os, will succumb to the pattern of "last hired, first fired."

In terms of hiring and promotion, Media Studies research has shown that, for example in the newspaper industry, editors would mentor those journalists who reminded them of themselves when they were young. This formed part of the unwritten rules. Because these are unwritten, they are harder to pinpoint and eradicate. This unwritten mobility rule tended to single out for mobility in the news organization mostly white males. A resulting set of strategies, activism, and research projects was that jobs had to be posted: otherwise the word-of-mouth practice – since it made use of insider social connections – excluded many from upward mobility within media industries. In the film industry, for instance, there is widespread nepotism – the employment of people along family lines. This means that if your family does not have a presence in the business, you are less likely to be hired and promoted. Of course, in family-owned media industries – something that is becoming less of an issue in the contemporary age of conglomerates – hiring and promotions, especially at the top levels, followed family lines. All of these practices functioned as barriers to entry for Latina/os and other minorities. Previously mentioned internship programs represent yet another effort to diversify the workforce, in terms of nurturing a pool of minority applicants. Research into whether these interns are eventually hired and whether they experience mobility once in media industries remains scarce.

In the workplace, not following written and unwritten rules quite likely means, at best, truncated upward mobility and, at worst, replacement, especially as there are so many applicants for each individual job, particularly at entry levels. Thus, the rules at the organizational level immediately impinge on the degree of freedom of individual communicators. Clearly, some individual communicators at the top of the organizational chain are possibly able to change, subvert, or ignore some of these rules and conventions. Chances are, though, that they reached that high level precisely by demonstrating their adherence to organizational rules. They were promoted partly for showing that they would not challenge production conventions. Most people, singly, cannot challenge the organization – it usually takes a critical mass, with representation at different levels of the organization, and/or previous success in ethnic and/or alternative media. As well, a support network beyond media industries, in the form of a social movement or a wider social acknowledgment that there is demographic and growing political presence, is needed. This time of ascendance in terms of numbers might signal just such a moment, so that media workers can draw on the wider acceptance of Latina/os elsewhere in society.

Other media practices, such as who becomes a source and is granted standing by journalists, guide the production of news and have great relevance to eventual coverage of Latina/o issues and/or Latina/os being used as sources, either in general stories or in Latina/o-focused reports. Sources are not picked at random but are the result of careful choices that most journalists would deny have anything to do with issues of race and ethnicity. In fact, journalists cite objectivity as a workplace strategy that is defined by lack of bias, not just in writing but in selecting stories and sources as well. Ericksen (1981) found Hispanics were allowed to be authorities neither on general issues nor on issues where Hispanics have the obvious expertise. Twenty-two years later, the findings of a more recent study (Poindexter, Smith, and Heider, 2003) were not that different. In addition to a finding of nearly no Latinos as anchors, reporters, or subjects in local television news, Poindexter et al. found that Latina/os were rarely if ever interviewed as news sources. In fact, if there was any minority as a news source, it was likely to be African American. Being a source is a powerful position because that person or set of people gets to represent entire segments of the population, and coverage is about representation. A key element of research is to find out how many Latina/os are sources in the metaphorical news rolodexes, and a corollary activist strategy is to advocate for more Latina/os in that rolodex. For instance, until quite recently, the Reverend Jesse Jackson was the person that national news interviewed for "minority issues." While he is an expert on a number of issues, there might be a person more knowledgeable about issues of Latinidad on a national scale. The recently contested Democratic primaries in the USA yielded a number of Latina/o spokespeople and sources as the Latina/o vote composed one of the crucial elements in a winning political campaign. Regionally and locally, one way to assert presence would be to acquaint local newsrooms with possible sources, so that, when they run a story on Latina/os, the community has had some input into who will represent them. This would reverse one component of racialization, which is that people who are racialized are treated with less authority and as if they have less expertise, even about their own situation. This potentially translates into Latina/os not being seen as credible sources, or being seen as less credible than a dominant-culture spokesperson. Sources, objectivity, scheduling, and hiring and promotion are all components at the news workplace, or organizational, level of analysis that affect how individual workers carry out their labor and also have to be understood within the context of the institutional level of analysis. In other types of media, such as magazines, advertising, television, popular music, and film production, we have to keep in mind what types of organizational rules and conventions might impinge on or enable the labor of Latina/os, and whether these have any effect on the representation of Latina/os and Latinidad in popular culture and, in turn, any influence on how people interpret Latina/os in the media, and the social effects of this representation.

Institutional level of analysis

Institutionally, the very values and norms that guide the production of media function as a last court of appeal for the public, individual communicators, and media organizations. Some of these values are local while others are national, and indeed global. One way to differentiate between the organizational and institutional levels of analysis is to think of the former as an actual place – a building with an address, such as *Latina* magazine, at 1500 Broadway Suite 700, New York, NY 10036 – whereas the latter is more of a set of ideas that guide the production of mainstream media in general but are not really centrally enforced, at least not in civil democracies.[8] Foremost within the institutional level of analysis is a free press, something that is central to the public discourse of the USA as a nation. In the USA, at least rhetorically, freedom of expression is cherished by both media industries and the public. Yet this is a highly volatile issue as efforts to concretize freedom of expression to include gender, ethnicity, and sexuality – to name some of the main vectors of difference – have been met with resistance. In *The Racial Order of Things* (2006), Mukherjee documents how the conceptual and political background for hard-fought gains from the 1960s have, by the 1990s, been literally turned on their heads. Whereas, in the sixties, calls for freedom of expression sought to include women and minorities in the public sphere, by the nineties public discourse, with accompanying public policy measures, treats these demands as the very antithesis of freedom of expression. From an administrative perspective that foregrounds marketing for profit's sake and the survival of our present economic system, understanding market forces explains the drive for greater audiences that in turn mean higher revenues from advertisers and a more stable economy. However, as critical political economists of the media – whose work will be discussed at greater length in the following section – hold, press or media freedom as a concept in the USA and most advanced industrialized countries is operationalized in a capitalist way, so that it is protected as a profit-making mechanism – as in freedom to make profit rather than a less market-driven and democratically informed version of freedom of the people to communicate. When we integrate Latina/os into this version of freedom of the press and the media, this translates into freedom to profit from Latina/os, for Latina/os and others, rather than freedom for Latina/os to include their ideas and creativity in the press and the media. Advertising-supported media, the norm in the mainstream, respond more to the needs of advertisers than to the needs of consumers. The very use of the term "consumer" instead of "the public" or "citizen," for instance, reveals how the profit motive, more than democratic principles, rules media production. Supporters of the market system argue that the press and the media maintain independence from government manipulation, thus reiterating the historical and philosophical roots that undergird so much of Western media policy development. Yet critical scholars counter that the potential for intervention from marketers and others who fund commercial media is great. Certainly, whenever you see the concept of "free press," you ought to ask "freedom for what?" and "freedom from/for whom?" The answers to these questions will yield much insight into the value of democracy in general, and of ethnic and Latina/o inclusion in particular. If diversity, in terms of ethnicity, is not a value at the institutional level of analysis, in terms of core beliefs, this has huge implications for the organizational level of analysis wherein media are produced, and for individual communicators who contribute to that production. The concept of "diversity" is the umbrella term that includes issues of difference in media policy and mainstream Media Studies. Indeed, under freedom at a structural/institutional level of analysis, McQuail (2005) lists three components: independence of channels, access to channels, and *diversity of content* which should lead to reliability and choice (p. 195, emphasis mine).

Diversity has historically been pursued within particular laws and regulations on US media. The public interest standard, a major component of broadcasting history in the United States, forms the basis for a claim of diversity in broadcasting. Given that broadcasting makes use of a public good, the electromagnetic spectrum – that is, the air we breathe – the Federal Communication Commission (FCC) since 1934 has granted broadcasting licenses on a local basis, "to serve the public interest." However, the history and current status of this public interest standard does not bode well for issues of diversity in broadcasting. Wible (2004, quoting Streeter, 1996) reminds us that "most appeals to 'the public interest' now are virtually ineffective" (p. 35). A long history of the "public interest" being defined as defending elite tastes or as lack of technical interference came to a hopeful moment in the late 1960s when the Kerner Commission suggested an increase in minority hiring, but not the more radical step of minority owner-ship. The development of cable as a parallel delivery option moved much of this minority production momentum into that new area of content delivery, while it simultaneously adopted the notion of the citizen as customer and the model of integration of minorities into mainstream production that reifies the types of economic arrange-ments that favor large industrial conglomerates. In this spirit, an FCC Minority Ownership Taskforce report asserted: "Unless minorities are encouraged to enter the mainstream of the commercial broadcast-ing business, a substantial proportion of our citizenry will remain underserved and the larger, non-minority audience will be deprived of the views of minorities" (Wible, 2004, p. 40). While these policies and reports potentially opened a space for media activists to make an intervention into the production of more diverse content and the hiring of a more diverse workforce, the impulse was integrationist and mainstreaming. Rather than supporting minority-owned and -produced media, this taskforce redirected efforts toward conglom-erates in the mainstream as the only viable option. Nonetheless, through this small window for making diversity claims, Latina/o media scholars and activists can appeal to the institutional level of analysis and the concept of diversity under the public interest stand-ard to make claims for representation in content and the labor force within media industries.

Mainstream media, which value objectivity at the institutional level, linking it to the "free press" notion through concepts of balance, deploy this value organizationally and at the individual level. Ethnic and Latina/o media have to assert the value of ethnicity while they also value objectivity. There is also an additional set of values that guides their existence and production: cultural resistance to main-stream media; cultural preservation, of whatever community they represent; and accommodation to the dominant society, especially if they are commercially supported, as they must get funding from advertising revenues as much as, if not more than, from subscription (A. Rodriguez, 1999, p. 11). Ethnic media occupy a third space that is difficult to maintain, because pulls from both sides lure them into the mainstream or into a more radical position. Alternative media might eschew the profit component and any semblance of objectiv-ity, especially if they propose a non-capitalist form of production. Yet in a situation of very small non-profit funding for such ventures, especially during an economic crisis, these media survive, if at all, on a shoestring. The communities they seek to represent are seldom wealthy enough on their own to support such production.

Political economy

Within Media Studies, the institutional level of analysis has most fruitfully been pursued by an absolutely essential political economy approach. In fact, we cannot understand how media are produced outside of this area of scholarship. Political economists extend diversity as a structural value to issues of ownership and control. Who owns the media? Do ownership and control of the media influence content and how workers orient their creativity? If there is such influence, can we say there is such a thing as a "free" press or media? In their highly influential propaganda model, Chomsky and Herman (1988) list five filters that, at the institutional level, guide media production: sources, advertising, flak, profit motive, and anti-communism.[9] As an unmentioned filter, usually missing from political economy scholarship, we might add gender, race, and ethnicity or white privilege, to complicate the economic with cultural aspects of identity, just as influential in the production of media (Lipsitz, 1998). Also, after 9/11, we have to add anti-terrorism to the fifth filter of anti-communism. Both of these additions have implications for Latina/os as a racialized component of the population whose skin surface appearance overlaps with the brown of the perceived terrorist. Moreover, immigration and border discourses have been collapsed into the terrorism paradigm so that, often, Latina/os crossing the border are treated as potential terrorists.

Obviously, foregrounding ownership as important implicitly suggests that ownership impinges on the way industries are run *and* the types of content that are widely available. Political economists and sociologists of the news and other production spaces of culture and the media have documented the low levels of ownership and control among both women and people of color, nationally and globally. At this broader level of political economy analysis of institutional values and ownership, we find that the mainstream media are owned by a small number of transnational conglomerates whose extensive media and other industry holdings allow them not only to engage in extensive profit-maximizing strategies of synergy and convergence, but also to present nearly insurmountable barriers to entry to other possible players in the global media game. In layperson's terms, how can an independent Latina/o television enterprise, perhaps supported by regional business investment with regional Latina/o products advertised, compete with Telemundo with its transnational media conglomerate backing? Thus, the competition so central to common sense perspectives of capitalism is not necessarily present in this area of the global economy[10] where we find the opposite: consolidation and monopoly tendencies. The shift to transnational capital is important as it allows for the participation of Latin American players, such as Televisa (Mexico) and TV Globo (Brazil), that are relevant to Latina/o Media Studies as they engage, compete, and sometimes supersede each other in the production and distribution of Latina/o content and employment of Latina/o labor. Whereas Jeremy Tunstall in 1977 could write a book entitled *The Media are American* because the USA was such a dominant participant in global media industries, by 2008 the revised update of that book is entitled *The Media Were American: US Mass Media in Decline*. By mid-2008, Latin American conglomerates had made significant investment in US Hispanic media, which had been increasing for over a decade and influenced both content about and employment of US Latina/os (A. Rodriguez, 1999; Sinclair, 1999). Political economic dimensions of the study of production must be taken up in the pursuit of Latina/o Media Studies as they largely explain what is available as well as the difficulties of intervening into the production of media and popular culture in our times. In fact, as in the rest of this book, the study of Latina/o media production is highly instructive for, and indicative of, larger global forces at play. What is happening to Latina/o media and Latina/o labor within media industries, in terms of ownership and control in the transnational setting of neo-liberal economic policies, is but an indication of global forces that affect or potentially threaten all workers in media production.

Trends toward transnational conglomerates serve to caution us to remember that a form of media being bilingual or in Spanish does not mean that it operates outside of market forces or transnational capital. That would be confusing language with economics. For the media conglomerate, as the demographic data show increasing numbers of Latina/os in the USA, the mere aggregate numbers of this audience augur well for market-driven media production. The additional fact that many members of the Latina/o audience have significant disposable income further increases the lure to try to market media products to reach them. The hipness and marketability of Latinidad, accomplished with or without Latina/o bodies, adds another wrinkle to the temptations of Latina/o media production. As the combined promise of these realizations reaches global media conglomerates, many of which are partly US-owned, the ownership and control of Latina/o media have shifted from Latina/o-owned and/ or -operated media to transnational and conglomerate ownership and control with hired Latina/o help, at best, and contrived homogeneous production by professional media personnel without much knowledge of Latina/o culture, at worst. Content diversity and local input often decrease as a result of transnational conglomeratization (Castañeda Paredes, 2003).

Because of their shared use of the electromagnetic spectrum, broadcasting of radio and television has, at least in the USA, been regulated by the same federal body since 1934, the FCC, and in their commercial manifestation they were originally held in a near-duopoly form by NBC and CBS, later to be joined by ABC when the Department of Justice (DOJ) found NBC Red and NBC Blue to be in violation of monopoly regulations.[11] In the past few decades, the advent of satellite effectively transformed local stations TNN and WGN into national superstations through their inclusion in basic cable packages, and thus unsettled the triopoly held by the three networks. The large-scale deployment of cable technology and internet networks now competes with the previous nearly guaranteed large audience shares once held by the three major networks, and potentially opens a space for increased diversity. Yet the increased availability of channels has not translated into increased diversity of ownership and control of media industries. In the contemporary global media climate of synergy and convergence, corporate owners hold radio and television stations as well as cable and internet properties. Many, if not most, of the increased available channels are absorbed into transitional conglomerate ownership. It must be noted that neither cable nor internet comes under the jurisdiction of the FCC, as neither of them makes use of the spectrum. Nonetheless, these technologies are entwined, not only in ownership but also in distribution networks, as cable packages include over-the-air broadcasting, and both radio and television can be downloaded on the internet. It is in this ownership and technological climate that we need to examine the rise of Spanish-language radio and television networks in the United States, with the rise of Univisión and SIN, later called Telemundo, being the most prominent.

Spanish radio stations number around 600 (Castañeda Paredes, 2003; C. Rodriguez, 2001; Subervi and Eusebio, 2005). Univisión is the largest Latino radio network. Clearly, Spanish-language radio is growing by leaps and bounds and not necessarily just in the traditional markets of the Southwest and the Northeast, but in places in the new Latino South, such as North Carolina. Formats and genres range from all sorts of music-specific stations – from Mexican, Texan, *norteña*, salsa and merengue, and *rock en español* – to news or sports stations, many of them with a much broader international perspective than mainstream English-language radio. Castañeda Paredes (2003) argues that, in addition to market forces responding to the demographic increase in the Latina/o population, two additional components must be studied: the growth of Spanish radio stations in non-traditional Latina/o markets and the consolidation of radio stations by Spanish-language media conglomerates (p. 6). The latter, all scholars agree, is part of a wider trend of consolidation in the broadcasting industry brought about by the Telecommunications Act of 1996, which allowed greater concentration of ownership and has resulted in larger conglomerates and fewer voices. This outcome primarily wipes out much of local input and programming, which historically had been a mainstay of Latina/o radio. As a consequence, Aparicio (1998) noted that the oligopolistic shifts in Latino radio have changed "listening practices of Hispanic audiences" (p. 94).

However, there are still some community radio stations left that continue to serve local needs. For example, a study by Graciela Orozco found that community radio was used as a mobilization tool during the immigration rallies of 2006. Especially, she found that Radio Bilingüe was important for "community discourse, outreach and organizing" (Social Science Research Council, 2007). Four themes accomplished these strategies: "¡Latinos unidos!"; "¡A organizarce!"; "¡Ya basta!"; and "What's happening?" Listeners felt united and empowered in expressing their opinions. Orozco underscores the importance of community radio as an organizational, activist, political, and cultural information tool. Chances are that the local case study carried out by Orozco could be replicated in many other communities. Radio being a portable, cheap, and non-literacy- or electricity-dependent media technology makes it an absolutely essential component of Latina/o media research and activism. Production of radio programming remains fairly accessible. It is no coincidence that, throughout the world, radio provides a key communication tool for a range of otherwise disenfranchised communities.

Television is an important component of a media diet, especially in the USA where saturation rates exceed 99 percent. Like mainstream television, Spanish-language television is organized in networks. In the USA, Univisión and Telemundo reach 97 and 91 percent of the US Spanish-speaking Latina/o households, respectively. This does not mean that all that is broadcast in those channels is produced in the United States, but that these channels target the Latina/o audience with whatever programming they can get their hands on. Merger mania, abetted by the Telecommunications Act of 1996, which allowed higher concentration of ownership, resulted in consolidation of Spanish television channels. While radio and television are historically owned by the same company in mainstream media, this was not necessarily the case in Latina/o media. That is, the NBC and CBS radio history, of radio ownership transitioning into television networks, was not replicated for Latina/o radio transitioning into Latina/o television.

Telemundo began in 1986, not as a product of Latina/o capital but through two media industry investors, Saul Steinberg and Henry Silverman of Reliance Capital Group, who saw a market niche under-represented by the mainstream. The original network, very similar to the *Chicago Tribune*'s incipient newspaper chain of *Hoy* newspapers, was brought together out of stations in New York, Los Angeles, and Miami, the locations of major Puerto Rican / Dominican, Mexican American, and Cuban American populations, respectively. On a sales graph that documents the increasing value of Latina/o media, Sony bought the network in 1998 for $539 million and, four years later, in 2002, NBC paid $2.7 billion for it (Journalism.org, 2004). As of 2008, Telemundo owned 15 stations and had 32 affiliates. Of note is the fact that mainstream capital investment undergirds this network as it merges with major global media conglomerates. Sony is one of these, with huge holdings in global entertainment ventures, ranging from motion pictures to hardware, popular music, and television. In 2004, NBC was acquired by GE, also one of the five largest corporations in the world, which owns, in addition to English- and Spanish-language radio and television networks in the United States, film and amusement park holdings as well as appliance and military products manufacturers. As you can see, Telemundo is part and parcel of transnational capital. It would not have attracted investors' attention and have been acquired by them if it had not demonstrated that there was an audience, with an identifiable set of products and services to be marketed to them, to make such a media venture profitable. Currently, Telemundo is the only one of the two Spanish networks producing telenovelas within the USA. Additionally, Telemundo sometimes provides English captioning in its Spanish programming, thus appealing to a more assimilated and upwardly mobile audience (Levine, 2001).

Similarly, Univisión began in 1961 as a small station in San Antonio, was purchased in 1992 from Hallmark by a consortium of buyers, and today reigns as the no. 1 Spanish-language television network in the USA, though Telemundo's audience is almost as large. As of 2008, Univisión owned 50 stations and had 43 affiliates. Its most popular programs come from Televisa in Mexico, Es Television in Puerto Rico, and Venevision in Venezuela. That means much of the production and content broadcast by this network is produced in and by Latin Americans. In 2002 Univisión proposed merging with the Hispanic Broadcasting Corporation, then the largest owner of Spanish-language radio stations. The Spanish Broadcasting System (SBC) sued, arguing that HBC-Clear Channel would prevent SBC from entering Latina/o markets. In 2006 the company was yet again sold for $12.3 billion, this time to a consortium led by TGP Capital, in a deal which left Univisión with a low cashflow-to-debt ratio. Like Telemundo, though not included in the top rung of transnational conglomerate capital, Univisión is part of contemporary global media consolidation, which means that fewer and fewer hands are controlling Spanish-language broadcasting, and much of the financial impetus is not in Latina/o hands. As with all media, when not owned independently but by a transnational conglomerate, the tendency is to develop chain pro-gramming, import cheap content, answer to stockholders rather than ethnic communities, take fewer risks, not conduct much audience research (as that cuts into corporate returns), and deploy formulaic approaches. This takes us right back to the findings by A. Rodriguez (1999), Castañeda (2001), and Dávila (2001), mentioned elsewhere in this chapter, that absorption of ethnic media into commercial net-works changes the content, input, and audience of ethnic media in general, and Latina/o media in particular.

In newspapers, we find similar developments. The circulation of Spanish-language dailies went from 140,000 copies in 1970 to 1.7 million in 2002; the number of Spanish-language newspapers has roughly tripled since 1990, from 232 to over 600. Ad revenues for these dailies have grown more than seven-fold in the same time period. All of these elements make Latina/o newspapers more alluring proper-ties for transnational capital (Journalism.org, 2004). In contrast, the circulation of English-language newspapers has steadily decreased since 1999. In what Castañeda (2001) calls the "remapping of Latina audiences" (p. 57), not only is the number of Spanish dailies increas-ing but also there "are presently thousands of weekly and monthly community oriented publications that serve local Latina/o readers in the United States" (p. 53). She adds that so alluring is the Spanish-language press that major mainstream English-language newspapers have launched parallel Spanish-language versions: *Al Día*, *La Estrella*, and *El Republicano* are versions of their respective English-language counterparts, the *Dallas Morning News*, *Star Telegram*, and the *Republican* (p. 53). Moreover, the relaxation of consolidation regulation has resulted in mergers within Spanish-language newspapers such as that of *La Opinión* and *El Diario / La Prensa* which combined in 2004 into one nation-wide newspaper chain, ImpreMedia (p. 54). Not to be outdone, mainstream media are also constructing chains, such as the *Chicago Tribune*'s launching of three newspapers named *Hoy*, in New York City, Chicago, and Los Angeles, to capture the audience in those major Latina/o markets. In fact, mainstream media now regularly include Latina/o sections and have begun to consider the Latina/o audience as part of the mainstream in some regions of the country.

As with news production in the mainstream, radio, television, and internet have become important sites of Latina/o-market news circu-lation. Not surprisingly, both Telemundo and Univisión have growing news bureaus, with the latter still ahead in this area as well.

The most extensive study on Latina/o news is America Rodriguez's

The Making of Latino News (1999). Her findings, among others, show that Latina/o news simultaneously denationalizes Latin Americans while it renationalizes them as US Hispanics. The Latina/o audience is conceived of as "racially non-White, linguistically Spanish speaking, and socio-economically poor." Her findings about the producers of Latina/o news are quite similar to those in Arlene Dávila's *Latinos, Inc.: The Marketing and Making of a People* (2002) – that is, the construction of a whitened pan-ethnic Latino is carried out by a transnational workforce that is not necessarily representative of the audience they construct, and then try to reach, through their media. Since the main product of advertising-supported media, dating back to Dallas Smythe's "blind spot" argument, is the audience that is being bought and sold in the marketplace, Rodriguez and Dávila emphasize that the Latina/o audience is an abstraction created in order to reach a segment of the population with a particular set of products.

Another medium that is widely available and fairly inexpensive to purchase, if not necessarily to produce, is the magazine. While the history of magazines is long and extensive, dating back at least a couple of centuries, for our purposes we need to know that the industry has evolved into a venue for reaching a broad audience – as in something like *Time* magazine – and also as a way to reach smaller yet committed target audiences with specific product and service needs, as in *Walking* magazine. As a preferred way to reach niche audiences, Latina/o magazines also exist in abundance. There are magazines such as *Latina*, *Hispanic Business*, *Selecciones del Reader's Digest en Español*, *National Geographic en Español*, *People en Español*, *Hispanic*, *Quince Girl*, *Playboy en Español*, etc. This very incomplete list demonstrates that not only the interests, but also the proven spending power, of at least a noticeable segment of the Latina/o population have generated both Latina/o capital ventures and transnational capital attempts to reach the Latina/o audience. The list also suggests a parallel development with mainstream magazines. That is, there are generalist magazines such as *People en Español* and more targeted ones, for example to adult women – *Latina* – or to teen Latinas – *Quince*. The number of Spanish-language magazines has nearly doubled since 1990, from 177 to 352. Yet, as with other forms of media, not all Latina/o magazines are Spanish-language or Spanish-dominant. Something like *Latina*, which claims to be bilingual, is much more in English than in Spanish (see chapter 3, "Audience and reception"). On the other hand, *People en Español* is fully in Spanish and focuses on Latina/o celebrities and Latina/o popular-culture matters. Nonetheless, there are magazines for women, girls, men, general audiences, business audiences, etc. Judging from the increase in available options, the Latina/o audience with middle-class levels of disposable income must be large enough to support most of these magazines, thus belying dominant narratives that all Latina/os are working-class. Most of these magazines are not free-standing enterprises. Like other media, many of the more successful ones form part of, or are derivative offshore of, mainstream versions owned by larger conglomerates. *Latina* magazine, for instance, is owned by CVVV. Yet, given their much more targeted audience, even those magazines owned by non-Latina/o enterprises hire Latina/o individual communicators and cover Latina/o topics, news makers, and celebrities. Additionally, as is to be expected, many of the Latina/o magazines cover Latin American and Peninsular topics, thereby providing a much more global and cosmopolitan fare than mainstream magazines.

Another area for mainstream production of Latinidad is the internet. When it was still a newer form of media, the internet had quite a bit of variety of ownership and production values. Thus it contains a wide range of Latina/o-oriented blogs, companies, and media ventures. While some prominent Latino websites have folded, including Quepasa.com and Latino.com, some mainstream sites are adding "Latin" flavor. Washingtonpost.com, for example, publishes a column by Univisión television reporter Marcela Sanchez, called "Desde Washington," in English and Spanish. Given that much of the internet has become a huge shopping center, one can find a huge range of Latina/o products and services, ranging from foodstuffs to Latina prostitutes and maids. Convergence in media industries means that on the web one can find cyber versions of all the previously mentioned media: newspapers, radio, television, magazines, etc. While similar in content, the internet allows for expanded capacity. Thus, archived images from the entirety of a magazine's existence are easily accessible. Likewise, one can search for news topics and the latest on breaking news of entertainment and hard news on Latina/os. It is hard to determine whether the labor force in many of these websites includes Latina/os, though something like perezhilton.com is at the very least spearheaded by a gay Latino who makes no pretense of either his ethnicity or his sexual orientation. For community and culturally grounded website coverage, one would think that someone embedded in Latinidad would generate such content.

Historically, different media resided with different owners. Other than radio and television, the latter of which develops out of the former, media industries such as film and popular music were parallel but separate enterprises. Nowadays, the film and popular music industries are huge and largely intertwined with each other as well as with other media such as broadcasting, cable, magazines, the internet, etc. While in film production Hollywood has been a hegemonic force for at least the last century, popular music production is rather more geographically dispersed. However, as previously mentioned, global media consolidation includes both of these industries, and thus major popular music artists such as Shakira and movie stars such as Jennifer Lopez work for and through the consolidated conglomerates. Their production and circulation is facilitated by these connections. Shakira is an instructive example as she crossed over into the USA, from her Colombian *rockera* career, through the Estefan machine located in Miami, Florida (Cepeda, 2003a, b). There, Emilio and Gloria Estefan function as a veritable entry and conversion point for Latin American popular music talent. This element of reconstruction is an important part of the production of Latina/o popular music. Artists are instructed not only in the English language but also in a sense of US mainstream aesthetics that will translate their Latin American popularity into one that appeals to the US Latina/o market, or, even better in terms of marketing, to the US mainstream. Once through Miami, Shakira became a Latina pop star who was then further marketed globally so that she ended up performing at the 2006 World Cup, a truly global event.

In terms of popular music, inclusion of new genres challenges industry values at the institutional levels of analysis. The values and norms that guide production in the music industry include standards as to what counts as music. These standards can, at least initially, serve as barriers to entry to newcomers with musical styles that may not get recognized as "music." Musical genres such as reggaeton encounter resistance within Latinidad as well as the mainstream – much like hip hop more than two decades ago.[12] One site of struggle has been the Latin Music Grammies, wherein the industry effort to characterize, categorize, and organize "Latin" music has met with some Latin artist input that the music industry may not have bargained for. Focusing primarily on "tropical" genres such as salsa and merengue, while acknowledging these other genres, has also slighted arguably more popular Mexican American music, such as *ranchera* and *norteña* music. The numbers of the audience for the latter are much greater than for the former. However, the disposable income of the former, as well as the crossover potential of the tropical into the mainstream, are larger. Even within tropical music, there has been both acceptance and resistance to reggaeton. Production of popular music is highly creative and potentially lucrative. The reception of such cultural forms, because it speaks to issues of community identity and formation, is inevitably embattled.

Contemporarily, popular music is distributed through new technologies such as the internet and MP3 players as well as through movies. Soundtrack placement is very important to the circulation of mainstream popular music. Latina/o musical artists and genres compose part of the mainstream and ethnic media. As such they appear in both

Hollywood and indie films. The indie global hit and Best Picture winner at the 2009 Oscars, *Slumdog Millionaire* (2008), ended with a Bollywood song in Spanish, thus combining the Latina/o aesthetic with the Indian, the British, and the global. The convergence with the movie industry and with global networks also has to include the huge gaming industry, whose size and profitability rival those of the popular music and film industries combined. The production of video and digital games is not carried out by the usual suspects but recent research into labor farming (Nakamura, 2009a) suggests that, in the gaming industry, we see a developing distinction between those who labor in games and those who play them for pleasure and leisure. This has implications for Latina/o labor in the gaming industry. There is clearly a need for more research into this new medium from a Latina/o Studies perspective.

Conclusion

This chapter began with many questions, some of which can be pursued by the study of production of the media – a research area that provides theoretical and methodological tools to explore how and why certain media are made. This chapter presented the research that combines the study of the production of media with issues brought up by Latina/o Studies. The presence of Latina/os who work in media industries in concert with the growing Latina/o audience and their increasing spending power – something that is absolutely essential in mainstream media driven by profit – means that the study of production is dynamic, complex, and ongoing. Given that media workers must balance the tensions between agency, their own input, culture, and identity against structure, and the institutional and organizational constraints – conventions in the workplace as well as norms and values of the media industry – Latina/o presence in the production of media can be said both to make a difference in some cases and to make less of a difference in others. Moving up the professional ladder helps in achieving greater degrees of agency. When Montecsuma Esparza and Jennifer Lopez achieve a degree of success, they can have more of a say in what they do, as well as intervene into media production. Esparza began as a pioneer in Chicano short films, but by the time he moved over to Hollywood production he was able to facilitate the production of big budget films with Latina/o actors and content. Similarly, Gloria Estefan began as one of the members of the Miami Sound Machine, a Cuban émigré musical group, but by the time she branched out as a successful crossover solo artist, and then in partnership with her husband managed incoming talent from Latin America, she had great power over the definition of popular "Latin" music. Having more numbers in these industries is also a development that opens up creative possibilities. Nonetheless, it is undeniable that there is a growing Latina/o media industry and that Latina/os as a percentage of the media workforce are making some inroads, though these cannot be taken for granted. It remains to be seen – though there are many hopeful signs – whether these two forces can change the way that media are produced and therefore make the media more diverse and amenable to social justice goals.

The production of media includes the production of new social and cultural categories. Therefore, the category "Latina/os" has to be produced. A set of signifiers or markers has to be gathered, an audience has to be identified and also produced so as to market both the media products and the products advertised therein. The production of this category, "Latina/os," comes from both within Latinidad and without. Further components of the production of this category will be examined in the following chapters on content and representation, audience and reception, and effects. In mainstream popular culture, it is difficult to determine whether Latina/o media are actually produced by Latina/o talent and/or Latina/o capital. This is indicative of an economy wherein the production of something is obfuscated from the circulation and aura of the final product.

Case study no. 1[13]

"The Homicide Report": the *Los Angeles Times* chronicles LA County homicide victims

The mass media have a liberatory and democratic potential. That they have largely become part and parcel of a process of global conglomeration and that their incessant production schedule – daily for newspapers – compels them to develop stringent production rules to fill a limited amount of column space does not mean that there aren't moments and spaces for that liberatory and democratic potential to be explored and applied. As well, committed individual communicators seek ways to try to make a difference. As the internet, in a sense, expands news beyond the limits of the printed page, it is only logical that it could be used to fulfill that potential. One such instance is "The Homicide Report" in the *Los Angeles Times*. On January 31, 2007, the blog was introduced by a reporter as an effort to have in one column a record of the weekly number of homicides in Los Angeles County, as reported to the LA Coroner. Given the size of Los Angeles County – over 4,000 square miles – and the large number of police jurisdictions – 89 municipalities – few of which coordinate crime statistics, the blog was introduced as follows:

Overwhelmed by the sheer volume, the Los Angeles Times, like other major media organizations, covers only a fraction of the more than 1,000 murders in Los Angeles County each year. Many violent deaths become, in essence, private homicides – catastrophic on a small scale, invisible on a broader one.

   Starting with this week's homicide report, however, The Times will list all homicides reported to the Los Angeles County coroner, plus additional information gleaned from street and law enforcement sources. This week's list is larger than usual because of a January crime wave, but otherwise fairly typical in terms of the ages and ethnicities of those killed and the manner of their deaths.

> *(http://latimesblogs.latimes.com/homicidereport/2007/01/index.html,*
> *retrieved April 28, 2008)*

In a further attempt to explain the blog, the *Los Angeles Times* explicitly mentioned limits on the production of media and the press as they affect their coverage of daily deaths:

> Selective news coverage is a practical necessity for most news organizations operating in a county where nearly 1,100 people die from homicide yearly. The Los Angeles Times, for example, is limited by the number of pages it prints, and in a recent year, found room for stories on fewer than 10% of L.A. County homicides, according to an analysis by a Times researcher. Such selectivity ensures that the people and places most affected by homicides are least likely to be seen, while the safest people are inundated with information about crimes unlikely to ever touch their lives. . . . With The Homicide Report, however, the Times seeks to exploit the advantages of the web to eliminate selectivity in homicide coverage and give readers a more complete picture of who dies from homicide, where, and why – thus conveying both the personal story and the statistical story with greater accuracy.

> *(http://latimesblogs.latimes.com/homicidereport/2007/02/welcome_to_the_.*
> *html, retrieved April 28, 2008)*

Thus began a blog that documented not only the violence in the county of Los Angeles, but also the particular communities and ethnic composition of the over 1,000 homicide cases each year. This blog is an important case study as it illustrates how one crime reporter, Jill Loevy, can intervene as an individual communicator and, through the blogosphere, not the prestigious front page, provide a voice and a space for that which does not receive much coverage in the mainstream press: the daily death toll among, mostly, the underprivileged. She says:

> "Your basic mission as a journalist, you bear witness, you see things that are unseen, . . . It's sort of awful to think of people being murdered and nobody seeing it."

> *(http://edition.cnn.com/2008/CRIME/04/18/homicide.blogger/index.html,*
> *retrieved April 28, 2008)*

Collecting information from official – the coroner and the police – and unofficial sources – the communities from which the dead come – Loevy challenged many of the established unwritten rules at the organizational level of production. In 2008, a year after her arduous work, Loevy was replaced by Ruben Vives, who is now listed as the official blogger on the *Los Angeles Times* website. Notice that the original reporter, Jill Loevy, was not Latina/o, underscoring her professional journalistic ethic as the reason for engaging in the activities that gave birth to "The Homicide Report." Her replacement, however, is Latino, perhaps decided by the *Times* in order to adhere more closely to established notions of authenticity, matching the ethnicity of the reporter to the story. One wonders if Mr. Vives's mobility in the newsroom will be enhanced by this assignment as Ms. Loevy's was. One further wonders whether a dominant-culture reporter is rewarded for venturing into "ethnic" coverage by promotion, whereas an ethnic reporter is expected to engage and remain in ethnic coverage.

The blog has generated much attention. It has become a resource for the police for a number of reasons. It provides a more or less comprehensive report of homicide across jurisdictions so that the police can spot trends, perhaps even the presence of a serial killer. Moreover, local communities have many reasons not to trust the police, and sometimes Loevy has been able to collect more information than would have been shared with the police, who list "normal office hours" as when they can be reached. As this chapter has noted, "normal office hours" presumes a middle-class work schedule and leaves out many who work nights and weekends or who cannot take time off in "normal office hours" to talk to the police. "The Homicide Report" has also spotlighted the racialized composition of homicides in Los Angeles. It has spurred academics and politicians to take note, analyze, and engage in some form of proactive measures. The report has generated the production of academic knowledge, as evidenced by this discussion. As well, it has made Loevy, and now Vives, news items themselves – the news are covering the news.

Case study no. 2

Jennifer Lopez

Jennifer Lopez represents a type of rags-to-riches success story. From her Nuyorican roots in the Bronx, she has risen to be the preeminent Latina star and celebrity of the moment. Parlaying her personal success into a brand, and thus turning her fame into a synergistic set of products that can be marketed across a range of arenas, Jennifer

Lopez has managed to turn her Latinidad into a marketable commodity. As such, she has produced herself into a brand – Jennifer Lopez is an individual communicator who works in both a creative and a financial capacity.

To begin with, Jennifer Lopez had to challenge the unwritten rule, in celebrity media, that representation of women in the mainstream had to involve women with small hips and very small behinds. One can only imagine the many magazine editors and film and video producers who wondered what to do with her image as it violated that unwritten convention of mainstream media representation of women. The size of her *derrière* challenged acceptable ideals of beauty in the mainstream. The fact that she got started in ethnic media – on the show *In Living Color* and as a back-up dancer for Janet Jackson on tour – suggests that these forms of media can sometimes contribute to changing standards in the mainstream, which may or may not be long-lasting. Still, her breakthrough role came as she played the main role in *Selena* (1997), and through the dead body of the Tejana star she crossed over into the mainstream (Paredez, 2002).

Jennifer's choices of media vehicles broadened her potential audience as she appeared in mainstream, Latina/o, and African American media. Her musical career in light hip hop and her movie career as an ambiguous ethnic increased her success and therefore her agency as an individual communicator. As she sought to expand her media and marketing reach, she developed synergistic products such as perfume lines and fashion. In both of these ventures, she created high-cost and more accessible products. As she gained notoriety and thus attracted more funding, she began to produce music and film. Her collaboration with her current spouse Marc Anthony has produced *El Cantante* (2006), a biopic about Hector Lavoe, "the King of Salsa," and a movie, *Bordertown* (2007), about the Ciudad Juarez / El Paso femicides. She has also produced a television mini-series, *Como ama una mujer* (2007), for Univisión. All of these productions focus on Latina/o themes and people and employ a wide range of Latina/o actors and other individual communicators. Jennifer Lopez is an individual communicator who, through her rise to success, has managed to intervene into the production of mainstream media and diversify the content available there, as well as to increase employment of Latina/o actors, musical talent, and overall Latina/o media workers. Her ability to garner audiences in the forms of movie-goers and popular music consumers has generated the profits that in turn allow her to engage in production and circulation of a wide range of products, beyond the media, but always circulated through the media. Jennifer Lopez is a paradigmatic individual communicator whose ascendance in popularity makes her an ideal case study in Latina/o Media Studies.

CHAPTER 2

Textual/content analysis

C AN you remember the last few times you saw Latina/os and/or Latinidad in any form of media or popular culture? Maybe at the movies you saw that Christmas 2008 release *Nothing like the Holidays*? Or have you been keeping up with the gossip about Jennifer Lopez and Marc Anthony's marriage and their twins? Or do you occasionally watch reruns of the *George Lopez Show* nightly on television's "Nick at Night?" Or do you like to listen and dance to reggaeton music and follow Ivy Queen as your favorite? Or when you read a magazine, do you keep encountering ads for products by El Paso and Ortega that represent Latina/o-looking families? Or are you driving by a billboard where the little girl on it looks Latina? These are all examples of the presence and representation of Latina/os in contemporary popular culture.

Of course, Latina/os are also present in the more realist genres of news and documentaries. Whether you pay attention to Latina/o or mainstream news, chances are that you have come across some Latina/o themes and/or Latina/o people and bodies. People are identifiable, and bodies are more anonymous but no less recognizable, as Latina/os in some cases. Within the news there are whole topics which are linked to Latina/os, such as immigration, and, increasingly, we have the minimal inclusion of Latina/os in general news topics, ranging from political elections to the economy. The fact that general themes and minimal inclusion represent Latina/os is a finding and advance in itself.

Out of all areas of Media Studies scholarship, content and representation analysis is by far the area in which there is the most research on Latina/os and/in the media. While content is the most accessible, it is also perceived as easy to study. After all, we consume so much media, voluntarily and involuntarily, from a very early age that it is understandable that so many of us feel like experts. Scholars study content and representation for a number of reasons, which differ depending on the theoretical framework that guides their work. To begin with, content is the most easily available piece of evidence in any relationship between people and the media. Everyone has access to media content – whether they want it or not. Whereas it might be difficult to find and study people as audiences or to set up an experimental and control group for an effects research project, and where it is in fact undeniably difficult to gain access to media industries and producers and study issues of hiring and promotion in the workplace, anyone can pick up a newspaper, buy a DVD, download a video or song, open up a website, play a digital game, or walk or drive by a billboard. In fact media messages are difficult to avoid, especially as formerly "public" spaces are becoming increasingly saturated by commercial and generalized media messages. Think of bus stops in major cities, public transportation, and the check-out lanes at the contemporary supermarket where a television monitor is activated by your presence. In all of these, Latina/os and Latinidad are likely to appear, such as Eva Longoria selling a cosmetic product, *Desperate Housewives* and *The L-word* peering at you from a bus shelter, or the Latina/o family on a bus poster.

You certainly do not have to go out of your way to experience media content, though some forms of content might be more difficult to find than others. What is available might not necessarily overlap with your interests or needs. For example in the inner US city, billboards of both African Americans and Latina/os consuming alcoholic drinks are plentiful, but those same residents who cannot help but walk, drive, or ride by these messages might have a far more difficult time accessing the internet or finding movies and/or informational materials about their country of origin or the health ramifications of alcohol consumption. Alaniz and Wilkes (1995) found that there are five times more alcohol advertisements in Latino neighborhoods than in predominantly white neighborhoods. Notably, Latino neighborhoods contained significantly more beer and wine billboards (23 percent) than White (6 percent), African American Black (5 percent), or Asian American (4 percent) communities (Altman, Schooler, and Basil, 1991). Although limited research exists examining the placement and frequency of alcohol advertisements, a 1998 survey conducted by the Los Angeles City Planning Department found that 80 percent of the billboards in their Los Angeles sample were within five blocks of a school and 7 percent of the 131 could be seen from the schools. Of those billboards visible from the schools, 80 percent showed alcohol advertisements (Mastro and Atkin, 2002). This is a concrete example of how content is everywhere but not necessarily in the form that we may want it.

For that matter, really anyone can be an amateur analyst of the content of the media as nearly all of us have common sense ideas about what we like, what we expect, and what is the "best." In fact, media industries draw on those common senses when producing content. That is how they decide how to release movies, television shows, popular music, etc., to coincide with what they see are our (as audiences) notions of what is proper, popular, and marketable. We go to a romantic comedy for example, because we expect it to have a romance and a happy ending. We have come to expect this plot and resolution from romantic comedies. Therefore, when Hollywood produces most romantic comedies, they also follow that general pattern. However, the analysis of content and representation, whether using quantitative or qualitative methodology, is not easy. Things are not always what they seem, and often what is just as – if not more – important is what is not there, what we do not see, what is missing. There are likely to be patterns about what is there in relation to what is not there.

Analyzing issues of ethnicity in general and Latina/os in particular has to take into consideration what is missing – as in "Why are there no, or so few, Latina/os in the media?" Or "Where are the Latina/o professionals?" Or "Are there any Latino male celebrities?" Or "Why do Latina/os only appear in certain types and themes of news coverage?" In terms of content and representation, until quite recently omission was more often the rule than not. From Media Studies we have learned that what is missing from media representations is not necessarily an indicator of that which is not present in our culture but rather a sign of that which we desire to ignore, extirpate, or marginalize. Thus, for centuries,[1] the fact that Latina/os have not been, or have barely been, represented in mainstream popular culture does not mean that they have not been there, nor that they have not contributed to the nation's culture, economics, and politics, but rather that, from a center-of-power perspective, they are not important enough to be mentioned. Representation, our presence in media content, speaks to issues of power, not of numbers. It is quite possible for a group of the population to be quite numerous, in absolute and proportional terms, yet lack representation. This has been the history of Latina/o representation in US media. Given the recent acknowledgment of the demographic presence of Latina/os in the USA, representation has begun to increase. Yet the increase does not necessarily mean that representations are improving in quality. Additionally, whereas in the previous chapter on production the challenge was to figure out what Latina/o-produced media are, in this chapter the challenge is to identify the Latina/o person or theme in the media. As with production, it is not an easy process identifying the Latina/o.

Studies of content and representation are not just about symbolic matter. Symbolic annihilation, a finding about gender and ethnicity in the media, signals the stakes. When groups of people are under-represented and, furthermore, sensationalized, victimized, or ridiculed, there are political, health, and educational results. The fact is that content and representations have real, life-and-death, implications.[2] The virtual absence of Latina/os throughout most of US history in the mainstream press, for example, means that they were not treated seriously as citizens and therefore endured discrimination and lack of access to the fruits of a democracy. At the very least, this virtual absence meant lack of knowledge about their lived experience and a lack of voice in public policy discussions. At most, this absence meant, for instance, that there was no coverage of such matters as labor conditions that led to the poisoning and death of many agricultural workers or health disparities that, again, resulted in unnecessary deaths. Latina/o lack of, or under-, representation also meant particular forms of treatment in schools, as well as no inclusion of Latina/o history and issues in the curriculum. The lack of content and representation, as well as particular narratives such as those of the criminal and illegal alien, have real-life repercussions for the lived experience of Latina/os and their ability to survive. The potentially negative ramifications of lack, or particularly racialized forms, of content and representation apply not just to Latina/os but to all brown bodies – and, indeed, to the entire nation – for they set up a climate of tolerance or intolerance for certain types of human beings that pervades social life.

Studying content and representation is a crucially important component of Latina/o Media Studies as it speaks to the fulfillment of the democratic potential of communication practices and technologies, and the themes and messages that we and others use to make sense of the world. While we may not use media content as a mirror or direct reflection of reality, we still use it as an indicator of reality. The tension between the traditional Berelsonian approach to the study of content – who said what to whom and under what conditions – and the more cultural or structural approach to meaning is usually talked about in terms of what is more important, the manifest (obvious) meaning of the content or the latent (underlying) meaning of the text. Rather than seeing these two perspectives as opposed to one another, it might be more fruitful to see them in relation to each other. Certainly it is very useful to look at, for example, the frequency of news about immigration on a yearly basis. The themes and missing components would only add to a fuller understanding of the raw numbers, as it were, and can be coupled with the study of narratives of immigration to come to a fuller understanding of content and representation.

Let me give some possible examples to illustrate the general statements made in the above paragraphs. You have probably heard about studies of Latina/os in the news, on television, in popular music, in

Hollywood film, in magazines, in websites, and in other forms of generalized popular culture such as ads and toy products. Take a moment to think about the last time you heard anything about Latina/os in the news. This might take you into deciding which news: print, television, or internet? Chances are you heard something about the immigration rallies of May 1, 2006 and thereabouts, in response to proposed bills in Congress designed to restrict immigration and the liberties of immigrants. In these rallies, given the relevance of the proposed bills to US Latina/os, of both recent and older provenance, the news foregrounded Latina/o participation. You may have actually lived close to where one of these rallies occurred, happened to run into one – as I and my family did on a random trip to Chicago – or have been integrally involved with the planning and execution of one of these rallies. If you had proximity to the rallies, you would have a special interest in seeing how it was covered, and depending on your own ethnicity you may have wanted to see how "your group" was represented. While some may have looked at this content as detached news, others may have wanted to see how something they participated in was mediated. This was a moment when there was significant coverage of Latina/os in both the mainstream and Latina/o press across the nation. Some of you may have wanted to see a range of numbers and statistics, such as: what percentage of front pages talked about the rallies?; what percentage of rally stories used Latina/o sources?; how many major city newspapers and which among the prestige national press had front-page stories about the rallies?; and how many television network news shows led off with the rally story, or how many minutes on average did the story last? Beyond numbers, qualitative questions might include: what types of people were pictured in accompanying photographs?; was there a tendency to talk about the rallies as an orderly and civil grouping or as a disorderly riot?; was the Mexican flag displayed as prominently as the US flag?; and were the photographs of the rallies representative of your experience in the rally? Some scholars have begun to pursue these questions. For example, Deb Merskin (2008) found that, in broadcast coverage of *A Day without an Immigrant* (May 1, 2006), there was an over-representation of photographs and scenes taken from a lower and close-up angle that showed Latina/os screaming, with their mouths open, in what could be construed simultaneously as an angry and potentially violent stance. This finding draws on a long history of research within Media Studies. The angle and close-up of printed pictures and broadcast shots is not innocent. Most often, people of color are positioned so as to appear threatening and disorderly. All of the research mentioned above required some form of content and representation analysis of a moment when Latina/os had great salience in the news. Yet there have been many decades and centuries where such coverage was much scarcer. Moreover, there still exists a tendency to under-represent, though – given the presence and activity of Latina/os – this under-representation is becoming more difficult to sustain.

However, it would be simplistic to suggest that, prior to the late 1990s, there was a total absence of Latina/os in the media. There have been small Latina/o booms preceding the nineties, and notable, if stereotypical, appearance of Latina/os here and there. Currently, in the last year of the first decade of the new millennium, 2009, there are sufficient representations for us to be able to speak about tendencies within particular segments of the media, and, given convergence and synergy between and within media industries, these tendencies occur in more than one medium at a time. In net terms, there is an increase in representation. As a corollary, we cannot also assume that representational increase will by itself generate social change. Media representation is an important and absolutely necessary component of social change. However, we cannot assume that social or media change is irreversible. Media form one important component of social change but not the only one. One of the reasons we study content is to ascertain types of representations and their change and/or durability. For instance, is the contemporary Latin boom yet another example of a temporary presence of Latina/os in popular culture or an indication that Latina/os are part of the national fabric and imaginary and therefore a lasting component of representations? Similarly, does the overwhelming narrative of Latina/os as "aliens" within the news show any sign of abating or does this continue to be the way that realist media, especially the news, represent Latina/os, and is it therefore part of the national imaginary?

Yet another reason to study content is that, many times, content analysis is the first step in the study of production, audiences, and effects. If content differs between mainstream and Latina/o media, then that generates production questions such as the agency and community connections of different types of individual communicators. What is the effect of transnational conglomerates on particular forms of Latina/o content or on the general representation of Latina/os and Latinidad? Likewise, when studying audiences, we have to show them content. The way we choose what content to talk to audiences about largely relies on studies in content and representation. Similarly, effects research follows content findings. For example, effects research suggests that, in a highly segregated society such as ours wherein people live in largely ethnically homogeneous communities, those least exposed to ethnic diversity are more likely to rely on media information to form their opinions about a particular group. Here content and representation in media are very important for the way people who do not come into personal contact with Latina/os think about Latina/os. Another relevant question about the relationship between content and effects is whether, if a general tendency in news discourse is to represent Latina/os as illegal aliens and/ or criminals, that has an effect on how the general population feels about Latina/os and/or issues of immigration? Does that in turn have a potential effect on the self-esteem of Latina/o youth? Before we could ask those questions, we had to have some sort of content analysis to guide it. After all, it is necessary to know what people are watching to examine the effects of the media. A major warning is that content and representation analysis is a guide to studying other areas, but cannot substitute for other avenues of research. You cannot decide what the effect of representation will be without engaging in an effects study. You cannot leap from a content finding to an effects conclusion. You cannot say, for instance, that, because Dora the Explorer is brown, this makes children think that Latinas are all brown. You would have to conduct a study that includes children, and you might find out that they do not even notice her skin color, that she is Latina, or even that she is a girl! Different children in the audience might notice different elements in the show, according to their own education, age, ethnicity, gender, etc. You have to conduct an additional piece of research, beyond content, before you can speak to effects or audiences. In sum, content and representation analysis are an absolutely essential component of Latina/o Media Studies, but they have to be conducted in concert with other methodologies to get to issues of production, effects, and audiences. To jump from content and representation data into any of these other areas is faulty scholarship.

Another lesson from Media Studies is that we have moved away from a binary approach of negative and positive images, a previous paradigm of studying issues of gender and ethnicity in the media. Positive and negative are judgment calls that cannot be guaranteed across a range of representation, audiences, effects, time, or constituencies. Before one can tell if an image is positive, one would have to study either effects or audiences to make such a judgment. When doing so, one usually finds a range of positions. Moreover, even something deemed positive can actually have negative ramifications. For example Limón (1973) bemoans the pervasiveness in film of the "unflattering" Chicano as "dirty, violent, treacherous, hypersexual and thieving or . . . cowardly, apathetic, and dormant," and the more positive "colorful, romantic figure full of rich, mysterious life forces" (pp. 257–8). However, the latter set of attributes stereotypes as much as the former, and indeed renders the Chicano in a distant cosmic location that also displaces the Latina/o presence within the national reality and exacerbates the perpetually foreign narrative. In other words, and to simplify matters somehow, what might be positive to you might be negative to me. What might be considered positive today might be considered negative next year. What dominant culture might consider positive might be considered negative by an ethnic culture. Because of the impossibility of nailing content or representations as absolutely positive or negative, this book takes the relational approach rather than the binary approach in discussing representations. From a relational approach, one would look at both sets of stereotypes discussed previously by Limón and ask how they relate to mainstream masculinity and film representations of a range of characters, whether they be white, black, mixed race, or whatever. One might realize that both of those stereotypes mentioned by Limón above speak to marked difference from the presumed, rational, modern subject. Neither "apathetic" nor "mysterious" describes the presumed rational, proactive individual.

In the USA a social scientific paradigm that relies on "objective" measurements and privileges quantitative data is the dominant way of conducting research. For many utilizing social scientific approaches, content analysis is seen as a way of accounting for what is there in the media. Content analysis research follows a more traditional social scientific approach in which elements are operationalized and their frequency is measured both in absolute terms and in relation to other variables. From this quantitative tradition of research we learn frequencies, percentages, and, whenever available, multiple regression analysis that points to the relationship, in frequency, between different variables, such as the likelihood that stories of Latina/os coincide with news about crime and immigration. Moreover, the theoretical impulse, implicit or explicit, assesses media content as a normative indicator of correspondence with reality. In other words, in the discussion of the results, many use quantitative results to declare that the percentage of Latina/os in the news, to use a random example, does not match the percentage of Latina/os in the population. Or, more insidiously, much news research finds that Latina/os are over-represented in news stories about social problems such as crime, drugs, obesity, and teenage pregnancy in relation to their percentage in the population.

At the most basic level in the study of content, we study frequency – meaning the absolute numbers and/or percentage of appearances of Latina/os people and/or themes. In Latina/o-produced and/or -oriented media, this is an easier task. The scholar knows that the material is about Latinidad and populated with Latina/o characters and actors. Those who are not Latina/os within this universe might be more challenging to discern. Yet in the mainstream, matters get noticeably more difficult. As basic as this type of analysis is, it can be very difficult to conduct. For example, we can look at by-lines of newspapers and see how many articles are written by people with Latina/o last names as an indication of how many Latina/o journalists are making it to that prestigious mainstream front-page reporting task. However, what is a "Latina/o last name?" The usual Garcia, Rodriguez, Gutierrez, and Martinez are likely to be Latina/os, but they also might refer to a person whose married name changed and her/his original name could have been Smith or Jones. Also what about Latina/os whose last names are Goldman, Behar, Smith, or Jones, who would not be counted as Latina/os if we were just going by the usual names? What about counting the number of Latina/os in a movie? Here you would have to decide if you wanted to count the actors themselves. So you would go into the cast and either know that a particular actor is Latina/o – Cameron Diaz or Raquel Welch perhaps – or again be sent back to the name-guessing game. If you took a visual cue as to what "looks" Latina/o, then you might miss Cameron Diaz altogether as she is tall, skinny (no booty here), blue-eyed, and blond-haired and does not play ethnic roles. Or you could listen for accent, and that might get you to an actor playing a Latina/o just as much as to a Latina/o actor. If you are looking at characters and settings in the movie, then you would have to look for "obvious" markers of Latinidad, which are there sometimes, such as the Virgen de Guadalupe or Café Bustelo in the pantry. This latter element was one that Rosie Perez, a "hot" Latina of the late eighties and early nineties, insisted be on the set to signify her Latina/o roots. However, what if you have no idea what Café Bustelo is all about, and it looks like any other brand of Italian coffee to you? Then you would miss that intentional marker of Latinidad. In another example, you might have a bunch of kids, or people in different scenes, whose ethnicity you could not ascertain. Maybe a kid dresses in a particular manner – but what is Latina/o style? Or maybe another is listening to merengue. But again there is no guarantee that a non-Latina/o would not be the one dressing like a Latina/o or listening to Latina/o music. It would be helpful to know something about the setting and likely composition of that geographic or cultural zone to be able to code it, yet the average viewer would not necessarily have access to that information. For example a commercial with tons of green VW Bug Beetle taxis might not mean that much to you unless you were familiar with Mexico City[3] where there are thousands of such vehicles. It is very difficult to gather frequency data unless they are very explicit and obvious, such as a cop with a thick Spanish accent, brown skin, a name like Ramirez, who tells us he lives in East Los Angeles. If he were corrupt and violent that would make it more explicit. Then we could code that character as Latino, although that would be a blatant deployment of a stereotype. Change enough of the elements to the stereotype and you return to an ambiguous ethnicity and right back to the difficulty of coding for frequency of Latina/os in audiovisual media. In fact, this is one of the reasons we study both effects and audiences because often people interpret characters and/ or situations differently from how producers might have intended or from how scholars think they should. Also, many times, a producer might intend a particular representation to be "positive" but it might not be interpreted that way – yet another reason to combine the study of representation with the study of audiences and effects.

Then there is the additional difficulty, in terms of measuring the frequency of Latina/os in media content, of the wide diversity of Latina/os. You cannot reduce, as discussed in the previous chapter, Latina/os to the "brown" race. In fact, Latina/os come in every shade of skin there is. So it is not as simple as telling a coder to count every time a brown person appears in a television show, for that person might not be Latina/o or the Latina/o may not be brown. The increasingly numerous portion of the population that is of mixed race – that is, from two or more racial backgrounds – complicates frequency coding even further. How is a coder to decide whether an Afro-Latina/o such as Rosario Dawson or Michelle Rodriguez gets coded as black or Latina? And whether someone like Cameron Diaz is coded as white or Latina? Frequency then – though a beginning step in content analysis that partly answers the questions "Are there Latina/os in media?" and "How many Latina/os are there?" – is very difficult to tally up. This is why I cautioned that this type of research is difficult at the beginning of this section. You might think that tallying up frequency, as in how many Latina/os are in media content, is the easy way to begin conducting research. But this is not an easy task at all.

One of the ways that scholars conducting content analysis of this sort attempt to arrive at some form of agreement is by striving for high percentages of inter-coder reliability. This means that when you have a number of people coding television, hip hop videos, movies, newspaper, digital game or social network spaces, websites, billboards, or whatever, you conduct pre-coding exercises so that those involved in the coding have a high degree of agreement about what counts as Latinidad, Latina/o, mixed race, etc. That way, at least within the coders in a particular content analysis study, there should be a degree of consensus, somewhere in the region of over 85 percent. If there is an inability among the coders to identify ethnicity, then those in charge of the study learn that in that case one cannot measure frequency of Latina/os just from the "looks" of them because there is no scientific validity in such measurements. Thus scholars strive for very specific definitions, operationalization, when measuring frequency. For example, Dixon, Azocar, and Casas (2003) operationalized crime as the following: behavior or information either pertaining to the commission of a particular law-breaking act, or social or legal reaction to law-breaking more generally. Only those crimes (e.g., murder, arson, robbery) tracked by the US Department of Justice were coded, to compare the depiction of crime in the news with crime data. So you can see from this definition that crime is related to the breaking of the law, and there is a whole range of crimes that potentially do not fit this definition. Nonetheless, scholars have to narrow down their operationalization, or very specific and replicable definition, so that coders know what to count, and are all counting the same things, roughly. Additionally, if another scholar wants to replicate the study or measure for the same frequencies but in another episode, movie, or whatever, the operationalization from one study should be replicable in another. Ideally, coders would have some form of grounding within the community that produces the content or which the content is about, so there is some sort of correspondence with the intended audience – e.g. they would have some form of inkling as to how that particular audience might interpret that particular form of content. But this is not always the case. Especially in matters of Latina/os – or most other ethnic audiences – the fact is that coders, being intellectual workers at the university level, cannot be assumed to represent or be familiar with Latina/os. Still, given our culture's preference for numerical data, frequency results are highly influential and likely to be circulated without much attention paid to the potential pitfalls of counting Latina/os and Latinidad in media content.

Nonetheless, as difficult and potentially problematic as it is, scholars try to tally up frequency. For example, Children NOW (2003) notes that, though youth of color account for 40% of the population under 19, their frequency on prime-time television is much less than that, with an over-representation of males to females to boot. You might remember from a previous chapter's discussion of disaggregation that this is precisely the type of data that, from a Latina/o Media Studies perspective, needs to be broken down in terms of particular ethnic groups. Children NOW does this. While there has been a doubling of Latina/o-credited characters since 1999 (from 3 to 6%), the presence of youth characters has not matched this increase. Youth characters were less ethnically diverse than the entire sample. Nonetheless, this is an improvement from previous research that indicated that Hispanics were largely absent from television in the United States (Greenberg and Baptista-Fernandez, 1980; Seggar, 1977). The Children NOW study coded for the following categories of characters: opening credits, primary non-recurring, secondary recurring, secondary non-recurring, and tertiary. The prominence of the character decreases from opening credits to tertiary. An opening-credit character would be George Lopez in the show of the same name. A tertiary character is less than a supporting actor. Tonantzin Esparza who played Marisol in five episodes of the 2002–3 season of the *George Lopez Show* would be a tertiary character. Obviously, the opening-credit primary character has much more salience than a tertiary character who is only mentioned in the closing credits. In terms of racial diversity of total prime-time characters, Latinos account for 6.5 percent, African Americans for 16 percent, and Caucasians for 73 percent. Nonetheless, the study notes that the presence of Latina/os in the total prime-time population has increased from 4 to 6.5% since 2001, and from 2 to 6% in opening credits. As with the research on African Americans, Latina/os show up most often in situation comedies. Furthermore, Latina/os continue to be cast in low-status occupations, with only 11 percent being cast as professionals. All other ethnicities had higher frequency of professionals: 37 percent of Asian American, 32 percent of Caucasian, and 26 percent of African American characters. When you couple this lower percentage with the lower percentage of Latina/o characters, you get a doubly small frequency of Latina/o professionals.[4] When interpreting these studies on frequency, one needs to read the entire range of data. For example, you could see a news story about this study headlined by "Television doubles frequency of Latina/o characters!" However, once you look at the data you would see that the doubling went from 3 to 6 percent of characters, still a woeful under-representation of the 15 percent of the total population composed by Latina/os.

Beyond frequency, the study of content involves a qualitative analysis of the ways that Latina/os and Latinidad are being represented. The figures above do not tell you how that 6 percent is represented, only that they are represented. Within the field of Media Studies, we have moved from using the term "images" to the term "representation." This is not just a matter of words, but a major theoretical step. "Images" implies reflection, as in "mirror image." The above study, for instance, concludes that prime-time television does not "reflect" the diversity of ethnicity in the USA. That is, media are not a mirror image of statistical proportions of ethnicities in society. Yet many scholars of the media note that popular culture, historically and contemporarily, has not reflected and does not – indeed is unable to – directly reflect any type of reality or experience. Media always use a shorthand or conventions to re-present something, whether in visual, written, or aural form – for example, a plane taking off to signify departure or Mariachi music to signify either specific Mexicanness or more general Latinidad. Indeed, representation is synonymous with mediation – which is what media do: they mediate. They re-present reality using shorthand. In doing so, in producing mediated representations, individual communicators make many decisions, implicit and explicit, conscious and subconscious, to re-present news or fiction. Again, returning to the above study, while the 6% of Latina/o characters may not reflect Latina/o numerical presence in the USA, it certainly represents how mainstream culture values Latina/os in relation to Caucasians and other racial categories. Thus, in Media Studies, especially as we move from quantitative to qualitative studies, we have largely stopped using not only the concept "image" but also its related verb "reflect."

Throughout this book you will notice the use of the terms "representation" and "represent." In fact it is quite unfair to criticize media for using stereotypes for Latina/os as media use stereotypes for everyone! It is their shorthand way of representing complex groups of people. At issue is not the use of stereotypes – that is nearly inevitable – but the reduction of a particular group to a small number of stereotypes that serve to marginalize or demonize a group of the population. Stereotypes, like myths, arise within a particular historical and social context, yet they endure long past their origin or even the lives of those who gave rise to such a stereotype. Nonetheless, it is very important to study the historical root of many stereotypes as these genealogies elucidate the development of racialized regimes of representation that circulate within our culture. Thus, research into stereotypes was one of the early forms – and an enduring one – of conducting content analysis of Latina/os in the media. Study on stereotypes fueled not only research in the academy but also activism, as diverse Latina/o communities began to make claims upon the state and the media.

Much of the work on frequency and representation dates back to the US Commission on Civil Rights (1977), more popularly known as the Kerner Commission, which found under-representation of minorities and suggested increased and better representation. Within civil rights coverage, people of color, including Latina/os, were used not as subjects but as objects. For example, predating the Kerner Commission, Sanchez (1973) found that newspapers in large Mexican American population centers were no more likely to have additional space devoted to stories about Mexican Americans than cities in other areas. Additionally, most of the stories about Mexican Americans were negative in tone, emphasizing conflict situations. Gutiérrez (1978) noted that newspapers increased coverage about Hispanics during times of social unrest, and that these stories would become increasingly unfavorable as the conflict went on. A slightly more recent analysis of newspaper content found that in newspapers in communities with a larger concentration of Hispanics there was a lower percentage of news stories about Hispanics that dealt with crime (Greenberg et al., 1983). However, in cities with fewer Hispanics, more stories about

Hispanics focused on criminal activities. Thus, in towns where Anglos might have less opportunity for direct experience with Hispanics, the press would either not mention their presence or over-represent them as criminals. We will read more about cultivation analysis in the effects chapter, but those depending on and watching a lot of television tend to have television answers for real-life questions. When you combine this effects paradigm with the content data above, you begin to see the implications of over- and under-representation of Latina/os. A 1993 Annenberg Study found that, whereas for every 100 good white characters there were 39 villains, for Hispanics the ratio was 100 to 75 ("20 years . . ."). Entitled "Out of the picture" (which has a stylized drawing of two male film producers on the cover) and "Don't blink," two consecutive National Council of La Raza (NCLR) media content projects (Navarrete and Kanasaki, 1994; National Council of La Raza, 1996) did not find great or varied representation in television and news. In 1999 the situation was deemed so outrageous – not a single television show in the prime-time line-up had any explicit minority characters – that a range of organizations, including the National Association for the Advancement of Colored People (NAACP) and NCLR, called for an audience boycott. In particular, the NCLR encouraged Latinos to join a "brown out" in the week of September 11–19. In sum, in a range of research on content of the media, Latina/os were either absent or portrayed as poor, of low socioeconomic status, lazy, with little education and with jobs reflecting that; as failures; and as criminals and problems to be solved. Much content analysis research references these benchmark studies. Additionally, results from these studies fueled community activism, government commissions, and further studies which in turn contributed to the creation of a critical mass of knowledge and groups to advocate for Latina/o rights in the USA.

When we move from frequency of Latina/os, to coverage of Latina/os in the news and television, to particular roles that Latina/os represent, we move to the classic Media Studies concept of *symbolic annihilation*. The finding of symbolic annihilation applies to Latina/os in all forms of mainstream media. Symbolic annihilation was first discussed in relation to women in advertising (Goffman, 1976) and applied to women in the news in particular and the mass media in general (Tuchman, Daniels, and Benet, 1978), but has since been found to apply to other segments of the population, and with increased virulence according to vectors of difference such as gender, ethnicity, class, sexual orientation, ability, and regional origin. For example, when studying white, dominant-culture women, the symbolic annihilation is not as intense as when studying working-class, lesbian, women of color. In the former, gender is the one difference from the assumed centrality of the white male subject of history. White middle-class women, since the sixties, have gained a certain degree of legitimacy and representation that the latter, working-class lesbian women of color – based on vectors of difference that combine gender, class, race, and sexuality – have not. This finding of symbolic annihilation not only applies to Latina/os, but does so virulently as Latina/os are often at least three times removed from centrality in our popular culture, by virtue of ethnicity, class, and gender. Indeed white middle-class women have been the main beneficiaries of much civil rights legislation, although the political-correctness discourse that penalizes people of color for their own discrimination seldom mentions this fact (Mukherjee, 2006). The extreme symbolic annihilation the latter encounter sometimes turns into outright omission.

Symbolic annihilation refers to both the under-representation of a segment of the population – for example, given that Latina/os currently compose 15 percent of the US population, they should compose 15 percent of news stories, etc. – and their criminalization, marginalization, or sensationalization when they do appear. Thus, you see an under-representation of Latina/os in prime-time television (the 6 percent already mentioned) and over-representation of Latina/os as criminal when they are represented. That second part means that, in the few instances when under-represented people appear, they are further marginalized through pejorative representation – for example on the very few occasions that Latina/o youth are represented in the news, they tend to be represented as deviants. For instance, Mastro and Stern (2003) found precisely that Latina/os are under-represented in contemporary television advertisements – making up only 1 percent of speaking characters – and that, when they are represented, they are negatively depicted engaging in "alluring behaviors and sexual gazing" (p. 645). Linking the discussion of symbolic annihilation to stereotypes of Latina/os, we find that, when there are Latina/o stereotypes that appear in the mass media, these tend to be pejorative ones such as the bandit, the spitfire, the Latin lover, etc. Thus, "negative" stereotype is the second part of a finding of symbolic annihilation.

Latina/o Media Studies scholars have traced the development of ethnic images in general and representations of Latina/os in particular to follow a sequence of portrayals formerly established with the depictions of African Americans and other minorities in mainstream forms of media such as the press, television, and popular music. At this point it might be instructive to consider Stuart Hall's discussion of the overlap between residual, dominant, and alternative cultures. Residual culture was once dominant but has been replaced by the currently dominant formation. Alternative cultures threaten or promise to become dominant, though it's difficult to tell whether they will unsettle contemporary dominant culture into residual status or whether they will fade from alternative status into oblivion. It is useful to keep these three distinctions in mind as we discuss Latina/o stages of representation. Drawing on the work of Greenberg and Baptista-Fernandez (1980), Mastro and Robinson (2000) detail four stages of ethnic representation: invisibility or non-recognition, recognition/ridicule, regulatory phase, and egalitarianism. You can have pockets of egalitarianism and non-recognition in different forms of media at the same historical moment. The first stage involves omission – what Mastro and Robinson (2000) call "nonrecognition" is a period of invisibility or lack of representations. This stage is followed by symbolic annihilation. To have symbolic annihilation, you need some form of representation, even if it is under-representation. The second part of this finding includes not only ridicule, but marginalization, victimization, sensationalization, and/or any number of pejorative strategies that serve to localize the under-represented population as different and aberrant. The third stage they call the "regulatory phase," when most roles are related to the legal system. Characters can be on either side of the law: as police officers or criminals. Mastro and Robinson warn that this phase of representation is likely to generate racial discord, though one could say that all stages that they identify have that potential. The fourth stage is the egalitarian stage in which "depictions begin to represent the value and diversity of the minority culture in a variety of statuses and contexts" (p. 388). That stage mostly remains in the utopian future. Were we to overlay these stages with Hall's dominant, residual, and alternative categories, we could see that both the second and third stages – recognition/ridicule and the regulatory phase – are currently dominant. The first stage, omission, while no longer dominant, is nonetheless residual. Egalitarianism, however, is not really in the alternative stage, but hopefully in the future. This stage also projects minority status into the future, something contemporary demographic projections do not necessarily support.

In my own research I have found a set of complementary stages that include not only realist but also fictional narratives. Concurring with the omission and symbolic annihilation component of some of the above stages outlined by Mastro and Robinson, I find additional tendencies toward binary and unequal forms of representation have to be factored into the stages. That is, when the world is shown in a black-and-white way,[5] with whites representing dominant and normal people and blacks the deviant and abnormal, that has to be considered a stage. My stages are the following: first is omission; second is binary, black-and-white; third is multiracial, with whiteness still being privileged and other ethnicities being represented in relation to the dominant white culture, and often in tension with each other; fourth is hybrid, with the black-and-white binary unsettled, with mixed race as a possibility, but with the still enduring privileging of whiteness; and fifth is a hopefully future stage where hybridity is more democratically represented, rather than in relation to the assumed superiority of whiteness.

Generally, scholars of ethnicity agree that representations have become less overt and more subtle. For example, Stuart Hall notes that overt racism has largely been replaced by inferential racism. Overtly stereotypical representations, such as the ones discussed in the early stages of the bandido type (discussed below) have largely, but not entirely, been replaced by more subtle and ambiguous ones. As you will see in the effects chapter, Latina/o Media Studies scholars have begun to explore whether and how these inferential and ambiguous representations generate an effect.

I agree with Mastro and Robinson that we are largely past the first/omission stage, though in certain cases whiteness is still represented as the main and only ethnicity. We still have movies, news, television shows, magazines, and websites where whiteness is pure and settled. For example, *Friends*, the huge television hit, was criticized for representing a nearly lily-white New York City reality. The second stage, of a black-and-white binary, with whiteness as normal and blackness as deviant, is still very much a component of popular culture representation. However, this binary is becoming less easy to sustain. Even mainstream television finds it difficult to produce shows such as Disney Channel's *Sister, Sister*, or NBC's monster hit *The Cosby Show*, wherein their nod to race and ethnicity consisted of discrete black shows on white television networks. Concurrently, many scholars and commentators still see the world in a black-and-white way as well. The word "race" still signs in for black, and that is partly why I use the word "ethnicity." For instance, Martín-Rodríguez (2000) notes that, in all the brouhaha about the racial politics in Disney's *The Lion King* (1994), all but one of the commentators cast the discussion in a black-and-white binary way, not noticing (or not considering important enough to mention) that Cheech Marin voiced one of the hyenas and that the hyenas could be interpreted as representing Latina/os and the border, especially illegal and unwanted border crossings. Thus *The Lion King* belongs in the second and third stages – depending on how you interpret it. It is in the second if one sees the conflict in black-and-white terms within a Hollywood film industry that still under-represents blacks, or in the third if one sees the tension as existing between whites and blacks/Latina/os. The third stage represents multiculturalism within a rainbow representation that includes Latina/os but still privileges whites in relation to all colors, and blacks in relation to all ethnically coded people. Examples of the third stage can be found in a number of television shows such as *Barney*, *That Seventies Show*, *Clifford the Big Red Dog*, *Lost*, etc., that include a range of ethnic characters yet the protagonists and long-standing characters remain the white ones. This is an instance in which the positive–negative dichotomy would not be as helpful as a relational approach, for while one could say that the multiculturalist stage is positive because it expands the ethnic register, that would not get at the fact that, relationally, white privilege is foregrounded and characters of color are backgrounded, and further demonized in terms of their inter-ethnic rivalries. The fourth stage I call "hybridity," and this can be found in certain segments of popular culture. More so than in content, we will encounter hybridity in the next section on audiences and interpretations. Beyond representing separate ethnicities, hybridity as a stage of representation challenges discrete categories of race and ethnicity and mixes ethnic traits. This is far more representative of the population than the discrete ethnicity approach in both the second and third stages, as the tendency with global populations has been toward mixture rather than racial purity. A paradigmatic example of hybridity as a representational strategy is the doll line "Bratz," with its ancillary television show and feature-length movie. Hybridity cannot be misconstrued as equating to egalitarianism, as many scholars (Molina Guzmán and Valdivia, 2004; Shugart, 2007) have noted that hybrid representations are still measured against an implicitly or explicitly white normativity. A less Eurocentric representation of hybridity, the fifth stage, also remains in the utopian future. The stages will be concretely explored below through the analysis of the most salient stereotypes of Latina/os: the bandit/bandido and the Latina maid.

The bandit/bandido as paradigmatic stereotype

Can you think of the most frequent way that Latinos (men) are represented in contemporary popular culture? If you are a fan of old movies (whether that means the seventies, the twenties, or the forties to you), you are probably also very familiar with this type. In fact, Media Studies scholars of content found this type in the earliest media forms that they had available to study: news and movies. Latina/os and Latina/o stereotypes have been present in Hollywood film since its early days in the 1890s. Likewise, in the news, there have been ways of representing Latina/os that have been more or less consistent in the past century and a half. None of this is meant to imply that there were many instances of representations of Latina/os in either form of media. Scholarship bears out the finding of omission followed by symbolic annihilation.

Looking at the available ways that Latino men have been represented, the bandit – or bandido – is the most enduring stereotype of Latinos. The bandido, begun in the press and traveling quite easily to movies, advertising, children's cartoons, etc., was found by Evans in Subervi-Vélez (1994) to date back to the 1880s as an "outgrowth of the Manifest Destiny" policy (p. 306). The declaration that westward expansion was God-mandated resulted in "banditry" from both sides: those heading West did not always do so in the most legally orderly ways and those being expanded into did not always take it passively. The tenuous legality of the transitional geographical areas led to many actions that could be coded as banditry. The coupling of bandit activities with a particular ethnic character resulted from the fact that westward expansion involved formerly Spanish and then Mexican lands. In the context of the era following the Treaty of Guadalupe-Hidalgo in 1848 – a watershed moment for the Mexico–US border and Latina/o Studies history, in which, after a war, the USA took over territory that included what is now California, Arizona, Utah, Nevada, parts of Wyoming, Colorado and New Mexico – the stereotype justified the US conquest of Mexican territory. Expansionist declarations about Latin America being the "backyard" of the USA date back to Thomas Jefferson, but the start of the twentieth century found the USA ascending as a global power exercising its backyard vision through repeated military, political, economic, and cultural interventions to safeguard US national interests. Thus, the whole Latin American region, especially Mexico and Central America, was represented as if full of bandits.

The bandit/bandido moved from news to silent movies and then the whole range of Hollywood film, often in an unkempt and less than intelligent form. This stereotype was used to represent both notable figures in the Mexican revolution such as Pancho Villa and Emiliano Zapata, and hordes of anonymous invading and marauding bandits roaming the countryside and threatening the calm and repose of an otherwise civilized setting. For an excellent compilation of early Hollywood film representations of the bandit, see Dee Dee Halleck's *The Gringo in Mañanaland* (1995) where she edits together eerily similar representations of the bandit. Similar to D. W. Griffith's representations of black masculinity in *Birth of a Nation* (1915),[6] many of the bandits in early movies represented the threat that the masculine and sexually demanding Mexican bandit posed to chaste white US femininity, the normal family, and thus to white masculinity. The usual scene showed a chaste white woman, who usually had a maid, on a ranch or somewhere similar as the bandit was not yet operating in the urban space, who is either notified of approaching marauders or surprised by them pounding on her door. Other movies included massive numbers of Mexican bandidos coming in like hordes, sometimes singing *Cielito lindo* as that is a component of the Mexican stereotype. Bandits were always male and "Latin." As such, this form of representation is gendered, for it singles out Latino men as dangerous predators and as a threat to the implicit purity of dominant-culture women. The early bandit gives rise to the more recent regulatory phase, for the implicit avenger of the threat to femininity has to be the force of law, usually represented by white masculine police power.

The bandido evolved according to the historical period. While disappearing from neither the press nor film, the type returns with virulence during the 1940s in the Los Angeles area, in what are now known as "the Zoot Suit riots." The public presence of Latina/o youth was covered in the mainstream press, such as the *Los Angeles Times*, within a panic framework, as if their mere presence threatened the safety of Los Angelinos. Criminalizing narratives in coverage resulted in real-life limitations on Latina/o youth's use of public space.

While most of the research focuses on Latinos in this process, in a historical newspaper analysis Escobedo (2007) carefully documents that girls as well faced discrimination, from both the dominant culture and their own community, as their perceived "dangerous sexuality" was contained by all involved: the Mexican Catholic community and the white anti-Mexican community. Some of these girls were turned in to the police by their own mothers. These Mexican American young women "rejected both traditional Mexican and mainstream [US] American culture" (p. 133). Some of the girls identified as "pachucas," the female version of Zoot suiters, were actually institutionalized for years as a result of their impertinent public presence and particular clothing choices, in addition to their assertion of sexual agency. In an article analyzing pachucas in Hollywood film, Fregoso (1995) affirms that the representation of these young women asserts a presence in the public sphere that is deemed dangerous and therefore demonized. The movie *Mi vida loca* (1994) presents us with an alternative version of girls who seek to assert agency and sexuality within a set of conditions not of their own choosing as they seek to survive in the Echo Park neighborhood of Los Angeles. Despite the overwhelmingly masculine nature of this character, feminist research demonstrates that Latina women were coded as bandits as well.

While not disappearing from popular culture in the following thirty years, the bandido made yet another noteworthy appearance from 1967 to 1971 when the Frito Lay company used the concept to create a cartoon, a mouse animated by Tex Avery and voiced by Mel Blanc, both iconic creative figures within US cartoon history, to the tune of *Cielito lindo* – the iconic Mexican song that goes "ay ay yay yay" – to sell corn chips through the fast-talking, heavily accented

Speedy Gonzalez, www.fanpop.com

mouse character who stole chips from unsuspecting consumers. Activist interventions by Latina/o groups such as the National Mexican American Anti-Defamation Committee first led to a toning-down of the most offensive elements and then to an outright retirement of the character in 1971. The Frito Bandido resembled Speedy Gonzalez, a Looney Tunes character that depicted a fast-running, fast-talking mouse, also with a thick Mexican accent. The huge yellow Mexican sombrero, red bandana tied around the neck, and peasant white shirt and pants are still often quoted in advertisements – albeit in more muted dimensions – such as a recent ad for Nabisco Oreo Crisps. A tablecloth that I bought in Xochimilco, the garden city outside Mexico City, also has embroidered figures in this vein, suggesting that the stereotype traveled back to Mexico and has been incorporated into indigenous handicrafts.

This latter example extends the finding of "blow back" to the area of ethnic representation. Blow back is a finding from international communications that refers to the process whereby the CIA or other such organizations will plant news items in Latin American news-papers that are in turn used by Congress as evidence of the need for continued or further intervention in the region. The original story is produced in the USA but planted in Latin American newspapers and "blown back" to the USA to become the basis for foreign policy. The bandido blow-back process is similar in that the stereotype was

Advert for Nabisco Oreo crisps, www.Adland.tv

constructed in the USA to represent a contact zone with a Mexican and Mexican American population. The imagery is exported south of the border so that indigenous producers incorporate it into their handicrafts and sell it to US tourists who bring it back to the USA as a form of authentic souvenir. It makes the bandido seem like an indigenous Latin American creation!

The stereotype of the bandit forms the basis for more recent representations of Latinos as criminals, the third "regulatory" phase previously mentioned in this chapter. Contemporary inner-city gangs, often involved in the drug trade, and consisting of violent thugs who threaten the virtue of dominant-culture women but also the safety of everyone in their neighborhood, have historically foregrounded Irish Americans, Italian Americans, African Americans, and now Latina/os. Indeed, this stereotype maps out US national-imaginary reaction to different waves of annexations and immigrants. African Americans and Latina/os now share the bandido stereotype while simultaneously sharing over-representation in the nation's jails, in rates that far exceed their proportion within the population. The two are related, though not necessarily in a causal relationship – that is, one of them does not singly cause the other. For example, M. B. Oliver (1994) documents the facts that Latinos are likely to appear as criminal suspects in programs, and more likely than other ethnic minority to be victimized by police aggression. Content analyses of reality-based police shows, such as *Cops* and *America's Most Wanted*, both hybrids of news and entertainment, show white characters are more likely to be portrayed as police officers and Latinos and blacks as criminal suspects – the latter being more likely to be the target of unarmed physical aggression by police officers (1994, p. 180). Additionally, in terms of the over-representation of solved crimes and justice served, televised crime over-represents white criminal suspects while news coverage of crime over-represents suspects as ethnic. Mastro and Greenberg (2000) found that the type of programming was linked to ethnic minority – 77 percent of Latina/o appearances (which make up 3 percent of the total) were in crime shows. The fact that there were so few Latinos and that they were concentrated in a few crime shows, like *NYPD Blue*, meant that if you missed the one show with Latina/os, you missed a third of their representation. Similarly, Dixon and Linz (2000a, b, c), in a set of studies that compared African Americans, Latina/os, and Whites as portrayed in television news in Los Angeles and Orange counties, find that Blacks and Latinos were significantly more likely to appear as lawbreakers, whereas Whites appeared as defenders drawing on "ethnic blame discourse." Dixon and Linz also found that more than a third of Black and Latino defendants were associated with prejudicial information. Moreover, ethnocentric talk became routinized in everyday experience in a context wherein Blacks and Latinos appeared as perpetrators more often than whites. In fact Latinos were found four times as likely to be featured as perpetrators than as officers. Mastro and Robinson (2000), in an article aptly entitled "Cops and crooks: images of minorities in television," in a two-week sample from the Fall 1997 season content analysis of prime-time television, found that police were more likely to use aggression against young people of color. As well, while Latina/os composed 4 percent of the police force, they accounted for 7 percent of criminals. These representations are just as likely to appear in the news, the movies, advertisements, television, video games, and popular music, as many of the videos accompanying the release of rap and hip hop, as well as reggaeton, show masculinist representations of gang-related youth. The issue with the latter is that they are often produced by Latina/o and/or African American artists. Linking this knowledge to the previous chapter on production suggests that, in some cases, the ethnicity of the producer does not necessarily result in less stereotypical content. The increase in representation, due in part to an increase in ethnic producers, reiterates the tropes previously present in film and popular culture and further circulates problematic representations of Latina/os.

I begin with the bandit/bandido stereotype because it dates back over a century, travels from realist to fictional media, from adult to children's programming, from young men to young women, from the USA to Mexico, from Mexico back to the USA, and from white to Latina/o-produced media, as in popular music and accompanying videos. This stereotype is enduring and morphs according to new social, political, economic, national, and global issues, and is taken up by both mainstream and ethnic media producers. As such it becomes a predominant way to think about Latina/os and thus potentially fuels contemporary concerns, such as immigration and the fear of criminal border crossers, and reinforces the perception of Latinoa/s as eternal and unassimilable foreigners.

Latina/o media scholars have documented many representational strategies beyond the bandit morphing into a modern-day criminal, usually but not always in relation to the drug trade. As suggested by the Mastro and Robinson stage approach previously mentioned, the third "regulatory stage" also includes police officers and Latina/os on the legal side of things, such as detectives and judges. We can trace this regulatory phase in television programming. *CHiPs*, premiering on September 15, 1977, included the adventures of two California Highway patrol officers, one of whom, Officer Francis Llewellyn "Ponch" Poncherello, played by Erik Strada, was the rookie "hot-blooded" one who needed mentoring to tame his temper and bring out his good qualities. Ponch was also a womanizer. Thus Ponch represented many of the stereotypical elements of the Latina/o dating back to early film depictions. In *LA Law*, nearly ten years later (1986), we find Jimmy Smits playing lawyer Victor Sifuentes, the Latino in a mostly white cast of lawyers that included women, an African American, and eventually a lesbian. Ten years later, in *Law and Order* (1996), Benjamin Bratt debuted as detective Reynaldo "Rey" Curtis. Like Jimmy Smits before him, he played a suave and debonair supporting character but left the show to pursue more central roles, a move that proved less than successful. By the time *CSI: Miami* premiered in 2002, and for the next five seasons, detective / private investigator Yelina Salas is a recurring character whose personal life includes abusive partners and their involvement in the drug trade, thus killing two birds with one stone: she is on the legal side while her husband is linked to the drug trade. All of these instances illustrate both the regulatory and the multicultural stages of representation in television entertainment, as all these shows combine white with a range of ethnic characters, usually African American and Latina/o. As well, in the news, the criminal and law enforcement officer tend to be over-represented. As of 2009 the regulatory phase, and new versions of the bandit, continue to populate mainstream culture as the preferred ways of representing Latino males and some Latina females.

While the above section concentrated on the bandit, another common type is the Latin Lover, a hot-blooded male who sensually tries to seduce women. Dating back to Rudolph Valentino in the twenties, the "Latin" referred to a broad swath of brown men ranging from Latin American to Middle Eastern and Mediterranean. Although Valentino passed away in 1926, the type has endured, sometimes in concert with the bandit. For example, Ponch from the *CHiPs* series mentioned above was both regulatory and a lover. Quite often it's the lover element that does a Latino character in. Contemporarily, Antonio Banderas has played the Latin Lover several times, including when he played Zorro, whose character includes the lover component. The Latin Lover is just as likely to be outside of the law as to be within the law, though the latter version sometimes overflows into the buffoon who is a simpleton. The types mentioned here – bandit, lover, buffoon – are identified by Ramirez Berg (2002) as the three recurring stereotypes of Latinos in Hollywood film. All three characters represent a deviation from normal (read "white") masculinity. The regulatory/multicultural phases bring up the fact that there is a fairly small range of male Latino types in mainstream entertainment.

The Latina domestic

While there is arguably a wider range of female Latina characters in mainstream popular culture, as usual more does not necessarily mean better. Ramirez Berg (2002) identifies three main types in Hollywood film: the halfbreed harlot, the female clown, and the dark lady. As with the male types, sometimes these characters bleed into each other. Lopez (1992) adds that each of the female characters represents a sexual threat. As well, all three of these characters represent a deviation from normal (read "white") femininity. However, one type that Latinas inherit from African American representation and that circulates widely in different types of media and popular culture is the Latina maid, formerly the African American mammy. You might remember the African American maid from *Gone with the Wind* (1939), or any number of other African American maids, in *Imitation of Life* (1934, 1959) to *Forrest Gump* (1994) and television shows such as *Beulah* (1950). Actresses Louise Beavers and Hattie McDaniel had entire careers playing this one role. Maids and mammies were not always the same. The former could be, as she was in *Gone with the Wind*, buffoonish and young, while the latter was large and motherly, caring for the white family more than for her own. Both of the types, however, were asexual so as not to threaten the white patriarchal family. The mammy/maid was the one female of the minstrelsy stereotypes, most of which were male.

The maid, as a type that combines elements of ethnicity, class, and gender, has largely, but not fully, moved into Latina representations. As with their African American predecessors, it places Latinas in a position of labor, usually in relation to white femininity's leisure. The Salas character in *CSI: Miami* alerts us to gendered representations of Latinas. As the extreme personal-life turmoil of Yelina Salas mentioned above as a character in *CSI* suggests, there is a tendency to focus on Latinas in the domestic sphere and/or as sexual threats. In fact, Jenrette, McIntosh, and Winterberger (1999) document both the under-representation of Latina/o family within daytime soaps and the over-representation of Hispanic maids within the same genre. The previously mentioned Children NOW (2003) study identifies "domestic" as one of the main credited roles for Latina/os in prime-time television. The Latina maid exists across a wide range of genres and media.

We might want to examine one prominent Latina-maid actress. While most of the coverage for the Latina hit movie *Real Women Have Curves* (2002) went to America Ferrera, who played its chubby lead character in a coming-of-age story where the Latina girl leaves her working-class neighborhood and family to go to the big city, New York, to pursue higher education, some may have noticed Lupe Ontiveros who played the role of her tradition-bound mother. If she looked familiar, it is because in her long career Lupe estimates that she played the role of maid in film and television between 150 and 300 times on-screen! Ms. Ontiveros, a US-born Latina, has played the maid in a range of movies from *El Norte* (1983) and *The Goonies* (1985) to *As Good as it Gets* (1997). Many times her performance has been delivered with a thick accent despite the fact that she is a native English speaker. Along the way, Ms. Ontivero also increasingly plays the role of either the *abuelita*, the self-abnegating Latina grandmother, or the controlling tradition-bound mother as she did in *Real Women Have Curves* and in her role as Juanita Solis, mother-in-law of Gabrielle (Eva Longoria's character) in the hit television show *Desperate Housewives*. Lupe Ontiveros is a highly accomplished Latina actress whose range is broad – for instance she played Selena's murderer, Yolanda Saldivar, in her crossover role – but she continues to be largely typecast.

Partly due to the fact that Olivares has played the maid hundreds of times, she was chosen as the narrator for *Maid in America* (2004), "a documentary about Latinas who clean your home and help you raise your children." Olivares claims that she gave her heart and soul every time she played the maid, as that is a job that many have to hold for a lifetime. She wanted dignity in that character. *Maid in America* defetishizes the maid – that is, it reveals where maids come from and the conditions of labor that they endure. It shows three women who come from Latin America, leaving their own families behind, to raise the children of those in the USA. Co-produced by a Latina, Anayansi Prado, this documentary show another face of maids – the children they leave behind, and the search for some form of income to send back to their children and family to provide them with an existence outside of abject poverty. The documentary gives another face to the story of immigration, which is so often represented in news discourses as one full of male lawlessness, and instead provides a full portrait of the cheap, underpaid female transnational labor that props, and indeed enables, the functioning of the upper-middle-class household.

Maids appear elsewhere in popular culture, and often linked to issues of leisure – for the white middle class – and unrepresented labor – for the Latina maid. For instance, www.maidinamerica.com is a website from the San Diego, California area that promises you more time with your family while others do the cleaning. The portal picture of the website is that of an Anglo nuclear family cavorting on the beach, presumably while a missing-from-the-picture Latina maid cleans their house (retrieved March 13, 2001). This is precisely the point made by Báez and Durham (2007) and Molina Guzmán (2009): spectacular Latinas are foregrounded while Latina labor is either backgrounded or altogether missing from the picture.

Another website, www.xquisitemaids.com, whose motto was "You've got it Maid, here!" (March, 2008) but changed in March, 2009, to "We get down & dirty to get what you need cleaned!!" features scantily clad Latinas promising to show you a good time singly or in groups (retrieved March 10, 2009). This website (see figure 4 opposite), whose posted address is in San Bernardino, California, utilizes the trope of the sexy maid combined with a Latina theme. Unlike the African American mammy, the Latina maid, because of Latinas' perceived hypersexuality and hyperfertility, does threaten the middle-class family and is represented in a sexually explicit or sexually threatening way. Damien Spry, an Australian media scholar of Japanese Manga representations, comments on this particular image:

> This characterization includes typical Japanese design elements popular in Manga (Japanese comic books and graphic novels). Firstly, the shape and size of the facial elements – small nose, small mouth, and large eyes – are tropes designed to evoke a childish coquettishness, and hence tap into (fetished) desires for youth sometimes referred to as the "Lolita complex" (Allison, 2006). Large eyes are also favored by Manga artists for their capacity to evoke different emotions, including passive, even submissive, sadness contained in the single tear shown in this picture, which again evokes childishness, a powerlessness that suggests submission, or a need for a protection – a (male?) savior. The maid uniform also directly corresponds to a fashion trend among young Japanese (mostly) women referred to as 'gothic lolita' – a variety of subgenres all based on the combination of the goth aes-

Picture from the website www.xquisitemaids.com

thetic (dark eye make up; big black boots) and a softer, more youthful yet similarly transgressive style that incorporates maid uniforms (or bo-peep dresses) and long hair in pig tails or similar (Winge, 2008). The uniform, here a maid, but elsewhere a schoolgirl, is commonly found in Japanese fashion and in comics, including pornographic comics and cartoons (Animé) often referred to as hentai. The similarities with Manga are many: her fetish uniform, her long flowing hair worn up, her plunging neckline, her short skirt coyly lifted to reveal her underwear, her childish bow and her long stockings, and the combination of the risqué and the slightly coy in the pose the maid is placed in. *The differences are around body shape. Japanese Manga sexualized female characters, while usually with unrealistically thin waists and curvaceous breasts and butts, are typically more slender and long-limbed than this image.* (Personal communication with Damien Spry, March 14, 2009, emphasis mine)

In sum, the representation in the figure above combines a style of Japanese Manga with big doe eyes and pseudo-Latina components, the big butt, the long brown hair, the bigger body, shorter limbs. It is truly a transnationally hybrid representation, using Japanese iconography in concert with narratives of Latinidad to generate a visual image for what is essentially a pseudo-pornographic service/product – the sexy Latina maid. The website includes a range of "services," and costs for those desiring a maid, and includes real photographs of the Latina maids who come to your household. These photos include the celebration of the Latina butt, although, given the nearly pornographic nature of this website, the butt is quite a bit larger than what is normally acceptable in Hollywood film, television, and advertisements. It is much more like the Hottentot butt than Jennifer Lopez's (www.xquisitemaids.com/entertainment, retrieved March 10, 2009).

In mainstream popular culture the Latina maid still figures prominently. Even the reigning Latina has played a maid in a major Hollywood-studio romantic comedy, co-starring Ralph Fiennes. *Maid in Manhattan* (2002), starring Jennifer Lopez, detailed the rags-to-riches story of a single mother hotel maid who lives in the Bronx and crosses the path of a rich politician who falls in love with her. Following the usual path of a romantic comedy – encounter, conflict, separation, and resolution – Marisa Ventura ends up not only together with her upper-class beau but also realizing her professional dream of becoming a hotel manager, and thus making the transition between working-class labor and upper-middle-class management. You could call this the successful maid story, with heavy-duty influence from telenovelas wherein the working-class heroine conquers class barriers through love. This is also one of the few movies in which Jennifer Lopez plays an explicitly Latina character – and within stereotype at that. However, Lopez is not the only contemporary Hollywood star to play a maid or nanny.

Other movies and television shows include ironic nannies, whose portrayals are a commentary on both representational strategies and the modern condition wherein the upper-middle-class family often depends on these nannies. In *The Nanny Diaries* (2007), Scarlett Johansson plays a reluctant nanny who is finding herself, between her undergrad degree and her decision to pursue graduate studies. Of course, her character, Annie Braddock, eventually quits her job and resumes her path of upward mobility. We expect no less of the white protagonist in a romantic comedy. However, as a nanny, she comes into contact and community with other nannies and domestics, the majority of whom are immigrant workers, from Latin America, the Caribbean, and Africa. In this movie, we get a glimpse of their conversations about their bosses as well as about the rich Upper East Side (New York City) women who employ them as laborers. To be sure, the former come off much more sympathetically than the self-absorbed and overindulgent mothers. Moreover, there is a bit of tension between Maria, the Latina domestic worker, and Annie, the Anglo nanny – Maria has no patience for Annie though she voices solidarity with previously fired nannies. A similar representational tactic – portraying the nanny/domestic as more sympathy-worthy than her employers – was present in the teen hit *Clueless* (1995). Here the domestic worker refuses to be identified as a Mexican, and asserts her Salvadorean identity to her clueless charge Cher, played by Alicia Silverstone.

As an aside, the nanny is an esteemed professional in the Old

World, serving as a surrogate parent for the upper-class offspring. Contemporary US television draws on this tradition and combines it with the make-over reality show. Shows such as *Nanny 911* import highly trained and organized British nannies to bring order and control to unruly, mostly upper-middle-class, US families. As such, they represent nannies as mobile, transnational, first-world professionals. One wonders what type of immigration status these nannies have as they are neither Latina nor any other form of third-world immigrant provenance.

Despite the upper-class nannies mentioned above, long-running television shows still draw on the Latina nanny, though, as with the movies, sometimes these are very ironic nannies. In the long-running hit television show *Will & Grace* (1998–2006), much-awarded for its portrayals of gays and lesbians, the maid, Rosario Salazar, played by Shelley Morrison, engaged in witty, self-reflexive dialog about maids with her boss, the wealthy Karen Walker, played by Megan Mullally. This maid had a mind of her own, and often demanded much more than her boss was originally willing to give. As well, this maid knew that her boss depended on her. The following witty dialog illustrates the relationship between these two women, a relationship that represents ways of treating maids rather than a real-life situation (the difference between representation and images):

From *Will & Grace*: "*Bed, Bath and Beyond*" (#4.7) (2001)

Karen: Finally, you're here!

Rosario: You know, if you're gonna leave me in the limo for five hours, the least you could do is crack a window.

Karen: What, and let you start yapping out at all the other maids so that they can come over and jump on the car? I don't think so.

Rosario: You better watch it, lady, because the next time you take a bath it'll be rub-a-dub-dub, I drop the blender in the tub.

(www.imdb.com/character/ch0019865/, retrieved March 13, 2009)

Will & Grace was a show that dealt with stereotypes and sought to break them. It remains to be seen whether the audience interpreted it that way (see chapter 3, "Audience and reception").

While the documentary *Maid in America* is much cheaper than a network television show, yet still much more expensive than any one person or grassroots group could produce, digital technology allows less financially endowed producers to intervene into media. One such media form is the alternative short video. Admittedly less slick than Hollywood film and shorter, it can still pack quite an impressive amount of meaning. One such effort, *Spanish for your nanny* (monkeywithashotgun.com, 2007), represents a critical analysis of the Latina maid and her employers. The video begins with a Latina teaching a room full of white middle-class women helpful phrases such as: "the cleaning supplies are in the closet" and "please use disinfectant before touching the baby." The scene turns hostile when the women interrupt, asking how to say things such as "I know you are stealing from me, I need to check your bag" and "I don't care if the bus was late; next time I'll beat you," which the Latina teacher, without losing composure, translates into "Yo soy una gringa puta de mierda" and "entrame palo con la escoba y metelo en mi culo, fuerte." The short video, slightly longer than two minutes, represents tensions marked by mistrust and impatience between dominant-culture women and their Latina workers. The documentary, major Hollywood film with the reigning Latina star, long-running and successful television show, websites for different types of maid services, and the alternative video speak to the fact that the Latina maid is very much a part of the social and economic fabric of the USA. The heterogeneity of representations of the maid speaks to the inability to harness such a stereotype. Many represent it for different purposes. Even within the mainstream, the Latina maid has become a tongue-in-cheek, an ironic, representation.

The Latina threat

The domestic/maid/nanny falls within the tendency documented by scholars to see Latinas in popular culture as a double ethnic and sexual threat (Beltrán, 2002, 2005; A. M. López, 1991). In *Spanglish* (2004), Paz Vega, a Spanish actress,[7] played such a maid, whose character and body represented a threat to the nuclear family for which she provided services. The father was attracted to her but the dominant-culture wife, represented as shrill and insecure, felt threatened. By the movie's end, the maid and her daughter move on, and the white nuclear family remains intact, heals, and returns to normalcy. This movie pitted the mother against the Latina maid, foregrounding the conflicted, yet sympathetic, male head of household. As such it is a profoundly anti-feminist traditional movie, as we are recruited to sympathize with the male while the women duke it out.

The Latina threat is represented in a number of ways. She can be a hot-blooded, hypersexual character such as the bulk of Rosie Perez's roles (Valdivia, 1998). For example, in *It Could Happen to You* (1994), Perez was the shrill Muriel, a money-hungry wife whose eventual replacement by good white girl Yvonne, played by Bridget Fonda, we come to welcome. As with *Spanglish*, we are recruited to sympathize with the hapless but good male character Charlie Lang, played by

Nicolas Cage. Similarly, in *Untamed Heart* (1993), Perez played a wait-ress character whose relational ethnicity within the working-class role sexualizes her in comparison to her co-worker Caroline, played by Marisa Tomei. Perhaps because of her thick accent, despite the fact that studios sent her to voice coaches, Perez did not cross over into major stardom and largely fell out of the limelight by the mid-1990s.

Many of Salma Hayek's roles have also reprised the hot-blooded Latina trope (Molina Guzmán and Valdivia, 2004; Molina Guzmán, 2006, 2007a, 2010). For instance, in *Wild, Wild, West* (1999), Hayek played the ever-clad-in-lingerie Rita Escobar. For some of the movie, she even spends some time in her bustier inside a birdcage-like structure. Indeed Hayek's first appearance in an English-language US movie, when she was attempting to parlay her massive telenovela popularity from Mexico into a Hollywood career, was as the discarded girlfriend in Alison Ender's *Mi vida loca*, previously mentioned in rela-tion to the pachuca version of the Latina bandido. In that role Hayek wore a skin-tight short dress and portrayed the shrill and drunken discarded girlfriend. In many of her roles Hayek reiterated the hot-blooded Latina, as in *Fools Rush In* (1997), wherein she is the volup-tuous girlfriend-turned-wife of Alex Whitman, played by Matthew Perry. However, here, as with *Maid in Manhattan*, we are witnessing a change to the biracial romantic couple representation. Whereas in the past these couplings ended in failure, often involving the death of the ethnic member of the couple, with the contemporary spectacular Latinas there is a happy ending. This signifies at some level, at least, the possibility of romantic coupling between a light Latina and a major white male actor. Previously, Rosie Perez in *White Men Can't Jump* (1992) had to roller-skate into the sunset at the end of the movie as the biracial male buddy couple, played by Woody Harrelson and Wesley Snipes, continued their friendship. Sometime between *White Men Can't Jump* and *Fools Rush In*, it became somewhat acceptable to envision biracial couples composed of white males and light Latinas experiencing a romantic happy ending.

Another representational form of the threat is the dark lady of mysterious and dangerous sexuality (Beltrán, 2005b; López, 1998). Most of the roles played by Dolores del Rio in the 1920s speak to this form of the threat. The dark lady is not as prominent as she used to be. On the other hand, the contemporary harlot, another female type, brings together the two previous types – the hypersexual and the dark lady – into a character with unbridled sexuality with darker tenden-cies. One such character was Mirtha Jung, played by Penélope Cruz[8] in *Blow* (2001). Mirtha, a Colombian woman who moves to the USA with her husband, a drug dealer, not only exudes sexual appetite but also becomes a cocaine addict and gets her husband caught by the police and neglects her child. Not a character to look up to, to be sure, but certainly one that delivers all of the elements of the harlot who threatens not only the family but society at large.

Within alternative films and videos there is a range of overlapping and contestatory types. There is a wide amount of scholarship, especially in regard to Chicano film, written by scholars such as Chon Noriega, Charles Ramirez Berg, and Rosalinda Fregoso. That is another entire area of scholarship that deserves its own separate treatment. Fregoso (1993) has documented the lack of women, either at all or in agent roles, in the early days of Chicano cinema. The opening salvo in Chicano film was Luis Valdez's *I am Joaquin* (1969), a visual adaptation of the poem of the same name, focused on a masculine perspective. Jesús Salvador Treviño's *Yo Soy Chicano/I am Chicano* again represented the Chicano experience from a male perspective. Both traced back the Chicano experience to indigenous roots through the recovery of male heroes. It took Chicana film producers to address the lack of gender sensitivity in what had been a masculinist ethnic movement. Esperanza Vasquez presented the importance of women and everyday life in *Agueda Martínez: Our People, Our Country* (1977), and Sylvia Morales expanded a slide show by Ana Nieto-Gomez into a film entitled *Chicana* (1979), in essence a response to *Yo Soy Chicano/I am Chicano*.

Since 1969, the short films have morphed into either documentaries or alternative feature-length films and videos. Benfield (forthcoming) finds that there is a lively variety of alternative production, especially now that video and digital technology make it less expensive to undertake such a project. For example, Lourdes Portillo has produced, directed, and/or written a number of documentaries, all of them about Latin American Women and/or Latinas. These include *Señorita extraviada* (2001) about the Ciudad Juarez / El Paso border-town femicides; *Corpus* (1999) about Selena – a very different take from Gregory Nava's *Selena* (1997) which focused on her rise to power guided by her father, instead exploring Selena's agency, her sister's view, etc.; and *Sometimes My Feet Go Numb* (1996) about AIDS. These documentaries are issue-specific and serve as both representation and activism. In these documentaries the previously discussed types dissolve into complex characters that refuse to be boiled down to one or two essential characteristics, the basis of a stereotype.

Prevalent themes

The previous research into the stereotype of the bandit/criminal, the maid/domestic/ nanny, and the Latina threat has been extended to the exploration of themes and narratives. That is, rather than focusing on particular character types scholars investigate the themes in which Latina/os appear solely or prominently. These themes are prevalent in realist and fictional genres, such as the news and movies, video and digital games, television, radio, websites, billboards, etc. Unsurprisingly, the study of themes is spearheaded by the finding of immigration and border-crossing as overarching narratives for talking about Latina/os. Immigration has been an overarching theme since the early days of the bandit stereotype, and, due to the moving border that not only changed the national sovereignty of massive amounts of territory but also separated families and communities into separate nation-states, this continues to be the case. Three major research studies document this tendency: *Covering Immigration: Popular Images and the Politics of the Nation* (Chavez, 2001), *Brown Tide Rising: Metaphors of Latinos in Contemporary American Public Discourse* (Santa Ana, 2002), and *Shifting Borders: Rhetoric, Immigration, and California's Proposition 187* (Ono and Sloop, 2002). In the first study, Chavez analyzes news magazine covers about Mexicans and Mexican immigration, and finds that while production is represented positively, reproduction is represented negatively. Xenophobic metaphors of war and invasion pervade negative coverage, and coverage subsides when immigration is not a political issue in Washington (1987–92). Santa Ana (2002) finds heavy usage of metaphors of invasion and animals, as well as of natural disasters – the "tide rising" component. Furthermore, guest-worker programs avoid the reproduction fear and therefore get better coverage, thus coinciding with Chavez's findings. Ono and Sloop (2002) explore the "sustained rhetoric of nativism and xenophobia" (p. 3) that surrounded the introduction, deliberation, and passage of Proposition 187 in California in 1994, a measure that denied undocumented immigrants access to basic services such as education and health care. The range of mainstream media analyzed in the above studies included magazines, newspapers, radio, and television. All these studies provide extensive historical background detailing US immigration laws and panics, affecting Latina/os and many other types of immigrants. As the titles suggest, that national imaginary rests partly on notions about where the borders lie, who belongs and who does not, ways of dealing with unwanted outsiders, and appropriate and accepted waves of migrant, albeit temporary, workers. Moreover, immigration rhetorics and politics are internally contradictory, as economic necessity, on the part of both the immigrant and the host society, fuels immigration, and elements in popular and political sentiment resent it.[9] Padín (2005) studied printed news in Oregon and found robust support for his "conditional whitening" hypothesis. News reports simultaneously portray Latina/os "as a social burden and a moral threat" (p. 68), locating them somewhere between normative whiteness and aberrant blackness. That finding suggests that the immigration frontier has yet to be ceded. Indeed, contemporarily, entire networks such as Fox, and daily shows such as *Lou Dobbs Tonight* on CNN, spew anti-immigrant themes daily, with "illegal aliens" being connected to every problem in the land, from terrorism to health infections to the global economic collapse of 2009.

Scholars also have found immigration and borders as a theme in media genres ranging from entertainment and fictional narratives, to adult films such as *Men in Black* (Ruiz, 2002), to children's animated movies such as Disney's *The Lion King* (1994) and Warner Brothers' *Happy Feet* (2006). Martín-Rodríguez (2000) interprets *The Lion King*, Disney's global mega-hit, as revealing social anxieties about the status of Latina/o immigration. *Happy Feet* (2006), a movie about penguins and overfishing, can be read similarly, with both movies exploring the tension between African Americans and Latina/os, at the margins. In *Happy Feet* the margin is represented quite literally, as in Antarctica, at the edge of survivability. In *The Lion King*, the flatlands, beyond the lion kingdom, represent the undesirable nowhere-land to which hyenas have been relegated. Both films incorporate themes of border and belonging. Whereas the border tensions in *The Lion King* are manifested through lions and hyenas, in *Happy Feet* emperor penguins represent African Americans, organized in relation to soul music, who in turn encounter the Adelie Amigos, a bunch of rock-hopper penguins, with their Latin beats and Spanish accents. Animated feature-length films, watched by children and adults alike, are important components of popular culture and, as such, include representations of contemporary ethnic politics.

Major Hollywood films and television shows, whether successful or not, also include themes of immigration and border crossing. Ruiz examines narratives of the border in films such as *Red Dawn* (1984), *Men in Black*, and *Traffic* (2000), as well as episodes of *The X-Files* and of news programs, in her discussion, and finds that "narratives pervading mainstream media construct undocumented immigrant bodies as diseased, contaminated, rapidly multiplying, and otherwise disorderly" (p. 42), resonating with the three previously mentioned studies about the discourse of immigration.

Not all films involving immigration reiterate the disorderly bandit trope. Films such as *Fun with Dick and Jane* (2005) and *A Day without a Mexican* (2004) represent other approaches to the representation of immigrants and immigration. In *Fun with Dick and Jane*, the protagonist loses his upper-middle-class job and eventually ends up at an immigrant corner, hoping to be offered a day job. He is unwittingly caught in a raid by immigration officers and deported to Mexico, thus joining other Mexicans who go through this involuntary border-crossing on a more regular basis. The protagonist's wife rescues him and as many Mexicans as can fit into their little car. Although the movie humanizes a few nameless Mexican workers, the focus remains on the travails of the main character. While the Mexicans are not represented as bandits, they are represented as illegal border-crossers. On the other hand, in *A Day without a Mexican*, a movie produced by a consortium of Mexican and US alternative production companies, the story is quite different. The premise of this film is that, one day, a cloud comes over California and one by one the Mexicans disappear. Only then do the state's non-Mexican residents realize how much they depend on Mexicans at every level of labor and experience in their everyday life – politicians, doctors, gardeners, journalists, clerks, etc. Actually, in every job and every setting, people/Mexicans begin to disappear, and the state comes to a halt, not being able to function without all the Mexicans. In a very witty scene toward the end of the movie, the state welcomes border-crossers, rejoices, and Immigration Patrol hugs them as they come back over the border. In yet another twist of the immigration theme, the major Hollywood blockbuster *The Day after Tomorrow* (2004) ends with the USA sending its citizens south of the border, as the Latin American nations welcome refugees after the USA suffers a mortal freeze. In this scene, the new US President (the previous one froze to death) thanks fellow American nations for accepting US citizens despite a history of blocking their north-ward trajectory in their time of need. The increased frequency of the theme of immigration in a wide range of movies does not necessarily reverse the fear and hysteria that usually accompany its appearance, but it does signify that immigration is becoming more prominent as an issue and that it is being linked to other national issues such as middle-class unemployment and global warming, making us members of one survival community. I might add that, in *Fun with Dick and Jane*, the temptation to pit the unemployed white male worker against the Mexicans, as in Michael Douglas against African Americans in *Falling Down* (1993), was not followed and the protagonist sympathizes with the Mexicans, though from a superior standing.

Scholars also examine a broad range of media – ranging from freeway signs to health campaigns that distribute materials as Public Service Announcements (PSAs). Ruiz (2002), for instance, points to another component of the immigration and border-crossing narrative – the gendered fear of hyperfertility from Latina women. Immigration discourses foreground the fear that Latina/os are reproducing out of control and will stress the ability of the state to provide basic services such as health and education, which takes us back to Proposition 187 which sought to restrict immigrant access to precisely those human

Border-crossing warning sign (Photograph courtesy of Roger J. Wendel).

services. Ruiz examines the California freeway sign warning drivers that border-crossers might literally be crossing their freeways (see figure). This sign is placed at several points on I5, close to the Mexican border, by San Ysidro, California, and close to the border checking-point south of San Clemente.

The sign foregrounds the child-carrying female figure and back-grounds the male, and as such can be seen as a representation of the fear of fertility. With the female/mother figure in the center, the foregrounding, placement, and size represent a gendered border-crossing. In a similar research project, examining the construction of a California teenage pregnancy campaign, Tapia (2005) notes that "while the official mission of the campaign had nothing to do with immigration . . . the signifying and interpretive material" fore-grounded "the pictures of pregnant brown women and young brown fathers" (p. 9). These resonated with other measures and discussions informing the common sense of that place and time. Public Service Announcements, distributed through local media, implicitly repre-sented Latina/o youth. For instance, one shows a brown young man pushing a stroller with a baby, against the background of a fuzzy pick-up truck, with the caption "are these the wheels you've been saving for?" Tapia notes that, in addition to the message of absti-nence implicitly targeted at Latina/o youth, the campaign articulated teenage pregnancy to reduced ability to participate in consumer culture. Powerfully distributed throughout mainstream popular culture, immigration discourse remains a major narrative about Latina/os in the media.

Connected to immigration, another theme is that of Latina/os and the body politic. Two major events have begun to generate research in Latina/o Media Studies. First, the war in Iraq and the coverage of Latina/o participation in that war bring up issues of belonging and citizenship, especially in relation to the fact that Latina/o non-citizens are taking part in the armed forces (Amaya, 2007b) and that there is an over-representation of Latina/o casualties in that war of attrition. News coverage of the local aspects of the war, especially in regions where there are many Latina/o recruits, cannot help but represent this side of the casualties. For example in San Diego, California, home not only to a large community of Latina/os but also to many armed force bases, the local news constantly covers stories about the Latina/o deceased and their families left behind. It is not that they necessarily set out to cover Latina/os but rather that, since Latina/os are dying in the war, the news cannot help but include them in their coverage. The second event was the presidential election of 2008. Especially in the 2008 Democratic presidential primaries, Latina/os have surfaced as a key component of a successful presidential bid. Subervi (2008) compared bi-partisan approaches to reaching out to the Latina/o vote and found a marked difference between the Democratic and Republican efforts at reaching Latina/o voters. In comparing party approaches to advertising and campaigning aimed at the Latina/o vote, Subervi-Vélez found the Democrats to be inconsistent and the Republicans to have a consistent long-term plan. Whereas the former focused on Latina/o issues, how these may have been caused by Republican policies, and how the Democratic Party might help resolve them, the latter consistently used an emotional approach emphasizing values and the promise of the American Dream to be delivered by the Republican Party.

Competing narratives of Latinidad: tropicalization and traditional Mexican

Beyond the major sterotypes – the bandido and the maid – and the major themes – immigration and immigrants – scholars assessing the field of media and popular culture have found there to be two competing narratives of Latinidad. These correspond to the two major groups of Latina/os in the USA: Mexican Americans on the one hand, and Puerto Rican and Cuban Americans on the other. The former cross over a land or river border from Central America, and the latter cross the Atlantic from island locations. Whether a result of fantasy or experience, these two different populations, despite claims that Latina/os are homogenized within mainstream popular culture, are generally represented in two different and identifiable manners. The tropical narrative has been identified as the ascending paradigm for representing Latina/os in popular culture. Aparicio and Chávez-Silverman (1997) proposed the term "tropicalization" to refer to the confluence of themes of island elements, salsa-driven, and dynamic movement narratives that characterize the hot bodies and cultures from the tropics. They specifically define it as "the system of ideological fictions which within the dominant (Anglo European) cultures trope Latin American and U.S. Latina/o identities and culture" (p. 1). This process of tropicalization can be found in all forms of media, from advertising to film, magazines, video games and virtual space, music, and news. Elements of this trope include near-turquoise-colored ocean waters;[10] hot, nearly combustible, colors such as fuchsia, neon yellow and green; tropical foliage such as palm trees and colorful ginger lilies; audio components of salsa, mambo, or merengue; sexualized situations and people, especially but not exclusively women – just look at a whole decade of representations of Ricky Martin following his "Livin' la vida loca" hit; movement and dance as part of the setting; and mostly urban, single, sometimes upwardly mobile, light-brown people.

The tropical narrative contrasts with the traditional Mexican narrative of stasis (remember the Limón image of the passive sombrero-wearing Mexican?); in a landlocked setting; with more muted colors of dirt brown, dull yellow, and pumpkin orange; barren earth and adobe instead of island waters; cacti instead of palm trees; *ranchera* or mariachi music instead of salsa; more religious iconography; extended and patriarchal family arrangements; working-class, and inner-city or rural, locations, sometimes including a donkey; and a darker-brown skin.

The picture opposite was taken in June, 2009, at a Mexican restaurant in Old Town, San Diego, and represents the Mexican narrative in mainstream US popular culture. Notice it includes many of the elements of this narrative: darker-brown skin, stasis, a donkey, a cactus, and some rural yet undetermined location.

Narratives include their own gendered elements. The overly sexual tropical woman, for example, has her religious and self-abnegating mother counterpart in the traditional Mexican discourse. The former is active and the latter static. They both differ from normal white femininity. One could say that the bandido is a Mexican narrative element, though in the urban space the bandido bridges from the Mexican to the tropical, including all Latino males. Relationally,

Stereotyped image of a Mexican on a donkey. Author's own image.

although both discourses mark Latina/os as different and ethnic, the tropical locates Latina/os within modernity while the latter locates them outside of contemporary forces of urbanism and progress. Both discourses of Latinidad flatten difference within – such as all Latina/os are hot within tropicalism and all Latina/os are lazy and rural within traditional Mexican discourse. While these two discourses account for most current representations of Latina/os in mainstream media, we cannot rule out their absence in some cases. It is also the case that these competing discourses on rare occasions become treated as one. The movie *Fools Rush In* (1997) is one such case as the protagonist played by Salma Hayek both comes from a dusty rural place in Mexico and dances to salsa in front of a huge fruit bowl, wearing tropical colors. *Dora the Explorer* includes the tropical music and island in the same place as a Mexican pyramid and the monkey. These discourses will be mentioned in the following sections as we explore contemporary representations across a range of media. Even the already-discussed prevalent theme of immigration includes elements of the tropical discourse, as illustrated by the fear of hypersexuality and therefore high fertility rates among the Latina/o population.

Spectacular bodies and backgrounded labor

The content analysis that yielded the bandit stereotype as it morphs into the present, especially of criminalized representations of Latina/os, demonstrated an over-representation of males in the regulatory phase. On the other hand, many contemporary feminist scholars explore the hypervisibility of spectacular bodies vs. the low visibility of ordinary bodies such as migrant and industrial workers – the former sexualized and individualized, and the latter massified and nameless (Durham and Báez, 2007). Spectacular bodies foreground Latinas in an effort to commodify their bodies, and any programming and products associated with those bodies. Commodification is the process whereby a product, process, or even a body becomes something that is available for sale and profit in the marketplace. Both ethnicity and femininity are highly commodifiable (Dávila, 2001; Halter, 2000). In a sense, this is a focus in analysis of media in general and Latinas in film in particular as the research on Dolores del Rio, Lupe Velez, Rita Hayworth, and Rosie Perez far exceeds that on the everyday lives of those who work to bring the stars to the spotlight (Beltrán, 2005b; Fregoso, 2007; A. M. López, 1998; McLean, 2004; Molina Guzmán, 2010; Valdivia, 1998). One can fairly say that in Hollywood film, regardless of ethnicity, the spectacular takes precedence over everyday life. Hollywood film seldom focuses on issues of labor as these are not seen as commodifiable.

The rise of the spectacular Latina is not a new development, as demonstrated by the partial bibliography above. The presence of these stars dates back to the 1920s and, as Beltrán (2008) has meticulously documented, their increased stereotyping is partly due to the advent of sound in Hollywood film. An accent was not an issue when films were silent, but became yet another element of stereotyping once sound was combined with the visual. However, there has been an ongoing spotlight on Latinas since the late 1990s Latina/o boom. Foremost on this list is Jennifer Lopez (see Case Study no. 2 at the end of chapters 1–4 in this book). There is a range of Latinas who have also been quite prominent in the 13 years since the death of Selena in 1995. Among these are Salma Hayek, Jessica Alba, Eva Mendez, Eva Longoria, Michelle Rodriguez, Rosario Dawson, Cameron Diaz, Christy Turlington, Christina Aguilera, Mariah Carey, and Shakira, to name some of the most prominent ones. Some of these stars and/or celebrities are more prominently "Latina," while others, such as Cameron Diaz – though Cuban American – because of phenotypic characteristics of white skin, blue eyes, blonde hair, and a tall and skinny body, are only claimed as such within Latina/o media such as *Latina* magazine. Outside of Latinidad, say within *People* magazine, their Latinidad is not mentioned. Some Latinas have recently come out of the closet about their Latinidad. These include Christy Turlington, a supermodel, whom *Latina* followed to El Salvador as she went "back home" with her mother, and Raquel Welch who only recently, and after her appearances in PBS's *American Family* and in the movie *Tortilla Soup* (2001), has been discussed as a Latina in the press. She claims that she never hid her Latinidad but that nobody seemed interested in that component of her identity – the Latina/o celebrity version of the US military's "don't ask, don't tell" policy. Other stars' and/or celebrities' ethnicities have been outed, especially on the web (Nakamura, 2007). Major recording stars Christina Aguilera and Mariah Carey, both of them part-Latina, have also spoken about their heritage and been covered as such in the Latina/o media. Moreover, actresses such as Penélope Cruz and Paz Vega, both of them Spanish, are often treated and talked about as Latinas in the press and celebrity culture. As you can tell, there is a wide range of women who are represented as spectacular Latinas.

Drawing on the representation of these spectacular Latinas, scholars have analyzed the Latina body as it represents broader national and global issues (Mendible, 2007). As Molina Guzmán (2007a) states: "the analytical focus is on how mainstream popular culture frames public understandings of Latinidad and Latina identity and how these representations speak to emerging contemporary Latina identity positions" (p. 118). One of the major components of the representation of Latina/os is the spectacular booty, often in reference to Jennifer Lopez (see case study at the end of this chapter) but also used to describe Latinas in general. The spectacular booty is both different and disciplined – that is, it is bigger than the flat white bootie but smaller than the African American booty. The representations of spectacular Latinas both reiterate some of the tropes of Latinidad and also challenge and disrupt them. Merskin (2007) finds that Eva Longoria's Gabrielle character in *Desperate Housewives*, the television show, while toning down some of the more egregious elements of the hot tropical Latina, nonetheless follows in that tradition, especially through situations and dialog. Báez (2007) makes a convincing argument for the multiplicity of feminist positions illustrated by Latinas in contemporary Hollywood film, pointing out that they "demonstrate the uneven intersection between Latinidad and feminism in contemporary popular culture and offer hybrid and multiple representations of Latina subjectivity" which "counter dominant archetypes of Latinas in Hollywood ... yet at the same time fit within the *tropicalized* trope of Latinidad" and offer a "taken-for-granted and often *commodified Latinidad* that is racially and ethnically ambiguous" (p. 126). In that same vein, Molina Guzmán (2007a) explores

Salma Hayek's purposeful assertion of agency and intervention into her public persona by both playing in and producing *Frida* (2002), as well as other movies, to disrupt her characterization as a bombshell or spitfire in previous movies. Molina Guzmán and Valdivia (2004) investigated the relationality between the representations of Jennifer Lopez, Salma Hayek, and Frida Kahlo in the mainstream and proposed precisely that all three women and their representations extend and disrupt narratives of Latinidad in the mainstream. This tension speaks to the dynamic relationality that Latinas represent in a period of turmoil of the national imaginary in the USA. That is, Latinas signify difference but not great difference. Latinas occupy that middle space of acceptance and difference between whiteness and blackness. Latinas are both feared, as the ultrasexual threat to the family and ultra-reproductive threat to social services resources, and also desired as the sexy bombshells, in relation to the normalized neo-Victorian sexuality of middle-class white women. Beyond gender, the fact that the USA needs migrant labor and has to acknowledge that it is not a binary racial nation contradicts the hysteria about immigration and racial purity. Latina representation in mainstream media and popular culture embodies all these internally contradictory tendencies.

If we take Paredez's (2002) assertion seriously – that is, that the Latin boom literally exploded over Selena's dead body in 1995, we can look at the Latina female body as a site of difference. One of the similarities, in addition to their common history of exploitation and marginalization within the USA, between Selena and Jennifer Lopez, whose break-out role as Selena crossed her over into the mainstream, is the presence of a prominent *derrière* (Aparicio, 2003). Indeed, much of the coverage and discussion of Jennifer Lopez initially centered on her butt, and that difference became the ethnic signifier of Latinidad. However, despite the huge coverage of Jennifer's butt (Aparicio, 2003; Barrera, 2002; Beltrán, 2002; Durham and Báez, 2007; Molina Guzmán and Valdivia, 2004; Negrón-Muntaner, 1997; Valdivia, 2007c), not all Latina stars are equally endowed or so treated. For example, Jessica Alba and Eva Longoria fit with the Anglo ideal of beauty, extremely thin, albeit with their long brown hair – that can nonetheless be dyed platinum blonde as in Alba's role as Sue Storm in *The Fantastic Four* (2005) and *4: Rise of the Silver Surfer* (2007). Bloggers such as Perez Hilton at perezhilton.com implicitly criticize Alba's distancing from her Latina heritage by calling her "Jessica don't call me Latina" Alba. The fact is that there is no purity within most of these spectacular Latinas, just as it is difficult to find purity within everyday Latinas. Just like Cameron Diaz's whiteness obscures her Latinidad, and Jessica Alba's mixed heritage calls her Latinidad into question, others such as Rosario Dawson and Michelle Rodriguez, with their mixed Afro-Latina heritage, do not get the prominent roles that more ambiguous and light Latinas receive. They are also more policed within celebrity tabloids – note the virtual spanking of Michelle Rodriguez for DUIs during her time filming the *Lost* series in Hawai'i. White Latinas are policed for being too white and Afro-Latinas for being too dark. Light-brownness remains the region of safety and authenticity for a spectacular Latina in the mainstream.

However, returning to the theme of reiteration and disruption, Beltrán (2004) notes that Michelle Rodriguez has consistently played "ballsy and physically active characters," and "she has thrown a punch in almost every one of her films" (p. 186). Beltrán feminizes the Latin American stereotype of the macho whose masculine traits are controlling, bordering on violent, and extends it to contemporary Latinas. The "macha" Latina has been played by Jennifer Lopez in *Anaconda* (1997), *Enough* (2002), and *Out of Sight* (1998). In the first, her character survives the jungle and treacherous mates; in the second, she has to train in martial arts to kill in self-defense; and in the third she is a gun-carrying police marshal/detective. In all three roles she functions as a bridge character, mediating between whiteness and Latinidad, or Latinidad and blackness. The macha shows up on television in *Lost* and even in the children's film genre, such as the role played by Alexa Vega as Carmen Cortez in *Spy Kids* (2001, 2002, 2003). Indeed, Beltrán finds that "Latinas have become prominently visible icons within the genre" of action adventure (2004). One could also interpret this representational trend as the feminine side of the regulatory phase. Latinas have entered into the legal and police realm through this macha character.

Latinas in the mainstream can be ambiguous and multiply cast if their ambiguity is malleable. This ambiguity factor also favors the light-brown Latina. This means that, if they are light enough, their bodies can represent not only Latinas but also Whites, Italians, African Americans, and indeed any ethnicity. Jessica Alba and Jennifer Lopez are two such economically ambiguous Latinas. Somebody like Raquel Welch was able to play within whiteness for decades until Latina prominence created a space for her to represent Latinidad. Salma Hayek's accent may have resulted in her playing more stereotypical roles within the discourse of tropicalism, but through her personal initiative she has managed to branch out. The fact remains that spectacular Latina bodies continue to occupy the mainstream stage. Despite dominant narratives of Latinidad, they disrupt as well as reiterate these in a manner that is not always manageable by powerful media industries.

Magazines and virtual space

There are at least two types of magazine research that need to be considered in Latina/o Media Studies. First, and less numerous, is the research that explores the representation of Latina/os in mainstream magazines. Banks (2005), for example, finds that, while representation of women of color has increased in teen beauty magazines such as *Seventeen* and *YM*, "Prominent models were more likely to be light skin than medium skin or dark skin; Black and Hispanic models appeared in more expensive advertisements than Asians and Whites; minority models were less likely to be seen in the workplace than whites but more likely to be portrayed in leisure places and school than whites" (pp. 6–7). Banks calls this the new racism in mainstream teen magazine advertising. Similarly Ricle Mayorga (2001) compared visual portrayals in *Latina* and *Glamour* magazines and found that "*Latina* constructed a homogenized and non-conflictive identity for Hispanic/ Latino women; an identity that supports U.S. dominant discourses on ethnicity and race and is subjugated to marketing practices" (p. 1).

Because magazines have become more and more target-audience focused, there are in fact a number of magazines that target the Latina/o audience. As the website Hispanic Media claims, there are over 600 such newspapers and magazine/publications from across the United States (www.allied-media.com, retrieved June 5, 2008). In addition many magazines include the representation of Latina/ os or target a broad multicultural audience that includes Latina/os. *People en Español*, as Paredez (2002) and Olivarez (1998) document, was begun as a direct result of the original *People* magazine, on April 17, 1995, for the first time in its history, releasing two different covers, one of Selena in the Southwest and another one of the cast of *Friends* in the rest of the country. When the commemorative issue after Selena's death repeatedly sold out, the magazine realized there was a large enough Latina/o audience that would buy its magazine and thus began the Spanish version. However, this was by no means the first Latina/o magazine. Indeed, Subervi-Vélez (1994) documents the existence of a wide range of Hispanic magazines dating back to the 1900s, and ranging from "culturally oriented magazines" to "political, social, educational, business, and entertainment topics" (p. 323). Contemporarily, there still are many community-oriented, as well as many commercial, Latina/o magazines. The latter illustrate the coming-of-age of a Latina/o market and include slick and well-funded examples, such as *Hispanic* and *Hispanic Business*, and more local productions such as *¡Que Onda!*, *Latin Heat*, etc. All of these magazines have online complementary websites.

Women's magazines are among the most numerous in this industry as they provide an ideal vehicle to circulate commercial messages about clothes, beauty products, home necessities, and decoration to women who have been culturally gendered as consumers. Not surprisingly, there is more than one targeted at Latinas. The most prominent one is *Latina*, a partially bilingual magazine whose circulation, size, and frequency has increased greatly since it began to be distributed in 1996 (M. A. Johnson, 2003; K. Z. Martinez, 2004 and 2008). *Latina*'s target audience is a heterogeneous pan-ethnic group of women whose bilingualism is stronger in English than Spanish and who have middle-class status and therefore represent a desirable audience for marketers. The components of the magazine that are translated are summarized in Spanish rather than directly and fully translated. The narrative thrust of the magazine is finding commonalities among Latina/os, supporting specificity, and promoting Latina/o role models. Martinez (2004) finds that *Latina* "makes an appeal to familial forms of identification, often presenting discourses of familial allegiances alongside calls for panethnic solidarity . . . *Latina* oscillates between celebrating the inclusion of Latina/os in the U.S. entertainment industry and speaking out against the criminalization of Latino men and the hypersexualization of Latina/os" (p. 155). Martinez (2008) further explores *Latina* in terms of the tension between everyday Latinas and the spectacular bodies, especially but not only Jennifer Lopez's, that grace the covers and many of the pages of this magazine. The magazine thus represents the tension already mentioned in terms of Hollywood film and popular culture at large, the highly commodified realm of spectacular Latina representation and the everyday lived experiences of Latinas as consumers of popular culture. Other magazines targeted at Latina women attempt to deal with this tension. For example, *Latina Style* magazine promises to cover issues of working women but, by "working," they do not mean working-class but rather women with jobs. In the women's magazine world, women with jobs are different from career women. The latter refers to upscale professional women, whose major focus and consumer choices do not necessarily revolve around the home and family. Perhaps the Latina audience does not yet demonstrate enough income and professionalization to support a career women's magazine. Other women's magazines are either extensions of Latin American magazines or mainstream women's magazine versions. *Vanidades*, a mainstay in Latin American women's magazines, is also distributed in the USA to a Latina/o market. Other magazines include *Moderna*, *Glamour en Español*, and *Marie Claire en Español*. The latter two, as is the case with *People en Español*, are hybrid mixtures of the original magazine and the more community-focused exigencies of ethnic media that result in the foregrounding of Latina/o celebrities and a pan-ethnic commodified identity.

Given the mainstream realization that girls and teens are an important market, it is not surprising that there are magazines aimed at Latina girls. There is *Quince*, a magazine solely devoted to the preparation for quinceañeras. These celebrations, of course, include a healthy amount for items such as dress, party favors, invitations, and all that a hyperconsumerist approach to that important rite of passage among a sector of the Latina population would entail. The online magazine includes the opportunity for girls to upload videos of their own quinceañeras. Articles in both the printed and online versions of *Quince* are not uniformly hyperconsumerist, and many discuss how girls and their families budget for this big date, echoing some of the themes of the more nuanced version of the movie *Quinceañera* (2005). That *Quince* is also an online website speaks to the fact the web allows for a broad range of online magazines such as *Latinitas*, a magazine by and for Latina girls, and *Teen Latinitas* (www.latinitasmagazine.org/). While the former represents the coming-of-age of the Latina/o audience as an attractive enough market to merit a specialist magazine, the latter is a non-profit effort whose mission is "to empower Latina youth through media and technology." You can draw your own conclusions from the difference in portal representations of these two websites.

Much research remains to be done about magazines. For example, S. N. Fernandez et al. (2005) compared the frequency and characteristics of cigarette advertising in magazines targeted at Latinas, in relation to men's and white magazines, and found that advertisers both target women differently from men and target Latina women differently from white women. Comparative research of advertising messages, their quantity and quality, within Latina/o media, in relation to mainstream media, would yield more information as to how the Latina/o market is being constructed and targeted and the potential implications for health and political access, for example. Comparative analysis of business strategies would also point to how Latina/os are being envisioned as part of the economic life of the nation.

Connected to the deployment of magazines is the wide variety of websites about Latina/os and by Latina/os. The already mentioned blog perezhilton.com foregrounds the webmaster's Latina/o subjectivity – that of a Cuban American gay man – and often deploys a Latina/o pride perspective on particular stars and events, as well as outing and disciplining closeted Latinas. The blogosphere is huge and deserves its own book, but there are chat rooms and blogs on almost any topic that might matter to a person interested in Latina/o

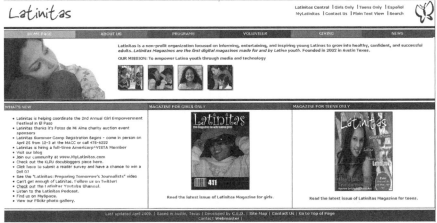

Images from *Quince* magazine online and from www.latinitas magazine.org

media issues, from an anti-reggaeton chat at www.terra.com on the site Foros Terra,[11] to a chat stream about Dora the Explorer in which participants attempt to decide where the show implies that Dora lives and what component of Latinidad Dora performs (Harewood and Valdivia, 2005). This latter task is all the more difficult to carry out given that Dora is one of those instances of media where both the tropical and traditional Mexican discourses are combined. Dora's island has both pyramids and palm trees; her music is salsa and and her pet Boots is remarkably similar to Mexican artist Frida Kahlo's painted pet monkey. No wonder that viewers write confusing entries about where Dora resides! Cyberspace is a whole new world of activity and research explores "the interrelations between representation in cyberspace, representation in other forms of popular culture, and representations of the body and the self" (p. 85). We need to remember that representation is multiply mediated in cyberspace as anyone representing themselves as a Latina/o could be putting forth a persona that does not necessarily correspond to their body and/or heritage.

Another area of media that is huge – video and digital games – has also begun to be studied in terms of representation of Latina/os. Most scholars find that game narratives are extremely racialized (Leonard, 2006; Nakamura, 2002, 2007, 2009a, 2009b). Children NOW (2003) found that black women were victimized and Latinas omitted. Latinos tended to be portrayed as athletes. Furthermore, the implicit space constructed in these virtual worlds itself invokes narratives of imperialism and tropicalization, so often present in other forms of media content (Magnet, 2006). Similarly Goldman (2004) discusses how the deterritorialized construction of Puerto Rico as island iconography is deployed in cyberspace. She concludes that the iconic value of the island is belied in practice as the Puerto Rican diaspora exists in a cyberspace well beyond the tropical location of Puerto Rico. Space is in fact a key component of the racialization in video games, as Leonard (2003) aptly entitles his article "Live in your world, play in ours!" The current controversy over the fifth installment of the game *Resident Evil* reiterates the usual positions. That is, defenders argue that race is not relevant as the game is now set in Africa and one would expect the heroes to mow down massive numbers of faceless hordes of dark savage Africans. Critics, building on media research, remind us that this is a traditional representation of Africa and brown people. It is relevant to note that previous installments of *Resident Evil* were set in Latin America and Spain after the first version began somewhere in the Midwest of the USA. Thus the game began at whiteness, went through Latinidad and is now in Africa.[12] The bridge role that Latina women play in popular culture is also something that Latinidad in general performs, between whiteness and blackness. Again, there is much research to be conducted into gaming. As Leonard suggests, much of the research so far has been on violent content, especially after it was revealed that high-school mass killers were fans of some violent games. However, there are issues of sexuality, sexualization, inter-ethnic conflict, children's games, etc. All of these remain to be studied.

Television

Until recently, television was a location where Latinidad and Latina/os were nearly absent. There was the occasional maid or working-class male: Rosario in *Will & Grace*, Chico from *Chico and the Man*, and Ponch in CHiPs stand out as examples. Some of the guys from *Welcome Back*

Kotter (1975–9), given that this was an inner-city remedial classroom, were Latino. Even Jennifer Lopez had a short-lived television series, *South Central*, for two months in 1994. PBS's *American Family* (2002–4) stuck fairly closely to the traditional Mexican discourse, being set in Los Angeles within an extended working-class, patriarchal family. The patriarch was played by Edward J. Olmos, an actor/activist who is as close to being typecast in that role as some female stars have been typecast in the dark lady or bombshell stereotypes. *The George Lopez Show* (ABC, 2002–7) was a popular prime-time sitcom with an all-Latina/o cast for its first five years, except for the part of his daughter. Also set in Los Angeles, the show revolves around his work and family situations. The show reiterated the usual location for Latina/os, although in a nuclear family setting, which is always a sign of acceptance in the mainstream within US television. With guest appearances by a number of major stars, the show was on the air long enough to guarantee its extended life on reruns. Another notable exception was *Resurrection Boulevard* on Showtime, the first Latino-themed cable television show. Drawing on Latina/o acting, writing, and directing talent, the show's location was also East Los Angeles, the family was also composed of a range of Mexican American characters, and other than the fact that the dad was a widower and boxing was a major part of the show, it corresponds with previous attempts to broadcast a Latina/o television show. Jesús Salvador Treviño, of long-standing reputation within Chicano film circles, directed many of the episodes and tries to walk the fine line between avoiding blatant stereotypes and making sure the show continued to be in Showtime's line-up (Wible, 2004).

The representation of Latina/os in mainstream television includes all Latina/o and mixed-ethnicity casts. The current hit dramedy *Ugly Betty* (ABC), an adaptation of the Colombian telenovela *Yo soy Betty la Fea*, brings together a multicultural cast of Latina/os, in the traditional Mexican mold, with Betty's sister Hilda performing the hypersexual foil to Betty's smart ugly-duckling role. This show is all about hybridity: it mixes the tropical with the traditional discourse; it has working-, middle-, and upper-class characters; it combines elements of the dramatic with the comedic genres; and it has characters who are Latina/o, white, African American, gay, etc. America Ferrera stars in this show, and she entered it fresh from her starring role in *Real Women Have Curves* (2002), a film that explored issues of ethnicity, gender, class, and ideals of beauty among a group of garment workers in Los Angeles. America Ferrera, like Jessica Alba, comes through the Disney young talent machine, and they both have a long string of made-for-television credits. Furthermore, America Ferrera is often spoken about as a representative for a more expanded ideal of beauty within Hollywood film, as she is a bit larger than most Hollywood stars. It must be noted that she is a size 8/10, hardly overweight, but nonetheless enormous compared to Eva Longoria's size 00. Much like Jennifer Lopez, as her success continues, America gets thinner and lighter. In fact Selena, who is often held out as an example of purity and authenticity, was actually planning to have liposuction in preparation for her crossover into the mainstream, which unfortunately came posthumously. This is consistent with crossover analysis: to cross over into the US market, stars have to adhere to, among other things, the US ideal of beauty standards, that include thinness, straight and light hair, and a general whitening that can be accomplished through make-up and relational placement in photographs and situations (Cepeda 2001, 2003a, 2003b). Shakira, another case study in crossover, lost weight, learned and began to tape songs in English, and became blonde as she entered the US market (Cepeda, 2003b).

Nonetheless, we have to acknowledge that the presence of Latina/o-themed prime-time television shows such as *Ugly Betty* and *The George Lopez Show*, as well as Latina/o-themed mainstream full-release movies such as *Nothing Like the Holidays* (2008), represents an expansion of the mainstream to include at least pockets of Latinidad. As much as we may want to criticize each of these media vehicles for particular characters or topics, they fact is they are available, and that would have been nearly unthinkable just over a decade ago. Lest we get too enthusiastic, and despite scholars calling attention to the rise of inferential rather than overt racism, we still witness regular instances of the traditional and explicit stereotypes. For example in popular reality television shows ranging from *What Not to Wear* on TLC, to *America's Next Top Model* on the CW, hostesses Stacey London and Tyra Banks, as well as the voice-over commentary, cast the Latina as a "hot tamale" or "fiery Latina." Thus, mainstream English-language television is currently a mixed bag in terms of Latina/o representation. There has certainly been an increase, which has, in turn, generated a range of themes and content, not all of which reiterates the traditional narratives but some of which does recycle the tried-and-true stereotypes.

Spanish-language television, Telemundo and Univisión, is no less embedded with the competing narratives of Latinidad. Levine (2001), in an agenda-setting essay, claimed that Telemundo represented the tropical while Univisión represented the traditional Mexican. In fiction there is the tendency to reiterate these discourses; however, in terms of the types of programs broadcast in these networks they both have more of a transnational diet. Mayer (2003a) notes that "*Telenovelas*, or Latin American soap operas, may not be the most popular programs among Latinos in the United States, but they are certainly the programs most targeted toward a Latina/o audience" (p.

429). Within this genre of soaps, traditional discourses of gender, class, and ethnicity predominate. Love conquers all in these narratives, with the usual process beginning with a working-class woman who falls in love with a man beyond her social circumstances. Telenovelas have proven to be a formidably successful genre, especially for Mexican and Brazilian producers who market them globally. The second most popular genre on both of these networks is the talk show, another feminine genre that combines therapeutic discourse with ethnic empowerment (Rojas, 2004). Rojas adds that "the most criticized elements of U.S. talk shows – pseudointimacy, dramatic confession, and moral judgment – also are part of the discursive strategies used by *Cristina* and *Laura* and the rest of the Hispanic talk shows." *El Show de Cristina* and *Laura en América*, two of the most popular talk shows on Telemundo and Univisión, are produced in Miami and in Peru respectively and distributed to US Latina/os. A significant part of the content of both of these networks is produced in Latin America.

A recent content analysis of Spanish-language television concludes that there are both gender and race tendencies (Mastro and Ortiz, 2008). First, males, especially older and larger ones, tend to have more power and exhibit classic gendered traits of assertiveness and toughness, whereas women are deferential and submissive. Men tended to have more professional roles while women were more often portrayed as home-makers. Second, light-skinned Latinos were found to be "more intelligent, articulate, and verbally aggressive than their darker on-air counterparts" (p. 117), while the opposite held true for light-skinned women who were less intelligent than their darker-skinned counterparts. Since only fictional programming was coded, the above findings draw heavily on telenovelas.

Also, especially in news and sports, both of the Spanish-language networks represent the global arena much more than the mainstream US English-language network. Spanish-language television has to represent the politics and economics of the Latin American region as so many of its viewers' lives depend on that regional dynamic. As well, for example during the World Cup, all fans know that they will find much better coverage on the two Spanish-language networks as their audience is more attuned to global sports such as *fútbol*/soccer than the mainstream English-speaking US audience. As with mainstream networks and magazines, both Spanish-language television networks also have slick and fully developed websites.

Another important component of television is children's programming. Here, the top-rated network is the Disney Channel, with Nickelodeon and Cartoon Network in second and third positions. However, all networks have children's programming and, given the convergence in media industries, Disney shows can also be seen on

ABC, and Nickelodeon on CBS. *Dora the Explorer* is a useful example. Originally a Nickelodeon show (since 1999), it was seen on CBS until 2006. It was also previously shown in Spanish on Telemundo and now can be seen on Univisión. Dora was conceived as a venue for teaching dominant-culture children some Spanish, but her success has made her into a global language pedagogue. In Israel she teaches her audiences English, for instance. She represents an achievement for Latinas and girls, as she is the explorer in her island world, with the help of her computer and her pet, Boots. She is drawn in the classic "brown" color and there is always a slice of her belly exposed between her shirt and her shorts, perhaps signifying rapid growth or a working-class lack of clothes that fit. Dora has been such a successful brand – one can purchase nearly anything "Dora," from gummy Doras and cookies to sheets, books, shoes, wall paper, furniture, music, books, backpacks, etc. –that she has spawned a related show *Go, Diego, Go!* As an eight-year-old animal rescuer, Diego provides a male counterpart to Dora's explorations. Both shows contain not only a small amount of Spanish language and music, but also cultural signifiers of Latinidad, across the two competing discourses, that demonstrate that the importance of this ethnicity, at this moment, has been extended to the world of children's programming.

One cannot talk about children's programming without talking about Disney. On Disney there isn't a "Latina/o" show per se, but there are some Latina/os running around. Disney's huge tween hit, the one that positioned it in the no. 1 slot in the children's television market, was *Lizzie McGuire* (2001–4), the paradigmatic white, blonde, upper-middle-class cutie. While the show starred Hillary Duff as Lizzie, her best friend was Miranda Sanchez, whose Latinidad was much muted. We were seldom privy to her last name, and only in a couple of episodes do we get to see enough of her home or family to deduce that she is Latina. Nonetheless, sidekick has been a usual role for ethnic characters in both Hollywood film and television. Disney has recently had two major monster hits: *High School Musical* (HSM) (2006, 2007, 2008) and *Cheetah Girls* (2003, 2006, 2008). In both of these franchises Latina/os figure prominently. In *HSM*, Gabriella Montez is a studious Latina, a math and science wiz, who falls in love with top white athlete, basketball star Troy. Her Latinidad is so ambiguous as to be nearly invisible unless you are looking for it. For example her mother looks Latina, but her role is so minor that you could miss it altogether. Gabriella is a fully assimilated Latina and as such her Latinidad nearly disappears. In *Cheetah Girls*, all the main-character girls are of mixed race. One of them, Chanel, is the rich Latina who describes herself to her friend Dorinda as "a little of this and a little of that." Her rich, perhaps Argentinean, mom is blonde, thus disrupting both the class and brown-race representation of mainstream Latinidad, but not the intra-Latina coding of Mexicans as brown and Argentineans as white (Dávila, 2002). In the second *Cheetah* movie, Chanel's Latinidad is much more prominent as the girls travel to Barcelona and she has to use her Spanish-language skills in that Spanish city. In both of these global Disney hits, Latinas are a component of a subtle mixed-race approach that is rather new in terms of ethnic representation. The subtle Latina girls are central to the narrative, though their Latinidad is muted. Their ambiguity can be recognized if you are looking for Latinidad, but totally missed if you are not. The mixed component is somewhat lost in successive Disney television hits. For instance, *Hannah Montana*, the monster hit that replaced *Lizzie McGuire*, exists fully within the terrain of whiteness. A newer show, *The Wizards of Waverly Place*, includes Disney newcomer and foregrounded hit girl Selena Gomez who plays Alex, and her mother Theresa who, according to the Disney website, is the children's "ambassador to their Latino heritage" (http://tv.disney.go.com/disneychannel/wizardsofwaverlyplace/about/index.html, retrieved March 15, 2009). The premise of *Wizards* is that the father is a former wizard, the mother is human Latina, and the kids have wizards' power. Trouble and hilarity ensue. The muted Latinidad of the family is present through occasional comments made by their Latina mother. The mother and the kids exhibit the slightest touch of Latina/o appearance – they all have brown hair and brown eyes, but really are light enough to be white. As such, they reiterate Disney's approach to Latinidad in particular, and ethnicity in general: keep it light, keep it white.

Public broadcasting also includes Latina/os in their television programming. *Sesame Street* had Latina/os from its inception in 1969 – remember Maria? Current shows include *Dragon Tales*, an animated show wherein two children, Emmy and Max, fly to Dragon Land to solve problems and spend free time. This is yet another case of ambiguous Latinidad as one would not know that the children are Latina/o unless one happened to be watching the few episodes where their mom calls out to them in Spanish-accented English. As well, the wise dragon Quetzal has an Aztec name and an accent that might not be noticed by most viewers and their parents.

In a similar spirit to *Dora*, also on PBS, *Maya & Miguel* is targeted at pre-school children, with a stronger component of Spanish language learning than their Nickelodeon counterpart. The twins, although a bit gender-typed – Maya is impulsive and Miguel is thoughtful – exist in a grounded Latina/o setting, a bit more territorialized than *Dora*'s ambiguous island world. One could say that *Dora* reiterates the trope of the eternal foreigner by living in that island somewhere, whereas *Maya & Miguel* live in the USA and therefore assert belonging. In other

PBS children's programming, such as *Barney*, the large cast of children includes one or two Latina/os. And even in *Clifford the Big Red Dog*, the cast includes two minor Latina/o characters. We can say that we are beginning to see a significant part of children's television with shows about Latina/os or, more often, that contain Latina/os, though usually as sidekicks or supporting characters that are barely recognizable as such.

Radio

Latina/o radio shows are multiplying in number; community radio still makes a difference, as was the case during the immigration rallies of 2006 when the word was spread through Latina/o radio about the rallies. As well, a number of community radio stations are forming "sister" relationships with stations in Latin America as a way to maintain contact between groups from that community who have emigrated and settled in the United States. Radio includes all genres of music as well as sports, news, and *radionovelas*, the radio equivalent and precursor of telenovelas, which are themselves the descendants of print-form *fotonovelas*. Latina/o radio is present in all major markets and many middle and minor ones, depending on the region. For example we can count on major stations in places such as Los Angeles, San Diego, New York, Chicago, and many cities in Texas and Arizona. While convergence in media industries means that many radio stations and programs are centrally produced and distributed by media conglomerates, research on Latina/o morning talk shows is very instructive. Casillas (2007) examines the hugely popular and largely masculinist shows available throughout the major Latina/o markets in the United States. El Cucuy and El Piolín in Los Angeles, El Vacilón in New York and Miami, and El Chocolate and El Pistolero in Chicago share "numerous discursive characteristics that frame them as working-class male personalities" (p. 162). All of these shows are ranked first in their Spanish-language markets, and are "largely dedicated to live conversations with callers, guests, and comedy skits" (p. 162). Casillas warns against treating these shows and their person-alities as the Hispanic equivalents of Howard Stern or Rush Limbaugh. These radio show hosts act as community leaders and present a tran-snational perspective on issues such as immigration, remittances, and Latina/o voting. Their participation in getting the word out to the community about the immigration rallies in 2006 was seen as decisive. However, their banter also includes an assertion of mascu-linity and agency often denied to Latinos in the USA, where they are marginalized and largely feminized. This assertion is accomplished at the expense of the women in the show. Casillas concludes that "women are relegated to the silent pause at the end of the show" (p. 177). In this element, these Latino radio hosts resemble Anglo shock jocks.

Conclusion

The area of content and representation analysis in Latina/o Media Studies is the most prolific one of the four – the other three being production, audience and interpretation, and effects. Beginning with stereotypes and frequency measurements, scholars in this area of research have also studied themes and narratives. While there are tendencies – and two competing discourses of Latinidad, the tropical and the traditional Mexican one, that tend to still be used in the mainstream – Latina/o representations, whether in mainstream or Spanish media, challenge and disrupt these themes and narratives. In a sense the tropical discourse is the ascending one and the traditional Mexican one the residual one. This exerts a near erasure of the most numerous segment of the Latina/o population, Mexican Americans, while simultaneously flattening the differences within Latinidad (Valdivia, 2004). However, as this chapter has shown, it is not that straightforward. Within and between these discourses there are contradictions, contestations, and active creations, especially on the web, that make the hold of these discourses, while still dominant, tenuous at best. Latinidad is too heterogeneous to be reduced to two narratives, and the commercial incentive to reach out to more members of this increasingly profitable audience will probably generate more possibilities, especially in reaction to increasingly likely activist interventions on the part of growing Latina/o communities.

The acknowledgment of the Latina/o presence in the United States has resulted in more representation. As mentioned at the beginning of the chapter, more does not necessarily mean better. Many content analyses of news and television shows demonstrate the enduring power of the bandido stereotype, as updated in crime news and fictional shows. However, as many Latina/os are moving up the ranks of entertainment production and participation, they are creating shows and narratives that disrupt the long-held stereotypes and constructions of Latinidad as the eternally foreign element in US popular culture and public life.

A final word of caution unsettles the very premise of this chapter. Given the heterogeneity of Latina/os, and the multiple forms of Latinidad, it is indeed nearly impossible to catalog or recognize all of the Latina/os in media and popular-culture content. In other words, the only way we can recognize Latina/os is if they explicitly dress, talk, or reside in some highly typical way or place. Latina/os need to ask ourselves, what is our goal in demanding increasing Latina/o representations, and what are the limits to these demands? Are we asking for more Latina/os that are recognizable as Latina/o? If so, does this mean we need the inclusion of elements that we recognize as Latinidad? Given that many of these elements are the result of long-standing stereotypes that serve to fuel discrimination against Latina/os and other brown bodies, how do we engage in a progressive activism that includes Latina/os but does not reiterate the demeaning narratives of the past and present? Can we envision another way of representing Latina/os? And does this actually amount to assimilation or a new hybridity of being? These are questions we might need to remember as we continue our analysis and resulting activism in relation to the representation of Latina/os in the mainstream.

Case study no. 1

"The Homicide Report"

"The Homicide Report" was an effort to address the fact that news content tends to focus on the unusual and extraordinary, the "newsworthy," rather than the everyday lived experience of people. It was, in effect, a successful effort to expand the range of representation for homicide victims in the Los Angeles area. Additionally, as this chapter has noted, one of the ways in which racialization is accomplished in the news is through the faceless and undifferentiated "mass reporting" about the other. The "Homicide Report" blog put a human face to the victims, the relatives, and communities of these victims. Moreover, the Report disaggregated the category "victim" into gender, ethnicity, and age. Furthermore, the specific location of each homicide also territorialized death – it pegged it to a particular geographical location in the immense Los Angeles County. All of these components are explicitly addressed in an early story in the *Los Angeles Times* about its own Homicide Report:

> The report seeks to reverse an age-old paradox of big-city crime reporting, which dictates that only the most unusual and statistically marginal homicide cases receive press coverage, while those cases at the very eye of the storm – those which best expose the true statistical dimensions of the problem of deadly violence – remain hidden.
>
> *(http://latimesblogs.latimes.com/homicidereport/2007/02/welcome_to_the_.*
> *html, retrieved April 28, 2008)*

The *LA Times* blog's first entry claimed to have a longer list "than usual because of a January crime wave . . . but otherwise [is] fairly typical in terms of the ages and ethnicities of those killed and the manner of their deaths" (http://latimesblogs.latimes.com/homicidereport/2007/01/index.html, retrieved April 28, 2008). Out of 17 reported homicides, 8 victims were identified as Latina/o, 6 as black, 2 as Cambodian, and 1, Filipino. Of these 14 were between the ages of 15 and 26, and all were from ethnic backgrounds. Some reports contained very little information: "a 24-year-old Latino man was shot at 14032 Oxnard St. in Van Nuys, and died at 1:31 a.m. on Jan. 27," or "was stabbed during an argument at 7530 S. LaSalle Ave. in LAPD's 77th Street Division and died at 10:32 p.m. Jan. 22." Other reports contained photos, and some gave detective names and contact details, asking the public to call in "during normal business hours" with tips and information.

Based on the details of each homicide, both the producers of "The Homicide Report" and a team of criminologists from nearby University of California at Irvine (UCI) have found that the violence seldom crosses racial lines, as in black on Latina/o violence or vice versa, but is most often within a racial group (http://latimesblogs.latimes.com/homicidereport/2007/09/blacklatino-vio.html, retrieved April 28, 2008). Loevy also found that even the most basic type of information – that is, the name of the deceased – was sometimes bungled by police reports. In one blog article, entitled "Bungled names, mingled ashes" (March 29, 2007), Loevy begins with:

> "Is the name really Ramirez?"
> In response, a detective shakes his head and shrugs. "It is now," he says dryly.
>
> *(http://latimesblogs.latimes.com/homicidereport/2007/03/bungled_names_m.*
> *html, retrieved April 28, 2008)*

In this blog entry, Loevy explores the differential naming practices within the Latin American and the US Latina/o communities. Middle names and two last names are important for a number of reasons, most prominently to differentiate among the thousands of Jose Ramirezes in any given setting. Also, seldom are Latin American and Latina women called just "Maria." Most of the time there is a second name as in María Isabel, María Teresa, María del Carmen, etc. Loevy points to police record forms that have not been revised to accommodate non-Anglo naming practices. Forms allow for first and last name only. Thus all sorts of *on-the-spot* measures are taken by police – from putting the extra names in the "alias" section or transferring some to the "middle name" slot. This has the effect of making it more difficult for families to find their missing relative, as they are not listed recognizably for them. It also erases from history many of the deceased, as their names are either entered into the wrong slot or wrong altogether. As the story begins, police are not exactly very careful in securing the right names for these victims. "Ramirez" will do for anyone. Undocumented homicide victims are even more difficult to enter into the police blog as very little effort is made to find their next-of-kin, and they probably are listed under a generic name such as "Ramirez."

The blog is accompanied by a lively discussion that merits research on its own. As well, a visual "Homicide Map" link (www.latimes.com/news/local/crime/homicidemap/) represents the frequency of homicides week by week and month by month. Frequencies of age, race/ethnicity, day of the week, gender, and cause of death add further details to the accounting of the dead. The map shows that the highest concentration of deaths is in the central Los Angeles area. In 2008, as of April 28, of 235 homicides, 129 (54.89 percent) have been of Latina/os (the largest number), followed by 73 (31.06 percent) of blacks, and 185 (78.72 percent) have been the result of gunshot wounds. Moreover, 199 (84.68 percent) of them have been male.

All of the components of the multifaceted Report represent crime and death in Los Angeles in a manner that had been impossible prior to the existence of the internet and its expanded capabilities for content. The Report represents the ethnicized character of homicide in the modern US city. Moreover, the Report represents the fact that death and murder have become a predominantly Latino occurrence in the Los Angeles area.

Case study no. 2

Jennifer Lopez

Jennifer Lopez began her appearance in popular culture as a back-up dancer, a Fly Girl, in *In Living Color*, a Fox network television show of the early 1990s that was produced by and to represent African Americans. From there, she moved on to be a back-up dancer for Janet Jackson in concert. After a brief and unsuccessful effort to appear in television (*South Central*, 1995), she made her successful crossover to the mainstream through the biopic *Selena* (1997). Featured prominently was her butt, representing Selena's butt. In fact, Jennifer herself claimed in *Esquire* magazine that "the world met my butt before it met me." Jennifer and her butt quickly became a powerful signifier of Latinidad in the contemporary USA. In fact, they were covered in the press and celebrity culture as if they embodied Latinidad. Because of this,

Jennifer Lopez on the cover of *Stuff* magazine, www.maxim.com

Molina Guzmán and Valdivia (2004) call Jennifer Lopez "iconic" – that is, she represents on a multiplicity of levels. She speaks for Latina women; she represents Latinidad; and she is re-presented as the essential Latina. Representing at three levels makes her iconic – more than just a simple representation.

As she crossed over into the mainstream, through Selena's dead body (Paredez, 2002), Jennifer Lopez was represented in relation to other white women through her curvy body. In all of her many movies there is at least one gratuitous scene – if not many more – when the camera lingers on her butt, as it takes center stage of the frame. At the beginning of *Anaconda*, she a scientist, is in her Amazon trailer working in a nearly see-through nightie when a co-worker comes to visit. She gets up to offer him a cool drink from the fridge and the camera lingers on her butt. In *The Wedding Planner* (2001), when she meets her white girl counterpart, Bridgette Wilson-Sampras playing the character of Fran, there is a scene when they both walk across an outdoor wedding and the camera, once more, lingers on Jennifer's butt, as it edges out Fran's slim and curveless silhouette. On magazine covers from *Stuff* to *Esquire*, her butt is foregrounded.

Latina/o Studies scholars were quick to analyze this attention to and the significance of Jennifer's Nuyorrican butt. The following six titles to scholarly material demonstrate how scholarship, like mainstream media, focused on Jennifer's butt: "Jennifer's butt" (Negrón-Muntaner, 1997); "Hottentot 2000: Jennifer Lopez and her butt" (Barrera, 2002); "The Hollywood Latina body as site of social struggle: media constructions of stardom and Jennifer Lopez's 'cross-over butt'" (Beltrán, 2002); "Brain, brow or bootie: iconic Latinas in contemporary popular culture" (Molina Guzmán and Valdivia, 2004); "A tail of two women: exploring the contours of difference in popular culture" (Durham and Báez, 2007); and *From Bananas to Buttocks: The Latina Body in Popular Film and Culture* (Mendible, 2007). This does not include countless essays presented at conferences, many of them submitted to journals, that echoed the themes already present in the above published material. Jennifer's butt became a fetishized component of contemporary Latinidad, and was amply documented as being so.

Concordant with narratives of Latinidad in the mainstream, Jennifer was not only sexualized in the typical tropical discourse, but was indeed reduced to that one body part. Scholars noted that in the mind–body, nature–culture binaries, being reduced to the butt placed Jennifer squarely in the location of body and nature. Not only was Jennifer reduced to her butt, but feminine Latinidad was also equated to this reductionist logic. Latina women became signified through the butt – a new element in the discourse of tropical Latinidad. The new equation became to be Latina = having a big butt. "Not so quick," said those who had a wider perspective – thus the invocation of the Hottentot. Latina representations fit between the Anglo ideal of beauty (no butt) and the fear of the African American component within the body politic. Jennifer's butt may have been big compared to the Anglo ideal of beauty, but it was decidedly smaller than the popular imaginary's version of an African American butt – the Hottentot Venus, whose butt was kept on display at the British Museum long after her death. Bigger Latina butts are present in hip hop culture and pseudo-pornographic websites such as the one mentioned and represented in the maid section of this chapter.

Furthermore, many noted, not only was Jennifer's butt not that big to begin with, but, as she became more of a mainstream star, her butt got smaller, her hair lighter, and her body thinner. Her crossover included crossing over into the Anglo ideal of beauty. Jennifer, already marked as different as she entered into the mainstream, became a pliable signifier. In her hip hop popular music ventures, she claimed an urban, mixed-race, African American- and Puerto Rican-inflected pop sound and persona. Her very public relationship with Puff Daddy anchored that side of her representation. In her Hollywood film career, she was able to portray a wide range of characters. In *Anaconda* (1997) she played an action adventure character, Terri Flores, with an ambiguously ethnic name. In *Out of Sight* (1998), another action-mystery plot, she played Karen Sisco, an Italian American police officer. In *The Wedding Planner* (2001), a romantic comedy, she played

In this picture, Jennifer representationally crosses over into whiteness. Her butt, proportionally, has decreased in size, her body is light-skinned and slim, and her hair blonde and long. There is not a trace of an element of Latinidad in the photograph. Author's own image.

another Italian American, Mary Fiore. *Enough* (2002) had her return to the action genre; her character, Slim Hiller, a white working-class waitress, kills her ex-husband in self-defense at the end of the movie. In *Maid in Manhattan* (2002), another romantic comedy, she plays Marisa Ventura, a Latina single-parent maid with an eye for business. In *Monster-in-Law* (2005), she plays Charlie Cantilini, a dog walker and aspiring clothing designer. In *Shall We Dance?* (2004), she plays Paulina, the heartbroken dance instructor who brings Richard Gere out of his middle-age crisis. Her roles reiterate three tropes of ethnicity in the US mainstream. First, she often plays a police officer as in the "regulatory" phase of representation. Second, when she is not playing a regulatory role, she has some pseudo-job (a dog walker?) but not a professional career. Third, and more connected to Latinidad, Jennifer Lopez marries or becomes romantically involved with white men in all of these films, a bridge role that Latina women play in mainstream Hollywood film (Valdivia, 2000).

Following her very public engagement and break-up with Ben

Affleck – the couple were named "Bennifer" in the celebrity press – and two poorly received movies (*Gigli*, 2003, and *Jersey Girl*, 2004), Jennifer seems to have re-embraced her Latinidad by marrying Marc Anthony, a Nuyorrican salsa artist with unambiguous Latinidad, and producing and acting in more Latina/o-themed movies such as *Bordertown* and *El Cantante*, both released in 2006. The former has Jennifer playing an investigative reporter in the Ciudad Juárez region where there has been a long period of unsolved femicides. The latter is a biopic of Hector Lavoe who is credited with bringing salsa to the United States. Her public persona has somehow changed to that of good wife/mother – in 2008 she gave birth to twins. She is also a business mogul as she nurtures fashion, perfume, music, and film-producing careers. Jennifer Lopez has successfully turned herself into a brand. Her representation still includes elements of the hot tropical Latina, albeit a somewhat tamed one now that she has entered holy matrimony with one of her own, a Nuyorrican man, and has settled into motherhood. Thus she represents the domesticated hot-blooded tropical Latina, who not only has crossed over into the mainstream but has reached a safety zone of family status within light Latinidad.

Audience and reception

Have you ever walked out of a movie and thought it was just great while those with you commented that it was an awful movie? You may have loved the excitement and girl-power feeling after watching *Enough*, wherein Jennifer Lopez, forced to defend herself from her abusive husband, takes charge of her life and confronts him. Yet as you walked out of the theater, you overheard someone commenting that it was yet another chick flick and that the ending was too violent and coded, once more, ethnic people as violent outlaws. Perhaps you love reggaeton music while whole governments attempt to outlaw or contain the lyrics and the beat that are precisely the reasons you love that music so much. Perhaps your family loves *The George Lopez Show* while you think it's lame and shrill. Or maybe you once participated in the production of some form of popular culture that you thought would resonate with a particular group, but it fell flat. Your intended audience did not respond as you thought they would. These are all hypothetical scenarios that relate to the study of audiences.

Let me give you a concrete example. *Crazy/Beautiful* (2001), a movie starring paradigmatic blonde, thin, white cutie Kirsten Dunst (Nicole) and much less known Jay Hernandez (Carlos), provides the audience with yet another version of the rich girl – poor boy romance with a Latina/o twist. In this case Nicole is the troubled daughter of a wealthy Congressman, and Carlos is a Latino straight-A student from the working-class part of Los Angeles. Even if you have not seen this movie, this bit of information is probably enough for you to begin envisioning the settings. As a member of the audience of countless star-crossed-lover films, and hundreds of television, news, and movie representations of poor and rich Los Angeles, you can piece together the rough details. Yes, Nicole lives in a house on a hill, reached by driving up a long beautifully landscaped driveway that ends in a circle in front of the house, with a great view of the city. Her house has plenty of large windows; the lack of clutter and dirt that is only possible with hired full-time help; and clean modern lines of expensive professional decorating. The house looks empty most of the time. On the other hand, Carlos lives in a block of small houses. Young people mill around the front yard and streets in his neighborhood. There are cars in various states of repair on the street. The house is dark, cluttered, and crowded. Women of his family are cooking in the kitchen. These are the spaces that signify to us, the audience, such binaries as rich–poor, White–Latino, the Hills – the *barrio*. I give all this background for at least two reasons. First, you probably recognize the elements here even without having seen the movie. Second, it sets up the scene that generates many audience positions. The girl is beautiful and rich but troubled. The boy is cute and poor but a great student. The girl can rely on wealth for the rest of her life. The boy must get into a good school with a scholarship to get ahead and help his family for the rest of his life. She is the recipient of unearned privilege. He is the one who must earn middle-class status to help his family, his community, and his people. At this point I want you to ask yourself, based on the information I have already given you, with whom do you identify and/or sympathize?

We move to the last third of the movie. At this point Nicole and Jay are a couple. They are having their "beach date." You know the one – where they go to the beach and the ocean and sun inspire them to make out and lose track of time. All of a sudden Carlos remembers something – today is his sister's quinceañera and he forgot about the party! This does not mean that much to Nicole, but to those familiar with this important Mexican and Central American rite of passage, we know he has messed up – big time! His family was in all likeli-hood planning this event for months. They spent money they did not have. Friends and relatives are attending the party. His mom and women-folk have been cooking for days. He must get home as soon as possible, and, given the geographic reality of Los Angeles, where those with fewer resources live freeways and many traffic jams away from the beach, this is quite a drive. Nicole asks to come along, to support her guy: "Do you want me to come in?" He is not quite sure – actually he may not have had the heart to tell her "no" and instead says "it's going to be kind of boring." So they both head to his home.

Picture this – everyone is dressed up in Mexican American working-class style at the quinceañera. Yet Nicole and Carlos are coming from their romantic day at the beach. She is wearing cut-offs. She is sandy. Her hair is all messy (after all they were making out at the beach). Plus, in that context, she is so clearly not Mexican. As soon as they arrive, the camera lingers on the whole party staring at her. Carlos is immediately whisked away by his mother to change his clothes. She glowers at Carlos and says "Porque ella está aqui . . . ya! vete a cambiar" (why is she here, already go change your clothes). Nicole is left behind to meet the family and friends. She offers to help in the kitchen but is

Author's own image.

rebuffed. She tries to talk to others but they are dismissive. After a brief escape to the bathroom where the mirror serves as a reminder that she is dirty and unkempt, she comes out to encounter Carlos and Luz, his ex-girlfriend, who is running her fingers down his chest and saying "You know you miss me." After some uncomfortable conversation between the three of them, Luz takes Carlos to talk to her mother and Nicole leaves the party. As she runs out of the house, we hear one of the party-goers whisper "sucia" (dirty) under her breath.

This is a rich scene to explore in terms of audience positions. There are a number of possible recognitions and identifications. At this point I ask my students: with whom or what do you identify? Many of the girls – since many students in this particular class are Mexican American – say "one of the girls or women at the party." Perhaps the sister whose quinceañera Carlos had clearly forgotten. Perhaps the ex-girlfriend who finds out her ex-boyfriend has become involved with someone from outside of their group – a *sucia* at that! Perhaps the mother who is exasperated that her son showed up late, under-dressed, and with a dirty *gringa*. Some of the white girls identified with Nicole. They did not like the way that Carlos left her to fend for herself as soon as they reached his home. They thought he should have warned her about dress codes for this occasion. They thought she was trying to be a good girlfriend by accompanying him to the party, even if she was ethnically clueless about the significance of this particular event. Yet one white girl said she identified with his ex-girlfriend. She had been in such a situation, and it was awkward. Some of the Mexican American boys name Carlos as the person with whom they identify. Some say that they could see themselves in that situation – forgetting about a sister's quinceañera because they were out with a cute girl. Others say that they identify with Carlos feeling "henpecked," but they do not relate to forgetting about the quinceañera. After all, your mother would not let you forget such an important event. Yet others say they identify with Carlos but they would not date somebody like Nicole, either for ethnic-pride reasons or because they just would not come into contact with such a rich girl. But one student, a very well-built African American, speaks out and says: "I identify with Nicole." At this point, the classroom is silent. After a while, one of the male Mexican American students replies: "But dude, she is the rich white chick!" To which the African American student responds: "I know, but I am not identifying with her skin color, her gender, or wealth but with the situation she is in. I always feel like I am the one who does not fit in. I always feel like people are looking at me like I am dirty or something. I am always the boyfriend parents did not want their daughter to have. I identify with Nicole's situation."

I spent a bit of paper telling you this story because it is elemental to the contemporary understanding of audiences. We cannot tell what the producers intended to do with this particular movie. Neither the writers nor the director are Latino. We cannot surmise their interests, other than increasing potential profit by reaching out to an expanded teen audience by including the light Latino angle into the narrative of the usual teen romance. By including a light Latino, producers hope to increase their ethnic audience without turning away the white mainstream audience. Also, by including a light Latino whose aspirations are education and whose character is very affable, the redemption narrative might take effect. In sum, despite the Latino twist, this begins as a Horatio Alger tale with a working-class Latino trying to pull himself up from the barrio. So we can hypothesize about the target audience in terms of the production of this movie.

The study of audiences also builds on the knowledge about representations. I had to tell you quite a bit of detail to get you to the point where students picked an audience position. Or maybe not. Maybe you decided pretty early on that: (a) you would never go to such a movie; (b) you knew exactly what that movie was all about and you either liked it or not, whether you had seen it or not; (c) you were intrigued about the plot and wanted to read more about it, and eventually would go out and rent the DVD; (d) you were familiar with such movies, and, knowing their patterns of representation, you would not recognize or identify with anybody in that movie because, as a Latina, you were used to Latinas being represented in the worst possible way; (e) you love teen romances, and, whatever your ethnicity, you go along for the predictability of the ride; (f) this movie had themes which relate to your job or research and therefore it would be useful for you to watch it. These are some of the possibilities for your personal position vis-à-vis my telling you a little bit about this movie. In fact, when people engage with media and popular culture, these are some of the audience positions that they take, and there are theories and methodologies that have been developed to take into account these audience positions.

Now let's go back to some of the students' interpretations of or allegiances to and with the movie. You may have noticed that, by and large, the girls identified with female characters and the boys with male characters. That is usually, though not always, the case. Gender, audience scholars have found, is a powerful element of identity, and it informs audience positions. You may have noticed that mostly, students identified with characters that shared their ethnicity. The Mexican American students knew that a quinceañera was a very important occasion that one should not miss, should not be late for, and should dress up for. The girls largely identified with the Mexican American girls and women in the quinceañera, and the

Mexican American boys largely identified with Carlos, the protagonist and only complex ethnic male character in the movie. Therefore the situation spoke to the Mexican American students in a very familiar way and along gendered lines. The white girls identified with Nicole and her situation vis-à-vis a boyfriend who was not supportive or informative enough. They totally thought being called a sucia was not fair since she had just come from the beach. She was sandy, not dirty. The most interesting audience position in this group was the African American student. He was very brave in stating his identification, as the entire class first looked at him like he was a bit crazy. He was crossing gender, ethnicity, and class lines in his identification. However, he explained his position situationally. His identification was not made on the basis of how similar a character was to him, but in terms of how familiar the situation felt to him.

As you can see from the range of identifications and recognitions discussed above, the study of audiences is intriguingly complex. From a production perspective, it is hard to anticipate audience interest. This is the reason that so much media content fails, either at the outset or after it has "lost" its audience. Believe me, if any producer had the answer to the audience question, they would rule the airways (if in broadcasting, that is). Who is in the audience? Why are they in the audience? What do they get out of media? Are Latina/os part of the audience? What do non-Latina/o audiences think of Latina/os in the media? Are media produced with a Latina/o audience in mind? What audiences are Latina/os part of? Which Latina/os are part of the audience? Audience analysis is one of the four components of media studies and is conducted from at least three perspectives, all of which illuminate and represent different interests: marketing, social scientific, and interpretive. McQuail (2005) reminds us that "audiences are both a product of social context and a response to a particular pattern of media provision" (p. 396). They are defined by place, people, medium or channel, content, and time. Only recently have Latina/os been seen as an audience, although within audience theory there was always the space for theorizing and studying individual or collective acts of identification.

From a marketing perspective, interest in audiences stems from the need to have knowledge about where to deploy advertising in order to fuel consumption. Much of the knowledge derived from a marketing perspective is proprietary – that is, it is conducted for or by businesses to increase their competitive advantage and therefore it is not shared with others, either in business or in academia. It is private knowledge, not available in journals or libraries. From a social scientific perspective, scholars seek to understand the uses and gratifications that the audience derives from the mass media. McQuail (1997) finds that users of the media are selective and choose media to fulfill needs. This active audience finding is in direct opposition to early media theory – not necessarily based on empirical evidence – which theorized audiences as easily malleable dupes – in other words, a passive audience. However, this early work did not really talk about audiences per se, but rather the replacement of the canon. The very notion of audiences is quite modern. That is, the way of thinking of people as audiences rather than as the public or masses is quite recent.

Qualitative/interpretive approaches to studying the audience are also very useful. From a more qualitative and interpretive framework of analysis, scholars – through either interviews, focus groups, or ethnography – engage with individuals and/or groups of audience members to understand how and why they make sense of the media in their everyday lives. For example, the vignette that began this chapter was an example of a qualitative approach. I selected a movie that contained the possibility of multiple audience positions. In particular, this movie showed the tension resulting from a romance between a Latino and a white girl. I showed the whole movie to my class but encouraged discussion of that particular scene because, based on my extensive research in this field, it was rich with possibility for understanding how members of the audience would relate to, make sense of, identify with, and/or recognize the characters and the situation. The "audience" in this case was a captive audience composed of the members of a Latina/o Popular Culture class. In that sense, this audience was highly informed about Latinidad and Media Studies as a framework of analysis. I could not have predicted all of the audience positions, though I anticipated many of them. For instance, the majority of students identified and sympathized along the lines of gender and ethnicity. But not all of them did. Of particular interest was the identification of a member of the audience who did not match the ethnicity of any of the characters in the movie. This is not unimportant, given that many times it is Latinos as members of the audience who do not coincide with the ethnicity of any of the characters.

Interpretive audience methodology finds that people have many ways of using and interpreting media and incorporating them into their everyday lives. This does not mean that everyone is an active and selective user of media. For example, while some Latina/o members of the audience might be quite purposeful when searching the net for news and data about Latina/o health, others might just turn on a television and have it on all day without any reason or selection. To return to the *Crazy/Beautiful* example, some students may watch that movie for entertainment purposes. Others might use that movie as part of a project on quinceañera celebrations in the USA, on representations of bi-ethnic couples, or on contemporary femininity in mainstream Hollywood film. Even more elementally, some people may have watched that movie to learn English or to understand how US culture works. Both the purposeful search for information from media and the collateral understanding of a range of issues in turn form part of the symbolic material that people, or members of the audience, use to make sense of the world and their everyday lives.

In the present, such a study is fairly straightforward, but how to recover the historical knowledge about audiences past? It is very difficult to conduct historical audience analysis. You really have to reconstruct audiences in hindsight. How would a scholar 20 years or 100 years from now go about finding out the meaning of a movie such as *Crazy/Beautiful* for audiences long ago? Talking to people about their previous audience positions would have to depend on memory, which has been found to be not terribly reliable. The particularity of questions and situations make the present a more amenable time to pursue such studies. This does not mean that people do not try to do historical audience analysis. For example Clara Rodriguez (2008) investigated audience reception of Hollywood film in Puerto Rico between 1896 and 1934, but she had to piece together newspaper reports, testimonies, and statistics in order to construct the audience perspective. Latina/o media scholars encounter additional challenges in this historical pursuit, given that sometimes records and documents have not been kept at all or have been stored in such poor conditions as to make them unusable. Archiving of historical materials is something that takes institutions and resources. Given that Latina/os have not been recognized as an important demographic group in the USA until quite recently, it is not surprising that major institutions such as the Library of Congress are basically playing catch-up in securing documents to build a historical foundation.

Even in the present, there are a range of difficulties in conducting audience analysis. Another relevant component of conducting audience research is that it inevitably involves dealing with human subjects. US university guidelines for conducting research on human subjects are subject to oversight by Institutional Review Boards (IRBs), making it rather difficult to interact with people, as one has to do in audience research. Due to earlier unethical research practices on medical research subjects, universities and scientific institutions have developed a set of codes of conduct to protect human subjects. For example, informed consent as a practice requires adults participating in a research project to acknowledge that they have been informed about it. However, the process of IRB clearance and approval may delay many audience investigations and sometimes preclude them altogether. Anonymous audience members – at least as they are represented anonymously in the published research – do not suffer the same risk of danger as someone being injected with a new untested drug. Yet IRB procedures sometimes treat the two situations similarly.

Moreover, finding audience members or communities whom one can study vis-à-vis particular media or media in everyday life can be daunting for scholars, especially if these audiences do not form part of the immediate community in which scholars function. Sometimes ethnic audiences have many logical reasons for refusing to participate in university research. They might be tired of being used as cultural capital for scholars, and the results of the research do not serve to improve their community. What often happens is that scholars descend on an ethnic community, gather their data, and then leave. They subsequently publish their research, and their careers depend on this cycle of knowledge production. However, the people of the community that they studied are left behind, and might feel used. If a project is conducted in a university space, such as a focus room or laboratory, ethnic audiences might not feel comfortable entering the institution to participate in research. Whereas most US universities are quite porous – that is, one can walk in, through, and out without having to cross a door or checkpoint – many people might feel uncomfortable or unwilling to navigate the university as a place. This has ramifications in terms of studies of ethnic audiences in general, and Latina/os in particular. Say you want to show *Crazy/Beautiful* to a group of Latina/o high school students from the local community. Or you may want to research how Latina/os navigate the internet, and you need to get them to your computer lab on campus. Neither group might want to come. Additionally your research group might not have the time or access to transportation to be able to get to the university. If you decide to conduct the study in the community wherein people live, then you have to gain access to a space therein, as well as to reach out to people to participate in whatever your project is. What is in it for them?

Researchers might not know how or where to find Latina/o audiences. They might not feel comfortable engaging with Latina/o audiences. In fact, most of the little research that has been conducted on Latina/o audiences has been done by Latina/o scholars. Overcoming these barriers, whether institutional or community-based, becomes part of the process of conducting audience research. Mayer (2003b) provides a brilliant example of the investment one has to make in order to engage in mutually productive research – for the scholar and the community. Mayer volunteered in a youth group and offered to teach media production skills. Through her engagement with youth, over a long period of time, she was able to develop a relationship that led to audience research in a setting that her subjects trusted. Youth research is particularly difficult to carry out as part of the definition of youth as an identity includes mistrust of adults.

All three of the research perspectives – marketing, social scientific, and interpretive – can be used separately or together in Latina/o Media Studies. A television network or a producer of soaps – for example the producers of *Ugly Betty* – may hire a market research firm in order to identify and reach the segment of the Latina/o audience in which they have interest. A scholar may show a group of elderly Latina/os a number of Public Service Announcements about aging and health in order to see which one is the most useful to the senior citizens, as well as the most efficient in delivering the message that the health provider wants to spread. Another scholar may hang out for a while with a bunch of Latina college students to understand the role of media in their every-day lives. This might include asking the students why they prefer this particular show; what other shows they like; who their favorite characters are, etc. Or all three perspectives can be part of the same project. For instance, a scholar can ask a group of teenage Latinas how they make sense of *Lost*, the television show in which Michelle Rodriguez acted (the interpretive part), and what they get out of it (the uses and gratifications part), against the backdrop of the inclusion of a Latina actress and character in the show, the ratings and particular audience component of the show, and the products that advertisers might be willing to market through the show (the marketing component) – perhaps fast food or feminine hygiene products whose ad includes an ambiguous Latina. If, as discussed in the production chapter, this show airs on a television network that is part of a media conglomerate, then synergies might be deployed, such as having the main actors appear in the talk shows on the network discussing the latest plot twist, etc. Audience analysis then can be done from an administrative perspective – to market products and figure out audience niches – and from a critical perspective – to understand people's relation to and meaning-making of media, and hopefully to use that information to make better media and make a positive difference in the world.

Construction of the audience

Before proceeding to Latina/os in/and the audience, a few remarks about the construction of the audience are in order. This chapter will focus mostly on advertising-supported media as those form the bulk of the mainstream media. Commercially produced media rest on the economic foundation of advertising support. Before advertisers commit to placing their ads within a certain television show, magazine, website, or to including their products in movies as tie-ins, or to placing a billboard, or to supporting a concert tour, they have to have some sort of proof or documentation – usually of the numerical kind supported by marketing and/or social scientific research – that their investment is warranted in terms of the projected economic return. From an administrative perspective, this is logical. After all, you have to demonstrate both financial viability and solvency in order to run a business. The media are big business (see chapter 1, "Production") and to account for the highly expensive production that is mainstream media (see chapter 2, "Textual/content analysis") producers and investors need to have some form of guarantee or positive projection of audience and profit. From a critical perspective, one that simultaneously does not take commercially supported media as natural or inevitable and explores ways in which media can make this a more democratic and just world, we ask what the limits and possibilities of a commercial system are, what the alternatives are, and how much agency audiences have vis-à-vis mainstream media.

Theoretical developments of the audience as a concept inform this chapter. Smythe (1977) theoretically explored the triangular relationship between audiences, advertisers, and the media and proposed that the real commodity – the product being exchanged in the marketplace – was not really the television show or the advertised products but the audience itself. That is, the audience was being bought and sold in the marketplace through – in his work – commercial television to advertisers who wanted to connect a product with the people who would purchase it. In other words, you and I are the product being sold. In *Crazy/Beautiful* the product was the attention of those who paid to see the movie or who subsequently rented it when it was available in a purchasable format. According to Smythe, the movie, television show, and the ad for widgets are just devices to connect you and me to advertisers. The plug-ins within movies, for example, use the movie as a vehicle to get us to pay attention to those products being subtly promoted within it. The people who pay for those products to be strategically placed within the movie, and sometimes as part of the narrative, are paying for our attention, so that will, hopefully, generate more sales.

Further critical work on audiences, drawing on the work of Raymond Williams (1974/1992), explored the fact that audiences are not out there, ready for media or advertisers to pick and target, at will. Rather, audiences have to be constructed by the media and marketers. This can be a symbiotic process. From a sender (media and marketer) perspective, a group of people, based on some form of perceived similarity, has to be addressed and then has to recognize itself as that group being addressed. This form of similarity could be based on gender, race or ethnicity, national origin, socioeconomic status, sexual orientation, etc. From a post-structural perspective, advertisers through the mass media seek to interpellate members of the public into a subject position as a member of a particular audience. That is, perhaps when watching *Crazy/Beautiful*, an audience member may feel like parts of the movie speak to their own lived experience. My student who identified with Nicole was interpellated into a subject position through that scene. His subjectivity was that of being the other, the one whom parents do not want their children to date. In everyday-speak, this means that, for example, you have to recognize a particular television show or magazine as somehow pertaining to your interests, preferences, or identity position and that advertisers have been shown that that particular show or magazine will appeal to people like you who are likely to buy the product that they want to sell. From a community or affinity-group perspective – say from a group of Latina/os – there could be an acknowledgment that they would like particular types of media products, and that these are not being offered. This could be anything from access to telenovelas, to particular musical genres, or even a language-specific offering. This in fact is the history of Latina/o radio, and connects to chapter 1, "Production". As Latina/o communities sought to create a space for their radio, and this proved to be successful, then mainstream radio and broadcasting industries noticed this previously ignored audience and sought to incorporate it into their marketing plan. To return to Williams's point, audiences are not out there waiting to be targeted, but rather a complex and symbiotic process between media and social groups results in the creation of an audience, which is not a permanent thing. Audiences are fleeting constructs.

From a Latina/o Media Studies perspective this means that the creation of the audience can come as a top-down initiative from the media industry or as a bottom-up grassroots activism. Advertisers have to be shown that Latina/os are in the audience and that it is worth targeting them as an audience with particular forms of media that in turn market particular products. In turn they, as ethnicized Latina/o members of that potential audience, have to recognize that a particular media product is speaking to them, through that ethnic component of their identity, and then maybe they will watch that television show and, even better from the perspective of marketers, they will not only pay attention to commercials but actually purchase some of those products now and in the future. Yes you do want to buy Taco Bell food or use El Paso salsa next time you whip up some home-made burritos or whatever product was advertised in that ad that made you remember your childhood. We can also make demands or begin our own media ventures, and if these are successful enough chances are that the mainstream media industry will notice. Maybe we see it as a partial victory that mainstream television shows even acknowledge our presence when either representing us or including ads to Latina/o products. The rub is that entering the mainstream usually means leaving behind more culturally specific and radical or liberatory tendencies. The fact remains that commodification of ethnicity brings in profits, and that ethnic audiences by and large prefer more, rather than less, representation in media. This results in a complex give and take in the construction of media audiences.

The audience has to be produced so it can then receive the marketing messages that are destined for it within a commercial media system. To do so we have to have contemporary understandings of the Hispanic audience and Latino media (A. Rodriguez, 1999, p. 46): "The construction of the Hispanic audience shapes as it creates notions of Latino race and ethnicity, U.S. nationalism, and cultural belonging. . . . Dominant construction of the Hispanic audience . . . is racially non-white, linguistically Spanish speaking, and socioeconomically poor" (p. 47). Latina/o media producers have to prove to marketers and retailers that the Hispanic audience is viable and commodifiable, not just a delinquent, hopelessly poor, and nomadic group of people.

Marketing approaches

Recent changes in the approach of mass media toward audiences have huge implications for the study of Latina/os as members of the audience. General market media aimed at a broad range of the audience that was implicitly conceived to be white and middle-class. Any reach to ethnicized segments of the audience was complementary or inadvertent but not the main impetus of the production. Traditionally, mainstream media did not think of Latina/os as members of the audience, just as they tended not to represent them or include them in the production of media. Likewise, Latina/o communities, especially those numerous enough, managed to have their own alternative pamphlets, newspapers, radio programs, etc., and interact through these media at the margins. However, as mainstream media have moved from mass marketing to niche marketing, Latina/os as a segment of the audience have become more important. This has to be considered in tandem with Census figures that make it impossible not to acknowledge that Latina/os are a statistically significant portion of the US population and that a segment of these Latina/os have the disposable income to merit the targeting of mass media if advertisers see them as a possible market for their products. Additionally, the fact that "Latina/os have larger households and are younger than national average" means that they "spend a bigger portion of their incomes on household items, supplies, and clothing" (M. A. Johnson, 2000, p. 234) – not to mention that it makes them the ideal target group for mini-van ads. If all of that is demonstrated successfully enough, there can be mass media products targeted at Latina/os. This is sound economic practice. Yet as we know from recent experience in a global financial meltdown, economic practices are not always rational. Wible (2004) underscores that this should mean that "television executives will target minorities only to the extent that, if at all, advertisers consider these audiences to be valuable targets for their advertising messages" (p. 45). Additionally, the Latina/o population is sufficiently large and diverse for advertisers, through mass media, to aim for different segments of that audience: the business community, older women, teens, teen girls, children, music genre groups, etc. Nonetheless, as A. Rodriguez (1999) and Dávila (2001) have documented, many are the anecdotes that have marketing executives listening to the data and remaining incredulous as to the Latina/o audience and their purchasing power. It seems that sometimes personal prejudice based on preconceived notions can be stronger than the power of scientifically derived verifiable numerical data.

There are many organizations, websites, think tanks, and university departments that document the spending power of the Latina/o population, whose annual spending power is estimated to be over $350 billion. Clearly, this appeals to a broad range of marketers. Population growth coupled with increased income projections leads to even more optimistic forecasts. For instance, HispanTelligence® estimates that by 2010 Hispanic market advertising expenditures will increase to about $4.3 billion, and urges marketers to attempt to capture the attention of this growing market (https://secure.hbinc.com/product/view.asp?id=159, retrieved June 5, 2008):

> Advertisers spent an estimated $3.3 billion to market their products and services to U.S. Hispanics in 2005, a 6.8 percent increase from the previous year. According to U.S. Census estimates, the number of Hispanics reached 41.8 million in 2005, an increase of 3 percent from the year before. The overall U.S. population increased by less than 1 percent over the same period. As Hispanics simultaneously make progress in educational attainment, their purchasing power represents an increasingly larger proportion of the U.S. total, reaching 8.9 percent in 2005. (Ibid.)

However, it is not as easy as growth in aggregate income and access to technology. For instance, while figures show that the numbers of Latino internet users are growing twice as fast as those of the rest of the population, Latino websites are struggling to survive (www.his

panicbusiness.com//news/newsbyid.asp?NS=1&idx=4960&cat1=news, retrieved April 16, 2008). The Pew & Internet American Life Project reports both that numbers of Latina/o internet users are growing at twice the rate of those of the non-Hispanic population *and* that those with lower incomes and less English proficiency are less connected. Putting these two bits of information together, we can deduce that Spanish-language websites will be less successful than English-language Latina/o websites as it is the English-speaking Latina/os who are more likely to connect to the internet.

Some excellent work on the construction of ethnic populations in general and Latina/os as an audience specifically, by America Rodriguez (1999), Arlene Dávila (2001), and Marilyn Halter (2000), in combination with more global approaches to consumerism (García Canclini, 2001), forms the background for studying the concerted strategies to market to Latina/os and the marketing of Latinidad. In concordance with Smythe and Williams, both Rodriguez and Dávila find that there is a tendency to construct the Latina/o audience in a homogeneous Spanish-speaking, working-class, large-family character. This may have been true even within the past decade. However, in another article, Dávila (2002) explores the differential representation and therefore audience segmentation of the Latina/o audience. Latina/os know that there are different types within Latinidad. Dominicans are constructed as black and Argentineans as white, for example, demonstrating an understanding that the Latina/o audience knows there are differences, even if those differences circulate Latina/o stereotypes inherited from Latin America rather than a US flattening of Latinidad (Mayer, 2004). Drawing on this work, Valdivia (2007c) explores the different branding approaches to Jennifer Lopez and to Penélope Cruz that suggest that the former speaks to a more working-class and the latter to a more upscale segment of the audience. The fact that each star was a spokesperson for a different range of products distinguished by price and cultural capital suggests that marketers realize that the Latina/o audience is not a homogeneous mass. All of the above scholars see the "discovery" of the Latina/o audience as part of a broader move to commodify ethnicity and difference.

Much of the difficulty in the construction of the Latina/o audience lies in the problem of the definition of Latina/o and Latina/o media. In an essay that begins by asking "What is Latino media?" Mayer (2001) proposes four constructions of Latino audiences: "segmentation, massification, pan-ethnicity, and fragmentation" (p. 291). Segmentation refers to developing a particular medium that appeals to a specific community. For example, Univisión begins as segmentation. With massification comes a broader market strategy. Pan-ethnicity usually includes the investment of multinational capital, such as was made into Latina/o television by Latin American media industries interested in expanding into the US Latina/o audience. Thus, while Univisión began as a segmented strategy, its success led to its becoming part of a massified approach. Finally, fragmentation applies to Latina/o audiences what is going on in the mainstream: the targeting of the most coveted sectors of the market. For example the December 2008 / January 2009 issue of *Hispanic* magazine includes ads for Chivas Regal whisky and American Airlines executive class, as well as for cheaper products such as Crest toothpaste and Comfort Inn. This glossy ten-issues-a-year magazine targets the upscale segment of the "Hispanic" demographic. Mayer concludes that these competing constructions of the Latina/o audience can be interpreted as a positive sign of growing multiculturalism and as a negative global trend to differentiate Latina/os by class. Those who cannot consume are largely left out of the target strategy. There is no magazine for struggling Latina/os though information in how to get by, etc., would be very useful to this group.

Within Latina/o media, there is a further need to differentiate between target strategies. For example Subervi-Vélez and Eusebio (2005) consider any program aimed at US Latina/o audiences, regardless of where it was produced – such as in Brazil, Mexico, Spain, or Venezuela – to be Latina/o media because it is targeted at the US Latina/o population. However, anything that might broadly appeal to Latina/o audiences, even if not based on Latina/o culture or Latina/o production, might also be produced to target this audience. Both Halter and Dávila remind us that marketers consider ethnic audiences to be very family-oriented. So any form of "family" programming can be construed as appealing to the Latina/o audience among others, and white television, for instance, has a history of family shows. Under this definition then, nearly all of television could have been considered as targeting ethnic audiences in general and Latina/os in particular.

Another recent development is that there are regional areas, such as in the Southwest, the Northeast, and Miami, where the minority population is large enough to compose the majority of that region or of large cities within that region. In this case, general-market or mainstream media also would have to be considered Latina/o media in that geographical area. The very use of "minority" and "majority" would shift, in complicated ways, in these situations. We cannot take for granted, or as a universal given, that the general market (the majority in the area) will remain one in which the mainstream (implicitly white) is more numerous. We also have to remember that numbers do not necessarily equal power so that even in markets where Latina/os may be the majority, their power might still be less, in terms of economic wherewithal and political representation, than that of the dominant culture. The mainstream media in those cases will not be representative of the majority of the population and will not seek to target the numerous and economically challenged segment of the audience.

Social scientific approaches

The audience has also been studied using social scientific approaches. In general, social scientists have found that the media fulfill functions for individuals and society. In an approach that is called "uses and gratifications," media scholars theorize that people use the media for a set of reasons. If they fulfill their reasons for using the media, then they are gratified. One of the reasons that ethnic people consume mainstream media, especially if newly arrived, is to understand dominant culture and perhaps to blend in. In that vein of thought, Subervi-Vélez (1986) found a relation between media exposure and Latina/o acculturation. That is, Latina/os who consumed higher degrees of mass media were more likely to become acculturated. Of course this assumes we are talking about mainstream mass media. You could study the *Crazy/Beautiful* audience in this manner as well. You could either find a group that had watched this movie and ask them why they saw it, what use they got out of it, whether they were gratified by this movie. Or you could include it among a range of options with a small synopsis of the plot and ask a group which movie they would find most useful and why. These are just two of many possible uses-and-gratifications projects using this movie. Of course you could get a null result: either nobody saw this movie or they saw no use in it. In social science, even a null result is a finding that tells us something. So if you had obtained a null result, you could conclude that the audience found this movie useless and that it fulfilled no gratifications.

M. A. Johnson (2000) lists the following as functions or uses that ethnic media serve: "the transmission of native culture, promotion of ethnic pride, political and social activism, coverage of community activities, terms used as identifiers, and evidence of social control" (p. 236). Dating back to Subervi-Vélez's (1986) germinal essay, we have evidence that Latina/os "use or prefer a variety of media (Spanish-language or English-language mainstream)" (Johnson, 2000, p. 232). These different types of uses can be linked to a number of variables including length of time in present culture, gender, class, education, and language proficiency. Whereas language has been identified as perhaps the single most important identifying component within Latinidad, in her extensive analysis of the functions performed by Latina magazines, Johnson did not find support "to the arguments that identity is language based" (p. 243). This is not as contradictory as it first sounds. This finding is actually consistent with research that shows Latina/o audiences like both Spanish- and English-language media, and Pew Foundation results that children of immigrants prefer to use English as their first language. Given that Johnson analyzed English-language-dominant women's magazines that are likely to be read by English-dominant speakers, it is not surprising that they still value their Latina identity, but in English. Hispanic users who prefer content in English over Spanish make English delivery of any media more likely to be successful in the mainstream. Given that these English-speaking users are the more upwardly mobile components of the Latina/o market, it is not surprising that the bulk of commercial Latina/o-targeted media is in English or in a bilingualism that favors English, such as the magazine *Latina*.

Research that explores Latina/os' relation to media in terms of cultural maintenance and assimilation finds, in consonance with all of the material leading up to this point in this book, that there is a great deal of audience heterogeneity within Latinidad. Against the backdrop of Subervi-Vélez's (1986) groundbreaking research into the twin forces of Latina/o media to foster both ethnic differentiation and social integration – his pluralism hypothesis – scholars engage in case studies to explore these forces. Ríos and Gaines (1998) combined a uses-and-gratifications methodology with a little work on the female of color in the audience that becomes more foregrounded in the next section, "Interpretive approaches," to explore the relationship between Latina/os, Spanish language, and mass media. The female of color part did not yield significant results so we will focus on the former, which, like much of the audience research so far, was carried out in the Mexican American Southwest. Nonetheless, in another study, Ríos (2000) found that Latina women used media both for self-preservation and acculturation to the English language and other elements of US culture.[1] The concept of "audience clusters" arises out of this research – that is, Latina/os segments of the audience cluster around variables such as language of user and of medium and strength of ethnic affiliation. In other words, scholars hypothesize that third-generation English-dominant Latina/os will cluster differently in terms of their media preferences from immigrant Spanish-dominant Latina/os. In fact the research shows that "cluster membership . . . was a reliable predictor of individuals' use of mass media for cultural maintenance" (p. 753). Low Latina/o-heritage people "expressed relatively unfavorable attitudes regarding Spanish, low knowledge-information regarding bilingual education, low ability in reading and aural understanding of Spanish (but not English), lack of identification with Latinos as a cultural group, and low exposure to media overall (with the exception

of English-language television, which had not been predicted"
(p. 754). The opposite was found for high Latina/o-heritage people
who although having high ability to read and understand Spanish
did not necessarily express favorable attitudes toward Spanish.

In general, social scientific research continues to support the early
finding by Subervi-Vélez (1986) that Latina/os use media for dual purposes. For instance, in yet another audience research project, Ríos
(2003) finds that Latina/o audiences of both US soaps and telenovelas
watch these for the functions named above: to keep in touch with
Latina/o culture, including the maintenance of family ties with those
left behind in country of origin or those in another US region, and
to become acquainted and keep in touch with dominant US culture
by, for example, using protagonists in US soaps as role models for
how to navigate a situation with different social rules. However, Ríos
also found that not all members of the audience liked soaps and telenovelas. This presages some of the research in the interpretive section
below wherein audiences do not like what certain genres suggest to
the general population about their ethnic group in general and their
gendered ethnicity in particular. In effect they are very critical of
hyper-stereotypes in Latina/o media precisely because of what these
representations might be telling the general population about Latina/
os, which in turn translates into being treated prejudicially.

A related and much more scathing finding is that as ethnic media
become financed commercially or by advertising, and thus incorporated into the mainstream, they lose their radical edge in terms of
ethnic pride and political and social issues (M. A. Johnson, 2000),
which translates into a light form of ethnic affiliation weighed more
heavily toward consumption than ethnic pride. The fear is that, as
audiences consume the commercially produced media that are more
widely available, they will not find ethnic pride as an option in their
use of ethnic media. Also, ethnic audiences will become more invested
in consumption as ethnic pride. That is, a Latina/o politics to, say,
make the political system more equitable will morph into an effort
to buy more products to be Latina/o chic. This fear resonates with an
older theory in media, the Frankfurt School, that suggested that commercial media diverted the working class from the revolution.

Interpretive approaches

The pursuit of interpretive knowledge about audiences of the media
was ushered into Media Studies research in the 1980s. While there are
a number of major projects that were produced during that decade,
two are of particular relevance to Latina/o media scholars, most of

whom have studied female audiences. In 1984 Janice Radway published her now canonical *Reading the Romance* wherein she studied actual female readers of romance novels to find out why they read these books and what these books meant to them in relation to their everyday lives. Previously scholars, including feminist ones, had dismissed both romance novels and their readers without studying what role romances played in the everyday lives of such readers. In 1988, Jacqueline Bobo published the first version of her canonical essay, later expanded into a book (1995), entitled "*The Color Purple*: Black women as cultural readers." In that essay, Bobo actually talked to African American women to find out how they interpreted *The Color Purple* (1985) and why they liked it despite its somehow problematic representations of African American men. I use the word "actually" because prior to this date people spoke for black women rather than talking with them about their media choices and interpretations. Common in these two touchstone projects was the acknowledgment that women were discerning consumers of media, and that they had reasons for their choices. They were not merely uneducated dupes consuming crappy forms of media and popular culture. Radway's project focused on white women and the romance and Bobo's on African American women and movies.

The eighties discovery of the audience involved a lot of work celebrating audiences as active and discerning. Some of this work drew on psychoanalytic theories and privileged the possibility of pleasure and resistance on the part of the audience. It was as if all of a sudden scholars were finding pleasure and resistance at every turn. That early tendency was checked by more careful research. Bobo, drawing on Hall's influential "Encoding/decoding" (1980) essay, reminded us of three audience positions. In the dominant or intended position, audiences interpret the media product as it was meant to be interpreted. If audiences are part of the dominant culture, they are more likely to interpret media from this perspective as it privileges their point of view. Prior to the Radway and Bobo research projects, many had assumed that women interpreted Hollywood film from a dominant perspective, that was masculine and placed women as either masochistic or plain dumb. In the second spectator position, the negotiated, a member of the audience will disagree with components of the media content but not its overall production. The third position, the oppositional, is one in which the member of the audience is at odds with the very production of the media content and thus enters the interpretive process in an "against the grain" stance. Bobo suggested that African American women attend Hollywood films knowing that this film industry has a long and steady history of either ignoring them altogether or representing them and their culture in demeaning and dismissive manners. These three possibilities were a definite expansion of and improvement on the previously accepted dominant or dumb/masochistic options for women in the audience.

Given that this chapter began with an extended discussion of *Crazy/ Beautiful*, it is logical to try to flesh out the three audience positions mentioned above in relation to this movie. A dominant reading would generate the intended and mainstream interpretation of that scene. So we could see that Nicole and Carlos had a difficult situation to face and Carlos should have stuck by his girlfriend's side when they got to his house and the quinceañera party. Usually the dominant reading is singular since it takes the position of mainstream culture. The negotiated and oppositional readings require the audience member to take a position from which to voice their negotiation or opposition. For example, the Mexican American female students read the scene in a negotiated manner in that they identified with the Mexican American female characters in the movie. They did not reject the entire premise of the movie, nor the system that produces such narratives, but they derived meaning and pleasure from identifying with the Mexican American female characters rather than with Nicole the white protagonist. Similarly the Mexican American male students identified with Carlos but did not reject the premise of the movie. One could say that even the African American student who identified with Nicole because of the similarity of the situation of exclusion to his everyday lived experience interpreted the scene in a negotiated manner. To have an oppositional stance one has to be at odds with the premise of the movie and/or the system of production that generates that movie. None of the students in the class articulated an oppositional stance. They produced either a dominant or a negotiated reading. An oppositional reading might come from a hypothetical student who is anti-capitalist and therefore rejects any Hollywood film as it is inescapably mired in capitalist forms of production hoping to generate capitalist forms of consumption. From a Latina/o activist perspective – similar to the oppositional viewers in Bobo's study who went to movies knowing that the Hollywood machinery would represent them in a negative way and therefore prepared to read movies against the grain – a hypothetical Latina/o student could have argued that s/he knew the movie would represent all Latina/os in stereotypical manners and therefore was prepared to watch the movie against the grain.

This encoding/decoding research phase largely preceded the bulk of work on Latina/o Media Studies of the audience. For a long time there was almost[2] no research on Latina/os in the audience. Valdivia (2000) warned against making generalizations across ethnic identities in terms of audience identification and positions but included no empirical analysis in that essay. In particular, she challenged the then dominant paradigm of pleasure, suggesting that women of color in the audience might have other responses, including frustration. Furthermore, reading against the grain added labor to the interpreting process. The dominant reading is easily delivered to audiences whereas oppositional reading took active work. The warning included, as with most Latina/o Media Studies research, a need to differentiate among minority populations – that is, we could not assume that African American women would interpret a movie in a similar way to Latina/o women – and within Latinidad. That essay was written after the influential Bobo work was published yet before any similar studies with Latina/o audiences were conducted. As with all other research in Media Studies, interpretive audience analysis followed the usual path of: focus on white mainstream audiences; focus on African American audiences in difference to white audiences; taking up a focus on minorities but with little attention paid to specificities within minority audiences; including Latina/os in comparative projects with African Americans; and finally paying attention to Latina/o audiences.

As an example of the comparative approach between African American and Latina girls, Rubin, Mako, and Becker (2004) interviewed African American and Latina female college students about their interpretation of ideals of beauty in relation to the body in mainstream magazines. They found that girls' responses urged a turn to considering body ethics rather than aesthetics. The girls spoke of a body ethic of self-acceptance and nurturance that rejects mainstream cultural pressures to reshape bodies to approximate aesthetic ideals promulgated in the media. The authors concluded that: "understanding body image concerns from the standpoint of body ethics, rather than body aesthetics, may be a more productive and inclusive approach to the study of ethnically diverse women's embodied experience. Ultimately it is anticipated that this will better illuminate the complex relationships among ethnicity, culture, and risk for body image and eating disorders" (p. 49).

Body image issues also guided Goodman's (2002) research project comparing Anglo and Latina interpretations of ideal-of-beauty issues in women's magazines. Goodman found, overall, negotiated and oppositional readings among the Latina women, rather than the more dominant reading of the Anglo women. Comparing Latinas to black girls, Schooler (2008) found that Latina girls' use of mainstream media resulted in acculturation and lower body image whereas their use of black media was associated with greater body satisfaction. This stage of comparative research between Latinas and other ethnicities, Black and White, overlaps with the more focused research on Latina girls and women in their own context and using more intensive qualitative methodology involving focus groups and ethnography. Furthermore this concern with body image signals the proximity between audience and effects research. Audience interpretations led Rubin, Mako, and Becker (2004) and Schooler (2008) to speculate about the health effects of eating disorders.

The relative newcomer status of Latina audience research – Mayer (2003a and 2003b) and Rojas (2004) ushering in the first wave of interpretive studies – meant that, unlike in other areas, such as content analysis, from the beginning there was keen attention paid to differences within Latinidad and an acknowledgment of hybridity as these concepts are now foregrounded in both communication and ethnic studies. This first wave of Latina/o audience research mostly includes projects that explore women consuming Latina/o media and Latina/o women and girls consuming media in general. Mayer's study of Mexican American youth in the San Antonio area (2003b) stands alone as including both boys and girls. The study of youth has proven immensely productive as, in a sense, they represent the border zone of contact between cultures and the rise of a hybrid lived experience (Bejarano, 2005). Both Mayer and Rojas generally conclude with a finding of hybridity, whether it be in the construction of identity by the audience or in the media diet that transnational audiences consume.

Before continuing to the focus of interpretive research, a few words about media access are necessary. While mainstream scholars can operate under the assumption that all media are more or less widely distributed, this is not necessarily the case for Latina/os, a significant percentage of whom still live in conditions of poverty or limited resources. Rojas et al. (2004) found that the digital divide continues to exist. Access to computers, in addition to cultural capital issues such as orientation to and habitus of computing, leaves many Latina/o youth untouched by the possible benefits of the digital age. Moreover, gendered peer pressure might predispose women toward office work and boys away from the computer world altogether as they see it as a feminine area. The gendered aspect should not take away from the fact that poor communities, Latina/os and others, do not have equal access to the technology upon which future success is predicated. Rojas et al.'s study of teens and their parents amply documents this.

Mayer and Rojas, though both studying audience groups – in San Antonio and Austin, Texas, respectively – worked within an inescapably transnational framework of analysis. "By showing how telenovelas mediate national and social identities," Mayer (2003a) "illustrates how Mexican American girls in particular integrate telenovelas into the rhythm of their daily lives" (p. 479). In a broader study Mayer (2003b) found that "Mexican American young people used global media texts to define who they were in relation to their friends, family, and community" (p. 119). Rojas (2004) studied immigrant and non-immigrant Latinas' interpretations of women on Univisión and Telemundo and found two outcomes for this relationship: ambivalence and distinction. In their interpretive strategies, the women Rojas studied sought to assert both agency and cultural capital. The methods these two scholars use vary widely. Mayer actually spent two years working in a youth center in San Antonio helping Mexican American youth produce media while simultaneously studying how they consumed and produced mass media: an ethnographic approach. Rojas interviewed 27 Latina women, ranging from working-class to college-educated and differing in immigrant status from citizen to what she calls "sojourner status" – that is, those who go back and forth – in relation to two particular television shows, El Show de Cristina and Laura en América: an interview and focus group approach. In an assessment of the broader range of Spanish television, Rojas found that most of the respondents "perceived that Univision and Telemundo networks fulfill an entertainment function more than being a service for Latinos. Too many soap operas, sensationalist programs, lack of television programming for children, little or almost no information about their countries of origin, an excessive propensity to air Mexican shows, and a controversial representation of Latino women" (p. 131).

This finding of Latina frustration with programming is echoed in Báez's (2008) study of Mexican American women in the Chicago area. Using the "ethnographic focus group" methodology, Press and Cole (1999) found that constructing a focus group with previous ties between its members, rather than randomly bringing together individuals who did not know each other, facilitated in-depth understanding between people with pre-formed relationships with each other. Moreover, focus groups were hosted by their members to further create that atmosphere of familiarity and ease. Like Rojas, Báez found that:

> the most recurring theme that occurred during the course of the focus group was frustration with the way that Latina femininity and sexuality are constructed in the advertisements and media in general . . . they took issue with the prevalent unidimensional images of Latinas as hypersexual . . . Through these types of comments the women contested hegemonic depictions of Latinas as mere racialized sex objects. (2008, pp. 264–5)

One clearly articulated reason for these objections, among the middle-class women, was that they feared that such overly sexualized representations of Latinas would be used against them in the workplace and prevent their upward mobility, while simultaneouly providing the wrong kind of role models to the next generation. As well, women in this study echoed another component found in Rojas's previously mentioned work (2004): ambivalence. In relation to representations of the "authentic" bottle-shaped Latina body, women critiqued this tendency and were simultaneously invested in some form of authenticity, thus expressing ambivalence.

Similarly Cepeda (2008), in a study of two groups of Latina college students, one in the Midwest and another in the Northeast, explored these women's interpretation of the racialized crossover aesthetics informing the global marketing of many Latina music stars, including Shakira, Thalía, and Paulina Rubio, among others. As noted in her previous crossover research, Cepeda (2000, 2001, 2003a, and 2003b) has found that there is a Miami-based crossover aesthetic where not only language change is attempted, but also an entire set of aesthetic components – such as blonder, lighter, and thinner versions of their former ethnic selves – is adopted. Using focus group methodology, Cepeda's study yielded decidedly feminist results. More so than any of the other research projects already mentioned in this interpretive section, the feminism of these findings, and the highly informed and sensitized nature of these responses, can be related to the fact that all participants in the study were university students. Cepeda's respondents were able to differentiate between their enjoyment of popular culture and their critique of the production of this culture. Like the work of scholars already mentioned in this section, these responses fit within negotiated to oppositional spectatorship stances. The respondents understood that these stars had to engage in aesthetic negotiations in order to survive in the cut-throat world of global stardom.

Another set of studies about transnational teen girls has been conducted by Lucila Vargas. Using a creative methodology of encouraging teens not only to talk about their biographies but to do so through media collages, Vargas has generated a groundbreaking and heart-wrenching set of findings. In her exploration of identity of transnational teens, Vargas (2008a) finds, in an approach informed by Judith Butler's notion of identity as *performativity*, that the girls perform a hybrid gender identity. Caught between US and Latin American expectations of gender and consumerism, expectations that limit their options, these girls do gender by creating a hybrid identity in order to survive in their new land. Vargas asserts that her research differs from other Latina audience studies in that she seeks "to explain how Latina teens' hybrid gendered identities are constituted in and through their media practices and in and through their talk about media and popular culture . . . to simultaneously express and 'do' a hybrid gendered identity" (p. 188). Vargas finds that, in their construction of a gendered identity, the girls have to continuously play gender discourses against one another.

In another part of her larger study, Vargas (2008b) explores how transnational working-class Latinas use media to navigate and deal with a loss that defies closure – that is the loss of a family member or significant person that they must leave as they cross the border without facility of return or back-and-forth transit. This study fitted within a broader type of Media Studies research that finds that people use media to cope with transnational phenomena, which they may or may not control. In the case of these teens, they have very little control over their mobility. Some of them may have prepared for it for years while others may have been woken up on their way to cross the border. She finds, like Mayer (2003a and b), a "use of media for recreating cultural spaces and for keeping connections across borders" (p. 50). However, that is the tip of the iceberg, as it were, in terms of Vargas's four major findings: first, girls use "media to resist the disjuncture of quotidian life and preserve a sense of historical continuity by reinventing old rituals"; second, they bring into play their "previous familiarity with global popular culture fare as a means to bridge two worlds"; third, they use "media to create a space of complete belonging"; and fourth, they perform a practice "with the purpose of bringing about the subjective experience of being with a loved one who is not physically present" (p. 50). Vargas concludes that the practices of today's transnational Latina teens are located within the larger social consumption of global popular culture and that "acculturation into the foreign can only occur within the territory of the familiar" (p. 51).

Notes from the classroom

Because media culture is so easily available, and students love to watch any form of media, especially if it means not listening to lectures, I have been keeping some notes when interesting and unexpected viewing experiences occur in the classroom. To begin with, most students do not want anyone to mess with Disney. I can show almost anything, and they are willing to entertain the possibility of multiple audience positions. When I get to Disney, they both love it – I literally hear sighs of joy from students and many of them know all the songs to movies such as *Pocahontas* and *The Little Mermaid* ("wish I could be, part of your world") – and hate the thought of speaking about possible audience positions. Eventually they are willing to admit things such as the fact that Pocahontas's hair is actually bigger than her body and thus becomes one of the main characters in the movie. It is interesting to note that the Disney princesses, though they include heroines of color, have not included a Latina. As we transition into Latinidad some of the more interesting moments have come in relation to movies such as *Crazy/Beautiful* but also the range of Jennifer Lopez movies and the movies such as *Blue Crush* (2002) that have a tri-color palette of white, Latina, and island native girl. Audience members, especially on the internet (Nakamura, 2007), like to out others as either ethnic or mixed race. In many new types of media and popular culture – from movies to television, popular music, and the internet – producers are using ambiguous ethnic, or light, Latina/os characters which encourage a range of audience positions, designed to interpellate as many members of the audience as possible, while alienating as few as possible. Thus the study of audiences is becoming more difficult when we take into consideration both representational and audience ethnic ambiguity and heterogeneity. We have to constantly remind ourselves that issues of identification and interpretation cannot be easily mapped in corresponding terms. That is, Latina/os will not always identify with Latina/os, and whites will not always identify with whites. Especially across ethnic lines, we have only just begun to explore what affiliations and connections audiences make with ethnic representations.

Conclusion

The work outlined in this chapter is still in its exploratory stage. This is the newest component of Latina/o Media Studies. This newness means that scholars working within this area of studies are able to take advantage of new concepts and theories that further illuminate this area of research, such as heterogeneity, hybridity, feminism, and transnationality. The changing composition of both Latina/os and Latinidad within the United States, the transnational character of Latina/os' media consumption and interpretation, and the changing character of regions and cities in the United States wherein the previous status of Latina/os has changed not only to most numerous minority but to outright majority mean that there is much work to be done in terms of understanding Latina/o audiences and reception of the media. The global circulation of most of the media mentioned in this chapter suggests yet another uncharted area of research. What do global audiences make of our ethnic media? How do they even understand our efforts to represent ethnicity? In a preliminary focus group study of girls watching *High School Musical* (*HSM*) in Spain, Báez and Valdivia (2008) found not only that these girls "loved" *HSM*, especially because the movie represented friendship and friends among different people, but that they could not articulate issues of race or ethnicity. These little girls, eight to nine years old, cosmopolitan and global in their outlook and experience, presage the future of an upscale transnational subjectivity. This is not the ambiguous loss group that Lucila Vargas writes about, but the target audience group in which global media invests.

Do global ethnic media connect to our representations of ethnicity? Issues of hybridity also open up new areas of audience research. Vargas and Rojas are already working within a paradigm of hybridity, but what does the increasing hybridity of the population mean in terms of audience choices and interpretations? Both of those scholars found hybrid choices and identity constructions, but what about audiences that cannot say they are Mexican American or even Latinas? How do we study these multiple affiliations and potentially disruptive identity positions? These are all questions that remain to be researched. In turn the work on audiences and interpretation promises to link the work in the previous chapter about content and representation with the work in the following chapter about effects of the mass media.

Case study no. 1

"The Homicide Report"

Whereas there has already been attention paid to "The Homicide Report" in terms of production, and of content and representation analysis, of the media, I know of no project that has attempted to study this blog in relation to audience and reception studies. This does not mean that a number of reception and audience studies could not be carried out. For example, at the outset, we could find out if Latina/os in the Los Angeles area are reading and paying attention to "The Homicide Report". If they are, and based on what we have learned so far about Latina/o media audiences – namely, that those who are second generation or later and have English proficiency tend to read English-language media – we would expect English-speaking Latina/os to be among the audience for the Report. A further study could be to ask these Latina/o audiences how they make sense of the Report, how they feel it represents them as a community, and what their hopes and fears are in terms of this form of representation and the way they are treated by mainstream culture. For example both Rojas's and Báez's respondents were wary of hypersexual representations of the Latina woman for what it might mean to them in terms of upward mobility. Similarly, Latina/o readers of this blog might have ideas about what this representation of violence and elevated death rates within their population might mean in terms of how they are treated in the workplace and, again, in relation to upward mobility. Whereas one of the functions of ethnic media is pride, this Report might generate another response, more consonant with Vargas's (2008b) work on loss, though not necessarily involving ambiguity (Cacho, 2007). Lisa Cacho writes about how certain lives are undervalued and treated as disposable, and we would want to find out if this Report reiterates that tendency or is actually interpreted as a resistance to that devaluation.

Also building on Latina/o audience research, our audience analysis would have to pay careful attention to the heterogeneity of the Latina/o audience in Los Angeles. Just as Mayer (2001) warned us not to generalize about Mexican Americans in the San Antonio area, the huge heterogeneity in Los Angeles would have to be brought into consideration. Maybe, and drawing on research conducted by Ríos and Gaines (1998), we would find more ethnic affiliation among those with high indicators of Latina/o heritage and vice versa.

Of course, it is not just Latina/os who are reading this Report, and the fact that the Report itself has become part of the news means that the Report, and news about the Report, are circulated nationally and globally, and therefore the audience is potentially far wider than Latina/os in the Los Angeles area. Within the Los Angeles area, the general multi-ethnic community reception and analysis of this blog might yield some interesting results. Maybe inter-ethnic alliances can be a factor in interpretation on the part of other ethnic communities. The fact that Latina/os account for most but not all of those murdered means that other minorities, notably African Americans, might have a specific interpretation of this Report.

From a pure marketing perspective, the *Los Angeles Times* is certainly also interested in finding out if this blog has increased their circulation and, more importantly for them as a profit-seeking medium, their ad revenues, and therefore their profit and that of their sponsors. Since it is only available on the web version of the newspaper, the revenue potential, as many newspapers are finding out, has to be explored in this new arena. We can expect that newspapers will either figure out how to profit from the possibilities of the internet or will disappear. The success of "The Homicide Report", in terms of its visibility and use – a uses-and-gratification hit, to be sure – augurs well for the expanded possibilities of the internet in terms of reaching out to new audiences with more relevant information.

Case study no. 2

Jennifer Lopez

For those studying Latina audiences, Jennifer Lopez is an inescapable name and therefore topic of analysis. For example, in largely Mexican American settings in Southern California, where most of my relatives live, there is explicit and long-lasting resentment that Jennifer Lopez got the part of Selena in the movie that propelled Jennifer's successful crossover into the mainstream. There is a long memory about this issue and not a lot of forgiveness. Many feel that a Mexican American should have played the Selena character. Furthermore, Jennifer Lopez's continued celebration of her Puerto Ricanness extends this history of resentment.

Being the most prominent Latina in popular culture means that Jennifer Lopez becomes part of the conversation about Latinas and the audience, even if the research project did not begin as such (personal conversation with Jillian Báez, 2006). Thus respondents question "why is she naked?" in relation to the Glow perfume ad (Báez, 2008, p. 265) and find that Salma Hayek is a more "authentic" Latina than Jennifer Lopez, invoking the burden of eternal foreignness carried by US-born Latinas (Molina Guzmán and Valdivia, 2004). Reiterating the finding of ambivalence in Rojas (2004), Cepeda (2008) found that her respondents both enjoyed Jennifer in *Maid in Manhattan* (2002) and criticized the fact that she represented that Latina stereotype, the maid. In fact Cepeda found that:

> the problematic nature of these depictions was further compli-
> cated by the fact that the focus group's participants then described
> Lopez's shifting public persona as the combined result of professional
> demands and personal conflicts. In other words, they recognized that
> the changes in hairstyle, clothing, and body shape were a reflection of
> the particular brand of survival aesthetics practiced by arguably the
> most visible Latina performer in the world today. (p. 250)

The findings above also remind media scholars of the finding of the burden of under-representation. This concept applies to any under-represented group. Given that there is gross under-representation, the few images available of, in this case, Latinas bear the burden of representing all Latinas. This means that a large range of Latinas, given the heterogeneity within Latinidad, will be frustrated with Jennifer Lopez since she cannot represent all of them satisfactorily. If there were a broader range of Latinas and representations of Latinidad, the burden would not fall so squarely on Jennifer Lopez's shoulders.

Jennifer Lopez continues to be a subject of audience discussions and interpretations, by Latina/o, mainstream, and global audiences. While

I was traveling in Finland, a male fellow communication scholar came up to me and said, "I want to meet your fellow country woman, Jennifer Lopez." For him she was not Latina or Latin American, just the most beautiful woman in the United States and the world. Conversely when I was talking to a South African feminist in a conference in Los Angeles, she remarked: "I am tired of all this US propaganda that is sent to my country. Personally I am most tired of Jennifer Lopez – is there no other star from this country?" Again, she was not interpreting Jennifer Lopez as a Latina but was complaining about her over-exposure, specifically in a conversation about the lack of African people in the mainstream media. This points to the possibility that, as she is marketed globally, Jennifer Lopez might very well be considered part and parcel of hegemonic US global culture, and her difference would be erased altogether.

CHAPTER

4   Effects and cognition

Aᶠᵀᵉᴿ pursuing the study of production, content and representation, as well as audience, reception, and interpretation, we finish with the pursuit of knowledge of the effects of the media and/on Latina/os. Why would we study anything about the mass media if we did not think or suspect they had some form or type of effect? Part of the impetus behind the production of media in a capitalist system is the desired effect of increased consumption. From a marketing perspective, the reason to construct and identify audiences is so they can be targeted with media that will hopefully encourage the effect of consumption. The production and circulation of *The George Lopez Show* is a great way to get a particular segment of the audience to be open to the effect of consuming products advertised in that show and also of developing an allegiance to George Lopez so that he can attract an audience to some of his other media ventures, such as his stand-up comedy on the Comedy Central network, and in turn expose you to messages that will hopefully continue to have the effect of fostering particular consumer choices. The very detailed production that results in particular types of content and representation is carried out with the implicit or explicit purpose of generating an effect. While consumerism might be one of the major effects desired, others include better nutrition choices, health habits, and interpersonal relationships. Thus, while we cannot really say that all of the audience engages in a purposeful interaction with media and popular culture, we can say that nearly all media produced in the mainstream hope for some form of effect. In the case of Latina/o Media Studies, some of this effect might be to reach the Latina/o segment of the audience and influence its attitudes, behaviors, and/or cognitions in some manner.

There is much research on effects of the mass media, and there are many types of effects to study. Do you think you are affected by the mass media? Usually when I ask this question, students answer that, while they are not affected, they suspect that their friends and family might be. Well this is actually a type of effect! It is called third-person effect when you think you are not affected but others are, as in "I can watch *Ugly Betty* but I am immune to the messages in that show and they do not affect me, but they sure seem to influence my friends' shopping choices." The third-person effect implies also that the reason we think ourselves immune is that implicitly or explicitly we are deploying a form of superiority over others we judge less able to resist influence. This becomes relevant at the individual and group levels in terms of ethnicity, as difference is often asserted through superior vs. inferior ability. Quite often dominant-culture people suspect that they are immune to such effects but that people of color are more susceptible, a form of infantilization of ethnic groups. Thus the third-person effect can occur at an individual and a broader social level.

How do we come to make choices about clothing, style, friends, political candidates, education, etc.? How do these choices, based on media influence, contribute to continuing or dissolving ethnic difference and identity? How do media contribute to attitudes and behaviors toward Latina/os and Latinidad? Is the way Latina/os are represented influential on Latina/o inclusion and self-esteem? Does the stereotypical representation of Latina/os increase discrimination against them? Mastro, Behm-Morawitz, and Kopacz (2008) assert that "the manner in which Latinos (and racial/ethnic minorities in general) are depicted on television is of import as these images may provoke a broader array of discriminatory responses than previously recognized" (p. 2). The concerns voiced by Mastro et al. refer to the effects of media on mainstream users who in turn might discriminate against Latina/os based on stereotypical representations.

Does the fact that Latina/os are heavy media users increase potential effect? Does the fact that some segments of the population do not come into contact wth Latina/os mean that they are more dependent on the media for their attitudes toward and about Latina/os? How do we study these questions? Well it is incredibly complex. If the media are among many contributing factors, to isolate the impact of media and popular culture, in relation to a broad range of dynamic variables such as nutrition, environment, education, location (to name a few possibilities), is really not a task for the faint-hearted. In this chapter, we consider what research there is connecting Latina/os and media effects, a rather new and understudied part of the field of Media Studies. While there are a plethora of studies of representation suggesting a possible effect, there are not really very many studies that pursue the methodology that results in an effects finding. Moreover, audience and effects research might be difficult to differentiate for a person new to Media Studies. Audience research explores interpretation and the inclusion of media in everyday life. Effects research, on the other hand, explores the implicit and explicit effects, at the conscious and subconscious levels, on individuals, groups, and society.

As McQuail (2005) notes in the beginning of his book's section on media effects, there is a great paradox surrounding effects. On the one hand, since the media contribute to our understanding of reality, nearly everyone – parents, educators, politicians, youth – is convinced that the media must have effects on individuals, groups, and entire cultures, if not on the global condition. On the other hand, it has proven very difficult to predict or even ascertain what these effects have been. In fact the long history of effects research takes us from a perspective, dominant at the turn of the last century, and not necessarily based on empirical evidence, that there must be very strong effects of the mass media, to a reaction in the form of a hypothesis of minimal effects, to a reaction to the reaction in a period and by a group of scholars returning to the hypothesis of strong effects, to a contemporary position of negotiated media influence. To be sure, all scholars agree that media by themselves can seldom be predictive of an effect. Media alone cannot make an individual or group be prejudiced against Latina/os nor can they, conversely, by themselves, do away with prejudice. Media are not causal agents – that is, the sole creators of an effect – but contributing factors to an effect. Especially given that prejudice is a rather large effect, media alone – and certainly just one instance of media exposure – cannot account for either the onset or end of prejudice. Maybe watching television late at night can make you want to eat more pizza if it's advertised, but prejudice is a much more complex chain of attitudes and behaviors than the occasional weakness that we experience while tired and working late at night. Prejudice might fit within third-person effects in terms of McQuail's paradox. That is, most people think that media might have prejudicial effects on others but not on them.

Moreover, media have been found to be more influential when they provide information about things which people have no personal experience of. This suggests that, for the many people living in segregated communities in the United States, the media's representations might form their only, or one of their few, contacts with people of other races or ethnicities. If we return to our discussion of prejudice and connect it to Mastro et al. (2008), then we can hypothesize that those who have few contacts with Latina/os and consume prejudicial stereotypes of Latina/os in media content are more likely to suffer an effect of prejudice. Without personal knowledge – say, of a professional Latina/o, an honest Latina/o businessperson, or a dedicated Latina/o teacher – people who rely on media to make decisions that might affect Latina/os are more likely to have a negative affect or attitude toward Latina/os. This finding alone has huge implications for

Latina/o Media scholars. Moreover, McQuail agrees with Carey (1989) that historically there might be certain periods of crisis in which the media have stronger effects than in more sedate times: "We can only speculate about the reasons for such associations in time, but we cannot rule out the possibility that media are actually more influential in certain ways at times of crisis or heightened awareness" (1989, p. 463).

If we see this moment – 2009, with a combined economic collapse and two-front war – as one of a period of, at most, a national identity crisis or, at least, a period of "heightened awareness" about ethnicity, when the imagined community that is the United States is coming to terms with not only its previously dominant binary, black-and-white self-perception but also the inclusion and long-standing presence of Latina/os, history may yet show that media perform a more influential role vis-à-vis dispositions toward ethnicity in general and Latina/os in particular. Research mentioned in chapter 2, "Textual/content analysis," suggests that Latina/os are represented in a particular manner, especially in relation to issues such as immigration, terrorism, and the drug trade. For effects scholars, the project becomes one of linking those representations with any potential effect on attitude, cognition, and/or behavior, either toward Latina/os or among Latina/os.

A definition of media effects can be succinct or lengthy. McQuail (2005) asserts: "media 'effects' are simply the consequences of what the mass media do, whether intended or not" (p. 465). Following this rather benign operationalization, McQuail then outlines a huge range of possible types of media effects research paths (pp. 467–70): planned and short-term, including propaganda, individual response, media campaign, news learning, framing, and agenda setting; unplanned and short-term, including individual reaction, collective reaction, and policy effects; planned and long-term, including development diffusion, news diffusion, diffusion of innovations, and distribution of knowledge; and finally unplanned and long-term, including social control, socialization, event outcomes, and reality defining and construction of meaning. Also, over time, the tendency to see behavior change as a result of changes in beliefs and attitudes has been largely discounted. People can explicitly admit or report having their attitudes changed but that does not necessarily translate into behavioral change. An example is that, although audiences might report that as a result of a particular type of media content they have more open attitudes toward minorities, when it comes to hiring or promotion they will still fall back on their tendency to privilege white applicants. Given that in the United States and some other places in the world, effects remains the dominant paradigm within

Communication Studies, each of the above-named types of effects has been and continues to be extensively studied. In fact, dating back at least to Bargh, Chen, and Burrows (1996) social psychologists have been exploring stereotypes in relation to "automaticity in attitudes and social cognition" (p. 230). They theorize, based on studies that include the elderly and black males, that we cannot assume that our behavioral responses are under our control. Selected stimuli, such as a photo or even a negative word, can trigger a hostile response not just toward the group being stereotyped but to anybody else coming into contact with the stereotyped person.

However, in relation to ethnicity and media effects in general, and Latina/os and media effects in particular, the amount of work is radically reduced. The above study by Bargh et al. (1996) studied African American males. However, the authors were not as interested in the particular ethnicity that they included in their experimental study as in the lack of control over behavior by individuals who are primed by a particular stimulus. As mentioned in previous chapters in this book, there is an abundant amount of research on dominant-culture groups, a much lesser amount of work on African Americans and effects of the media, and an even smaller amount of research on Latina/os. In fact, if one looks at the major journals in the field, such as the *Journal of Communication*, *Communication Theory*, *Communication Research*, and the *Howard Journal of Communication*, we continue to see a steady amount of work on African Americans and the effects of the media, but a near "brown out" on Latina/os. A recent issue of the *Journal of Communication* on agenda setting and priming (2007, 57:1), two related areas of research within which there has been some very productive work on matters of ethnicity and effects of the mass media, contained no research on either African Americans or Latina/os. Indeed, Latina/o Media Studies scholars are just beginning to flesh out the area of effects studies.

M. B. Oliver (2003), speaking on the topic of the effect of representations of race and crime in the media, suggests that: "most scholars from a media effects tradition enthusiastically embrace the notion that viewers' selection, interpretation, and memory of media content play central roles in the influence that media portrayals may have on attitudes, beliefs, and behaviors" (p. 422).

Of importance to note here, while also mentioned in chapter 2, "Textual/content analysis," is that, while a content analysis is usually a first step in a project about effects, an additional step must follow that usually involves experimental methodology exposing a control and an experimental group to different types of media content. As McQuail warned us above, effects are fairly difficult to predict, so just looking at content cannot form the basis for predicting effects.

Nonetheless, these two areas of Media Studies are inextricably linked. For example, M. B. Oliver (2003) devotes the first part of her analysis of effects of race in crime coverage to a literature review of representations of race in crime coverage. Similarly Casas and Dixon (2003) begin their study of effects of counter-stereotypical representations of Blacks and Latina/os with an overview of the representation of race in the news. Still, many studies, for example Mastro and Stern (2003), conclude a lengthy content analysis with a section on possible impact on audience, based on social psychology theories but not on the empirical research derived from an experimental study. Similarly, Mastro and Robinson (2000) use content analysis of television to transition into cultivation effects, hypothesizing that the long-term, cumulative effects of over-representation of violence in relation to people of color on television over time will have a strong impact on heavy television viewers, especially those with little personal experience with people of color. Finally, in a content analysis of Spanish-language television, Mastro and Ortiz (2008) suggest that, based on social identity theory, group-based outcomes might include the twin forces of associating power with men and youth and attractiveness with women. Again, this study can only hypothesize since the research connecting the content analysis finding to an effect has yet to be carried out. Navarrete and Kamasaki (1994), whose findings can be summarized as classic of the symbolic annihilation approach – that is, Hispanics are virtually invisible, and, when present, are represented negatively and stereotypically – suggest the following as effect implications of such content analysis findings: damage to a group's public image and the public attitudes that may accompany them; negative stereotypes of Hispanics held by non-Hispanics to coincide with media portrayals; "negative stereotypes reinforced by media contribute to actual discrimination against Hispanics [which include educational, job, credit, and health discrimination – in terms of access and how they are treated by professionals]" (p. 6); policy implications in terms of lack of identification and support for Hispanic issues; negative self-image, especially among Hispanic youth; and under-representation of Hispanics in employment in media industries. This is a wide range of possible effects, none of which are pursued by Navarrete. Some of these concerns or areas of possible research are taken up in the literature that will be discussed below. In sum, while scholars warn against making a methodological and theoretical leap from content analysis data into effects conclusions, many of them hypothesize just such a leap. One of the reasons that effects research is conducted is in case of a counterintuitive finding. We cannot assume that our hypothesis will match the research results.

Additionally, most of the existing research revolves around effects of television given the medium's prominence in US culture, concerns about its tendencies in terms of representation, and fears (and outright moral panics) in relation to its perceived negative effects on society. Since the 1960s, US Media Studies scholars have been concerned about the effects of television since television access and ownership rates reached a saturation point. You have probably heard figures showing how there are more televisions than toilets or beds in the USA. Much of this early television research was concerned with negative effects on children and the effects of televised violence on youth and society at large. Most of this research implicitly, and until recently unreflexively, focused on white middle-class normativity. That is, the research assumed the white, middle-class, nuclear family to be the norm, and measured all others in relation to their deviation from this norm. If minorities are hypothesized as deviant or pathological, the very assumptions of the research will inevitably generate a body of knowledge that does not necessarily serve to illuminate the complexity of media effects on the population at large, much less on segments of this population. Contemporary research on minority effects promises to disrupt this tendency to pathologize. Further research on effects on and by Latina/os also will disrupt the minority literature tendency to focus primarily on African Americans. Mastro (2003) argues that, despite the number of research articles documenting under-representation and stereotyping, "only a paucity of research exists examining the relationship between media exposure and subsequent social perceptions of Latinos" (p. 98). Research on other ethnic minorities, especially on Asian and Native Americans, is even more scarce.

As a partial corrective to the dearth of research on television, effects, and Latina/os, Mastro et al. (2008) tested two theories, aversive racism and social identity theory, to explore the effects of television portrayals on mainstream audiences. Beginning from the standpoint that "only minimal attention has been paid to investigating the socio-cognitive effects of exposure to those images on consumers" (p. 1), Mastro et al. deploy these two theories not generally associated with media effects. Although media effects research is inescapably social-scientific, there are many points of congruence with more interpretive approaches. For example, both Bargh et al. and Mastro et al. can be said to explore the notion that racism is much more inferential than overt, as suggested by Stuart Hall. Indeed, Mastro et al. suggest that "more subtle race based responses are likely to emerge when media messages provide sufficient ambiguity for the expressions to be attributed to race-irrelevant rationales" (p. 2). The theories of aversive racism and social identity function at the inter-group level. Aversive racism posits that "evaluations of racial/ethnic minorities are characterized by a conflict between Whites' endorsement of egalitarian values and their unacknowledged negative attitude toward racial/ethnic out-groups" (Gaertner and Dovidio, 1986, in Mastro et al., 2008). Social identity theory refers to in- and out-group discrimination, studying "the *minimal* conditions that would lead members of one group to discriminate in favor of the ingroup to which they belonged and against another outgroup" (www.tcw.utwente.nl/theorieenoverzicht/Theory %20clusters/Interpersonal%20Communication%20and%20Relations/ Social_Identity_Theory.doc/, retrieved March 20, 2009). This subtle effect combining these two theories can be studied through an experimental design that exposes dominant-culture participants to ambiguous situations in which "their actions can be attributed to factors other than race" (p. 4). As a result the racist participant in the study is able to sustain their vision of self as egalitarian and thus maintain their self-concept and self-esteem. For example a television show that contains ambiguous characters will likely generate responses favoring the in-group for whites precisely because their responses cannot be attributed directly to race. The result of the empirical study revealed that self-esteem within the in-group was increased after exposure to narrative ambiguity which in turn allowed them to advantage the in-group. While the findings of this study did not bear out all of the hypotheses, they supported the effect and uses of ambiguous data in the maintenance of racist attitudes. While aversive racism is a finding that had previously been applied only to blacks and the media, this study (Mastro et al., 2008) extends this paradigm and shows effects in relation to Latina/os and the media. Furthermore, the authors of the study acknowledge that their project continues the patterns of exploring white responses to mediated images of Latina/os. It would be interesting, they note, also to explore the responses of racial minorities to mediated images of racial minorities.

Given the roots of Latina/o Studies in the USA, one would expect there to be a rich foundation for the study of effects of the mass media on Latina/o audiences and publics. Issues of representation, belonging, and cultural citizenship have been central in the field of Latina/o Studies. Another reason that one might expect there to be a future wealth of effect studies on Latina/os, now that they are acknowledged as a significant part of the population, is that, given the racializing tendency to see any ethnicized population as different if not abnormal, one might find attention paid to issues of deviance among this racialized population – studies on effects of violence, food and obesity, smoking, general health and exercise, children, sex role models, and political influence are all within this paradigm. Studies of effect include issues of ethnic stereotyping as they influence people's notions of crime and capital punishment. Migration policy is also influenced by coverage of the border in the news. As well, health discourses are greatly affected by narratives of infections crossing the border, and health panics are partially an effect of media coverage of the health risks associated with particular segments of the population. From a more gendered perspective, we wonder if body images affect Latina women and girls differentially from the effect on white middle-class women. Last, but not least, given the demonstrated heavy viewing of television by Latina/os, and the fact that Latina/os, especially from the second generation after migration onwards, consume mainstream media, we have to keep in mind that the effects of the media need to be studied in relation to dominant-culture members, as well as Latina/os and members of other minorities.

Media effects and Latina/os

This chapter explores both the existing research on Latina/os and media effects, and the implications of gaps and concentrations in that research. Within effects research, there have been influential theories that have guided research for decades. Among these are cultivation analysis, selective exposure, priming, agenda setting, and third-person effect. Much as in chapter 2, "Textual/content analysis," there have been themes that are foregrounded in the study of effects. In fact we often discuss content and effects together precisely because effects are studied against the backdrop of content. The bandido stereotype foregrounded in chapter 2 endures today in the form of the criminal element, in both news and entertainment content. Not surprisingly, based on this long-standing content and representational analysis of the bandido, one major area of media effects research as it overlaps with Latina/os is the effect of over-representation of Latina/os as criminals on general audiences. It must be noted that, within social cognition theories, stereotypes have a particular definition: "Stereotypes are cognitive structures or categories that affect the encoding and processing of information, particularly information pertaining to groups to which the perceiver does not belong (i.e. out-groups). . . . These structures or schemas direct attention to some stimuli and away from others, influence categorization of information, and help us 'fill-in' missing information, and influence memory" (Casas and Dixon, 2003, p. 483).

In other words, stereotypes are cognitive shortcuts. Our brain uses these shortcuts to facilitate cognition and understanding. Media use them because it is not feasible to represent fully a person or situation as in lived experience. From this perspective, stereotypes are inevitable. So it is not stereotypes per se that are objectionable but the constant deployment of stereotypes that serve to demean and discriminate against segments of the population.

Out-group people are perceived in terms of their shared group characteristics rather than their individual personal attributes. Scholars build on extensive ongoing research on the effects of over-representation of blacks as criminals to make a connection between these schemas and cognition, attitudes, and behavior. Translated into Latina/o Media Studies, if whites perceive criminality as a stereotypical dimension of Latina/os, they will default to that when they see Latina/os in the television news. There is little research conducted on ethnic minority stereotypes of other ethnic minorities, and this is clearly a gap that needs to be addressed in future research.

Cultivation theory

Cultivation analysis is a theory of long-term cumulative effects. While originally studied in relation to television, it has come to be studied in relation to mass media in general. This theory, which has tinges of acculturation analysis, posits that heavy television viewers will develop television views of their reality. That is, they will give television answers to questions about their lives. For example, Faber, O'Guinn, and Meyer (1987) found that white heavy television viewers felt that, generally, Latina/os on television were treated equitably. Similarly Mastro, Behm-Morawitz, and Ortiz (2007) found that "increases in television consumption strengthened the influence of TV representations of Latinos, particularly when viewers had less closeness in their real world contact with Latinos" (p. 362). A heavy television viewer is likely to overestimate the prevalence of equality if that is the only version of reality they view, or the incidence of crime in their neighborhood, because crime is so over-represented in both news and entertainment content. The former might lead to a belief that racial equality is a reality, and the latter might "lead to greater feelings of fear and insecurity" (M. B. Oliver, 2003, p. 426). If a viewer has personal experience of prevalence of crime, the effects are stronger. In the same study mentioned above, Faber et al. (1987) also found that Latina/os were less likely than whites to rate television depictions of Latina/os as fair. This can be explained by the fact that the whites in the study lived in segregated communities, with little or no contact with Latina/os, and therefore believed the very few instances wherein Latina/os on television were shown to live in equitable conditions. In contrast, the Latina/os, who certainly had personal experience with their own lives, judged the television coverage in much less positive terms.

Similarly, for someone who lives in a crime-ridden area, the cultivation effects are likely to be stronger as those people have personal experience with crime. Clearly, cultivation as an area of effects research has implications in terms of Latina/os. Drawing on the material presented in chapter 2 on content and representation, Latina/o criminal characters are over-represented in realist and fictional content. Scholars are concerned with the cumulative impact over time, not just a single exposure. Heavy television viewers believe a television reality. M. B. Oliver (2003) lists three reasons why cultivation of attitudes and beliefs is particularly worrisome in terms of news over-representations of people of color as criminals. First, US individuals list news as their primary source of information. Second, the representations of minorities and crime appear mostly in reality-based programming which has been shown to have stronger effects on attitudes and beliefs. Third, given the long history of stereotypes, these are already in viewers' minds to function as interpretive schemas for new portrayals of stereotypes. Portrayals of crime, especially some of the highly sensationalistic violent material available in police shows and hybrid police-docu-drama genres, might lead to increased fears of crime and violence among heavy television viewers. Given that Blacks and Latinos tend to be over-represented among criminals, there is a problem. Therefore, people with heavy television diets are likely to fear Latina/os as criminals, regardless of their own personal experience either with criminals or with Latina/os. If we add the possibility that many of these heavy television watchers may live in areas where they seldom come into contact with Latina/os and therefore have little information based on personal experience, then the effect of the overwhelming amount of criminalized representations might be even stronger.

M. B. Oliver (2003) suggests disposition theory in conjunction with the cultivation analysis above. "Disposition theory suggests that enjoyment of entertainment is largely a reflection of viewers' dispositions toward media characters and the outcomes that media characters experience during the course of entertainment" (p. 426). In essence, people side with particular characters based on previous dispositions. Within this theory, when characters for whom individuals have a positive disposition enjoy a positive outcome and, vice versa, when characters for whom individuals have a negative disposition suffer a negative outcome, then the enjoyment for the individual is the greatest. In relation to crime Oliver reminds us of the interaction between viewers' dispositions and issues of race: "because reality police shows routinely feature portrayals of Black and Latino criminal suspects being aggressively punished by police, these programs should be particularly appealing to viewers who not only harbor punitive dispositions, but who also harbor negative racial attitudes" (p. 427). Thus cultivation analysis can be used in tandem with disposition theory. Both of them suggest disturbing effects as a result of content and representation patterns regarding Latina/os.

Selective exposure

Selective exposure theory is rather self-explanatory – that is, people expose themselves to the types of content that they are already in agreement with. Thus their exposure to media content is unlikely to change their views and much more likely to reinforce previously held beliefs and attitudes. According to this theory, we would hypothesize that those who already have beliefs and attitudes supporting racial tolerance will expose themselves to media content that is supportive of diversity. Conversely, those who already hold racist beliefs and attitudes will select material that reinforces such a worldview. A key element of this theory is that people are familiar enough with media content to make decisions prior to exposure to any type of content. For instance, a study of selective exposure by Melican and Dixon (2008) exploring use of news sources on the internet found that those who viewed "non traditional sources as more credible also score higher on a modern racism scale" (p. 151). Once more the findings are rather disturbing in that the room for social change is reduced if people select media according to pre-existing beliefs.

Third-person effect

This is a distancing type of finding. Scholars find that, while most people believe the media have effects, they also do not believe the media affect them personally. However, they are quite willing to believe the media affect others, including those around and close to them. In terms of Latina/o Media Studies, people might be willing to believe that others are affected by things such as over-representation of Latina/os as criminals, but they do not believe themselves subject to such influence. Moreover, people might take a group third-person effect position. That is, they might think that certain types of people are more likely to be affected than people of their own social or cultural group. Scharrer (2002) found that, based on out-group stereotyping, some social groups are more likely to be perceived as negatively affected by television violence than others. While her project explored children and teenagers, those with less education, and lower-income groups, one could see both the intersection of some Latina/os with these three categories and the extension of out-group status to ethnic minorities including Latina/os.

Priming

Social cognition theory posits that representation can influence beliefs and stereotypes. This type of research derives from psychological efforts to study how people make sense of information (Lashley, 1951). The concept of priming refers to how visual and/or aural cues literally prime our understanding, interpretation, and judgment. In more scientific terms, priming describes how pre-existing schemas or cognitive structures, which we have stored in our brains as a result of previous experience, influence the interpretation of new information such that recently and/or frequently activated ideas come to mind more easily than ideas that have not been activated once perceivers encounter similar stimuli. For example, if your school had a clock atop the blackboard in every classroom, chances are that, after exiting a classroom, you might say there was a clock there even if there wasn't because your brain is so primed to associate that clock with a classroom setting. While priming is a useful tool for evaluating political figures in public opinion, it has also been of central importance to scholars of stereotypes of racialized groups and audience effects of this stereotypical representation, who have found that exposure to negative racial imagery in the media adversely impacts subsequent evaluations of minorities. You can see how the unending representations of Latina/o criminals might prime a viewer to interpret a Latina/o character as criminal, given that extensive media history. Worse than that, the extensive and repeated exposure to Latina/o criminals in the mass media might prime a person walking down the street to fear for their safety if they see an identifiably Latino man walking toward them. In an extensive literature review of priming as it pertains to news of crime and race, Dixon, Azocar, and Casas (2003) note that effects are stronger when viewers agree with the represented stereotypes. Worse, priming effects can happen even if the viewer does not endorse the stereotype. Moreover, not only do people make judgments and experience enjoyment when primed by racial stereotypes, but also "people may make judgments about race-related social policies based upon their racial perceptions" (p. 502). Sniderman and Piazza (1993) have demonstrated, for example, that the stereotypical belief regarding black laziness is associated with the endorsement on social welfare spending for African Americans. A range of research associating blacks with laziness has been found to be related to support of conservative social policies. Media effects scholars connect these stereotypes and predispositions to issues of race and the media. M. B. Oliver (2003) concludes that "for priming effects to occur, it is necessary that the viewer have the mental associations in place that connect cognitions, attributes, and feelings. In other words, for media to prime racial stereotypes, racial stereotypes must exist – otherwise they cannot be primed" (p. 432).

A growing group of scholars (Bargh 1999 in M. B. Oliver 2003) is now suggesting that exposure to stereotypes is so widespread throughout mass media and other forms of culture that we are all subjected to their effects, explicitly or implicitly, and therefore that media activate stereotypes in everyone, even in people who do not explicitly endorse or support them. This is a wider type of social effect that takes us into the next theory, agenda setting.

Agenda Setting

A logical extension of priming is agenda setting. Like priming, which developed as a way to study political communication, agenda setting can also be applied to the study of race and ethnicity in news and entertainment. Whereas priming refers to individual effects or particular types of content, agenda setting is a broader type of effect. In Media Studies, students learn the agenda-setting lesson early in their education: *the media do not tell the public what to think, they tell them what to think about.* The second-level finding of agenda setting is how the media tell us to think about issues of relative saliency. In other words, agenda setting is a measure of relative saliency in content as it affects the public agenda. Agenda setting is also related to framing, a way of organizing content and suggesting "what the issue is through the use of selection, emphasis, exclusion, and elaboration." Their convergence is relevant "because it links the framing of news content with the effect of that content – that is, how people of color are covered in television news may influence how they are perceived by communities across America" (Poindexter, Smith, and Heider, 2003, p. 526). Agenda setting can be a useful tool for the study of Latina/os and media effects as it could be applied to the study of issues such as immigration and saliency, not just in news but in media at large. Scholars of agenda setting straddle the areas of effects and production of media as agenda setting crosses over into a practice in the newsroom and in other sites of media production.

Another area of agenda setting is the influence of salience on pedagogical models in general and teachers in particular. Reyes and Rios (2003) examined the "impact of mass media on teaching and on knowledge about teachers and students" (p. 3) – linking representation not only with how the public thinks about Latina/os but with the very way (dominant-culture) teachers treat them in schools and in the classroom. Their research is bi-modal. They begin with a representational analysis that finds that the public is left with little information about what a Latina/o teacher can be. Although the piece is methodologically unconventional for agenda setting – it consists of a conversation between two Latina/o Studies scholars – the piece speaks of impact or effect on the curriculum and of treatment of Latina/o students in that teachers neither use appropriate pedagogical resources nor know how to deal with the Latina/o students. Agenda setting leads scholars to wonder whether a change of representational narratives might lead to a more progressive agenda. The next section sheds light on that possibility.

Effects of counter-stereotypical representations

As a logical extension of both priming and agenda-setting research, scholars have sought to find out if counter-stereotypical messages will generate a less problematic and less racist effect. Much of the work in this vein is inspired by the canonical *Enlightened Racism* (Jahlly and Lewis, 1992), which showed that, despite the liberal politics and attempt at positive representation of African Americans in *The Cosby Show*, the counter-stereotypical representations served to reinforce global audiences' pre-existing racial dispositions. In particular, those who already held racist attitudes and beliefs saw in *The Cosby Show* a reiteration of black inferiority and white superiority. This finding suggests that changing racist attitudes and beliefs will be much more difficult than anticipated. Whereas Jahlly and Lewis focused on attitudes and beliefs about blacks, some research has begun to be conducted, within the same approach, on Latina/os. In an unusual study – because it focused on magazines and women of color, instead of on television and disaggegrated gender issues – Covert and Dixon (2008) found that increased representations of professional women of color elevated "the expectations of women of color among white readers but not people of color" (p. 232). While for Whites the images might have served as a "stand-in," for Latinas it was a reminder of occupational blocks in their way to professional advancement. Casas and Dixon (2003), in a study about counter-stereotypical effects of viewer perceptions about Blacks and Latinos in the news, found that any news viewing triggered White perceptions of Blacks and Latinos as failing to take responsibility for their actions, even if these representations were counter-stereotypical. This area of study is still in its preliminary stages but findings so far suggest that just changing stereotypes by itself will not be enough to reverse what amounts to centuries of deeply held stereotypes repeatedly reinforced in mass media and culture at large.

Health effects

One of the major components of media effects research has been into health campaigns and other related effects of media, on either positive outcomes of media content – such as proper nutrition and safe sex – or negative outcomes – such as underage smoking and drinking, obesity, and unsafe sex. Given that minority communities in general are singled out as having unhealthy practices and that reduced resources and contact with a new culture place people at health risk, it should not be surprising that Latina/os would be included in some of this research. Indeed, from a Public Health perspective, there have been health campaigns since at least the 1980s. For example in 1988, the Center for Health Promotion Research at the Houston University of Texas Health Science Center, with an eye to reducing future occurrences of cancer, conducted a campaign targeting Mexican Americans in the Southwest with anti-smoking and cessation of smoking messages. Similarly, although at the time Mexican Americans were not seen as a high-risk population for AIDS, a San Antonio program in 1988 included Public Service Announcements on local television hoping to reach Mexican American youth with safe-sex messages. Alcalay et al. (1999) utilized a multi-media bilingual intervention to reach Latina/os with information to generate lifestyle and behavioral changes, including "television telenovela format public service announcements (PSAs), radio programs, brochures, recipe booklets, charlas, a promotores training manual, and motivational videos," with post-broadcast research showing that the target population "were substantially more aware of risk factors for CVD, and had greatly increased their knowledge of ways to prevent heart disease" (p. 359). All of these projects hoped for positive outcomes in which healthier choices would be made by the target population.

There is little research to be found linking media, health, and Latina/os in the effects literature. Brodie et al. (1999) compare the perceived effectiveness and relevance of general-market media versus Black- and Latino-oriented media as sources of information for ethnically diverse segments of the audience. While they found that "Whites, African Americans, and Latinos rely heavily on the media for information about health and health care, take personal action as a result of media health coverage, and would like the media to expand its coverage of health topics," they also found differential use of media sources according to race and ethnicity. Though there was more reliance on mainstream media by African Americans and Latina/os, their trust of these was low. The authors of this study suggested that these findings indicate the need for more coverage of minority health issues and more sensitivity to issues of race and ethnicity.

In terms of effects of particular types of messages on particular outcomes, Weintraub Austin, Pinkleton, and Fujioka (2000) included Latina/os in a study about the effects of media exposure on underage drinking and though they found some differences and particularities with Latino boys, who were found to be more attracted to beer logos, they suggest less attention to exposure-based effects research and more focus on logical and emotional components of young people's decision making that might influence how and when they make the decision to engage in underage drinking. In terms of the relationship between alcohol advertisements and the availability of alcohol in a neighborhood, Alaniz (1998) suggests that alcohol outlet density can be a stronger predictor of homicide and violence, among inner-city populations that include Latina/os, than is race or ethnicity (p. 286). The whole process is rather tautological as there is an over-representation of alcohol outlets in poor racial or ethnic communities; and, not surprisingly, alcohol outlet density is a determinant of alcohol advertising in a community. Mastro and Atkin (2002) studied the connection between beliefs and attitudes of Mexican American youth and their exposure to alcohol billboards, drawing on Bandura's social cognitive theory and the finding that Mexican American youth are disproportionately exposed to alcohol billboards, living in urban areas with large numbers of such signs (Alaniz, 1998). Mastro and Atkin (2002) found that, while the consumption of alcoholic beverages has decreased for the White population, it is increasing for Latina/os, especially Mexican American men who report not only higher drinking rates than either White or other Latino men but also a steady heavy drinking rate after reaching middle age. Mexican American men have much higher drinking rates than their female counterparts, who exhibit some of the highest abstention rates, but also overall drink more than Cubans and Puerto Ricans. While the media are not seen as a causal agent – that, is they are not the sole reason that Mexican American men drink heavily – the amount of alcohol advertising in their environment and within their media diet, combined with family and peer pressure, results in high drinking rates. Moreover, the youthful character of the bulk of this population, the element that makes them such a seductive market for both alcohol and cigarette marketers, has long-term implications for health care issues and costs.

Television and Latina/o youth

Given the relative youth of the Latina/o population, and the ongoing concern within Media Studies with the effects of the media on youth, there has been some research on this topic. Rivadeneyra (2005) asserts that "as a growing segment of the U.S. citizenry and as avid media consumers, Latino adolescents represent a critical population for the study of media effects" (p. 468). Teenagers are also more likely to consume media in general and television in particular, and Latina/os are also heavy consumers of television. As well, Latina/o teens watch both Spanish- and English-language television. All of these findings suggest that studying Latina/o teenagers and television might yield important effects. Investigating whether gender-specific expectations within Latinidad would generate gendered uses of media and stronger cultivation effects, Rivadeneyra (2005) found that girls who are heavy viewers of both English-language television – talk shows in particular – and Spanish-language television, prime-time comedies and drama, exhibit more traditional gender role attitudes. In another study, using constructionist theory, which holds that what the viewer brings to the message affects what is taken away, Rivadeneyra (2006) sought to understand Latina/o teenagers' perceptions of television messages. Her two-pronged study was to ascertain whether Latino youth were aware of the ways they were represented and, if so, to find out what they took away from that. Latino youth noticed negative representations, but more of them in English- than Spanish-language television. Girls liked different content from boys who preferred a show called *Gata Salvaje* that girls found demeaning. Unexpectedly, Rivadeneyra found that watching Spanish-language television may actually act as a buffer to the perception of discriminatory stereotypes on English-language television. In terms of general self-esteem, Rivadeneyra, Ward, and Gordon (2007) found that, among Latina/o teenagers and college students, heavy television users exhibited lower self-esteem socially and as regards appearance, with women and strong Latino-identity youth showing more pronounced results.

Ideal of beauty

Especially within gender and feminist studies, scholars have explored the effects of the circulation of an unattainable ideal of beauty on the female population, in particular youth. The prevalence of eating disorders among the white, middle-class, young female segment of the population – estimated to be at 25 percent – has been partly blamed on the effects of media's glorification and over-representation of this unattainable ideal of beauty. In fact Rivadeneyra (2005) – above mentioned – noted that the finding that heavy television viewing among Latina girls generated more traditional gender roles potentially predisposed these girls to adhere to ideal-of-beauty standards. While people assume this ideal of beauty does not affect women of color, scholars are beginning to investigate whether this is true. Goodman (2002) found that, though Latina women interpreted the ideal of beauty as "lacking curves" and reported growing up around women with larger bodies, some of them still aspired to the ideal – maybe not as thin but certainly not flabby. They chose a model that was muscular but still quite thin. In a sense these findings suggest third-person effects as the Latinas claimed a different ideal of beauty yet admitted that the ideal was still influential. Goodman concludes that Latinas

> were aware of the positive judgments, attention, and economic successes received when conforming to the mediated ideal. Both Latina and Anglo women pursued the mediated ideal through diet and exercise, although the Latina women more often cast this in terms of health rather than weight loss. Indeed, Hispanic culture provided many Latinas with an alternative lens on thinness. They were more critical of the mediated ideal, knowing that their physical differences excluded them from attaining the ideal and that their culture and Hispanic men appreciated a more voluptuous female form. (p. 725)

The "alternative lens on thinness" did not shield girls from the pursuit of the ideal of beauty. This is yet another example of attitude change not necessarily translating into behavioral change.

Similarly Schooler (2008) found that despite negotiated and oppositional audience readings on the part of Latinas, their attitudinal resistance did not always translate into behavioral difference. Some still policed their bodies and engaged in eating and exercise practices to achieve the hegemonic ideal of beauty. The growing area of Girls Studies, which is just beginning to branch out into ethnicities beyond whiteness, also promises to shed light on some of these ideal-of-beauty and self-esteem issues among Latina girls.

Conclusion

Despite effects being the dominant paradigm within US Media Studies, there simply is not enough research on Latina/os and media effects. Study after study that could have included ethnicity in general and Latinidad in particular is published in myriad journals. Admittedly, when using quantitative methodology, adding another variable makes for a different study. However, ethnicity and Latinidad need to be considered not only as other variables but as theoretical and ontological refinements in effects research. The existing research is strong enough to provide a base for future research, and the following are just some ideas of where to go. Latina/o Media Studies scholars can expand effects research to include Latina/os and Latinidad. The findings about ambiguity in relation to aversive racism and social identity theory suggest that paradigms that have been applied to African Americans need to be tested with the Latina/o mediated images. Given that ambiguity is a rising form of representation, this opens up a window to study issues of aversive racism and social identity theory whose effects have been found in relation to ambiguous stimuli. Another caveat of the Mastro et al. (2008) study was that we need not only to branch out from studying Whites in relation to African Americans by including Latina/os, but also to study effects among Latina/os and between Latina/os and other ethnically coded segments of the population. Moreover, and drawing on theoretical models of the circuit of culture, we need to explore not only the influence of mediated messages on activating and perpetuating stereotypes but also how media affect inter-group relations. Large-scale effects such as prejudice, and smaller-scale effects such as in-group protection and self-esteem enhancement, contribute to a climate of hostility toward Latina/os. We also need research on whether positive mediated images increase self-esteem among Latina/os and other minorities. In sum, effects research is really in its infancy in relation to Latina/os.

Some questions that remain to be answered are: Does the over-representation of teenage sexual activity influence Latina/o youth attitude toward recreational sex? Does advertising literacy mediate the effects of obesity on Latina/o children? How do peers and media influence adolescents' sexual attitudes and sexual behavior? What are the media effects on the beliefs about the health consequences of smoking and age of smoking onset for Latina/o youth? What is the relative effectiveness of comparative health campaigns targeted at Latina/os in the areas of AIDS, smoking, weight, heart disease, cancer, etc.? What are the effects of sexually objectifying media on self-objectification and body surveillance in Latina/o college students? These are all titles from recently published articles in communication journals that I have amended to include Latina/os and Latinidad. The range of possibilities suggests that future research is likely to be plentiful and, hopefully, illuminating.

Case study no. 1

"The Homicide Report"

The Report falls within a long line of mass-media texts that over-represent violence among communities of color. It is a realist text, and that has implications in terms of effects, given that people have been found to attribute more truth value and legitimacy to realist texts. In fact, it is as realist as it gets. It represents death in a particular geographic location. From such a finding of content, effects scholars usually begin to build an experimental research project. As far as I know, none has yet been carried out on the Report, but there are a number of possibilities, for effects have to be considered within a wide range of settings.

First, does this Report fall within cultivation, priming, and agenda-setting findings? In terms of cultivation, for heavy media consumers, including those who now rely on the internet, will this Report contribute to their view of the world as a violence-ridden place, where crime and violence are mostly ethnic? We could hypothesize that those who have little or no contact with Latina/os and African Americans and who consume a heavy media diet will be primed by the results of the Report to fall back on their stereotypes about people of color. Also, we would need to study the effect of this content on Latina/os. Especially for those living in the communities reported on, does the Report reinforce their perception of living in a dangerous community and increase their fear of crime?

Second, given that agenda setting is a related effect to priming, are there any agenda-setting effects from this Report? Is there any effect in the communities themselves – that is, the communities where the bulk of homicides are being committed? Does the Report contribute to an awareness of the pervasiveness of death and the particular character of those deaths: involving firearms and young men of color – mostly Latino, but also African American? Does the knowledge effect some sort of community effort to intervene into that cycle of death? Does the knowledge contribute to some form of activism or community outcry over the uneven distribution – for lack of a better term – of death in Los Angeles County?

Despite some concerns about the possibility of intra-ethnic tension as a predictor of violence and death, the Report shows that the overwhelming majority of homicides occur within the same ethnic group. Does the Report serve to assuage concerns about intra-ethnic violence? Does it generate some form of inter-ethnic solidarity?

In the larger community of Los Angeles County, does the Report serve to insert the issue of homicide deaths into the political agenda? Scholars found that respondents in effects studies tended to blame ethnic individuals rather than social systems of discrimination for crime statistics. Does putting a face on the deaths have any effect on this blaming-the-individual response? In some ways the Report could be seen as counter-stereotypical coverage, but in other ways it reiterates the usual narratives about ethnicity and violence.

The blog has also had reported effects in other sub-communities.

For example police forces in the 57 jurisdictions that compose Los Angeles County are beginning to look at the Report as a source of information to be shared across police precincts. They are able to see patterns and maybe even discover a serial killer that they might not have identified had there not been a composite Homicide Report. This effect has led to more sharing and cooperating across police districts.

In terms of effects on the news process itself, this Report has shown that there is a way to use the expanded capability provided by the blogosphere to enhance coverage and widen the public sphere. There might be long-term effects in terms of coverage and beats[1] in the news-gathering process. This would, as effects research ultimately promises to do, take us back into production issues of the media.

Case study no. 2

Jennifer Lopez

What effects has Jennifer Lopez had on media audiences in particular and culture in general? She has definitely foregrounded the Latina body as a site of contestation and negotiation, and that is no small feat. However – and at this point, most of the evidence is journalistic and anecdotal – she has contributed to a reformulation of the ideal of beauty. Cosmetic surgeons report an increased demand for booty lifts and booty implants. The cosmetic industry, ever solicitous to comply with any beauty trends, has responded by making available a range of products that promise to lift that behind without surgical procedures. It is now hip to have a prominent booty. Other stars, notably Beyoncé (Durham and Báez, 2007), are being discussed in terms of how they unsettle ideals of beauty. Girls are writing in to magazines reporting how they feel more comfortable with their body after this expanded sensitivity. Jeans makers in particular, and pants makers in general, are marketing a broad range of options ranging from booty-lifting jeans to ones with padded behinds. Even the women in *Sex and the City* discussed booty lifts in one of their episodes. Granted, a booty lift still falls far behind breast lifts and implants in terms of popularity of cosmetic surgeries, but it is now part of the radar. In sum, Jennifer Lopez has managed to have an effect on the cultural landscape in terms of body shapes.

From anecdotal evidence, we would need to study this effect via social scientific methodology. We might find third-person effects in terms of girls saying they would not want to increase their booty but they think others might. Or we could find that a booty, despite its popularity, still signifies difference and abnormality. People might say they accept, have a new attitude toward, this new standard of beauty, but they might not act, or behave, as if they do. For example, at the level of hiring and promotion of on-air newscasters, all other things being equal, we might find that employers still decide to hire the less curvaceous job applicant. At this point, this is all merely speculative. From our knowledge of content and audience, we would need to devise social scientific experiments to teste a range of hypotheses. The representational and audience analysis would form a backdrop to this enterprise but could not replace it.

Other less embodied effects might include the expansion of media industries to branding by a broader range of celebrities. Jennifer Lopez is a profitable brand. Many other celebrities attempt to cross over from individual communicator to brand. Many fail. The fact that someone so coded within ethnic and Latina/o discourses manages to brand herself across a wide range of products in the mainstream might have positive implications for other ethnic celebrities seeking that expanded profitability. The long-term effect might be that ethnicity is not coded as such a marker of difference but as a marker of the centrality of hybridity and mixture to our national imaginary. This latter set of speculations, like all effects issues when taken to a broad cultural level, take us back into issues of production and thus form the full circle of Media Studies analysis.

Conclusion

WE encounter Latina/o media everywhere and Latina/os in the media in previously unlikely places. For example, John Leguizamo, a Colombian American, who began as a stand-up comic of Latinidad (he was known for a skit where he "outed" Latina/os in the public sphere, as in "Barbara Bush, Latina!"), moved to a major Hollywood film, *To Wong Foo Thanks for Everything: Julie Newmar* (1995), a movie in which he played the Latina/o drag queen in relation to the black drag queen played by Wesley Snipes and the white drag queen played by Patrick Swayze. Thus he moved from one realm of media, stand-up comedy, and its circulation through cable networks, to mainstream film. Later, after being in many movies, he played one of the doctors, Dr. Victor Clemente, on the television show *ER* in the 2005–6 season. He moved from the margins of mainstream media, as a Latino comic doing Latina/o jokes, to the multicultural relational palette of mainstream Hollywood film, as the Latino in a movie with a white and an African American in the three leads, to a subtle Latino in a prime-time television show with a one-year term – not becoming one of the recurring characters in that long-running show. His career has somewhat followed the path of Latina/o inclusion in mainstream media. We do not know the decisions that were made on the road to his becoming one of the doctors in a show that once starred George Clooney. Was there some Latina/o in the production chain who thought it prudent to include a Latina/o given that the show has had men, women, lesbian, African American, and Asian American characters? Was it a response to some activist intervention that brought to the attention of the producers the lack of any Latina/o character in the professional roles in that long-running series? After all, there had been plenty of derelicts and stereotypical Latina/os coming in as patients, but none as doctors. Did the producers decide to include a recognizable Latino, to most Latina/os, but in a subtle ethnic role so as not to alienate their mainstream white audience? We do not know nor have access to those decisions that resulted in the inclusion of John Leguizamo and the character that he plays. But the issue of the very subtle Latina/o takes us from production into content and representation. In any given episode in that show, do we, who watch the show, find any clue as to his Latinidad? If you are an occasional viewer – say, for example, you stumble upon the show one night while in a hotel room when you would not normally be watching television and there he is, playing alongside Parminder Nagra, the British Indian actress from *Bend it Like Beckham* (2002) – maybe you do not even recognize him at first and then you see him go through the *ER* motions of saving patients from death or declaring them beyond help. He is just another one of the doctors in a hospital show. If you follow the show and watch for minor clues, you might be able to discern a bit of Latinidad in his character. Maybe he wears a Virgin Mary pendant around his neck to signify Catholicism or he mutters under his breath in Spanish, as he did in *Wong Foo*, but maybe not. Or, if you know the actor and his long career, you bring that luggage to your interpretation of his doctor character. You might look really hard for Latina/o symbolism, or you might just decide he looks Latina/o and you know he is Latina/o and therefore that makes him a Latino character for you. But really, when the credits roll, it does not say "Latino doctor" by his name, Dr Victor Clemente. What might be the implications of his career trajectory and his inclusion in a major prime-time network television show? Does it make audiences more accepting of Latina/os, especially if they are included in that most sensitive of professional occupations, that of the doctor? Does the audience for the show expand once one of the main characters is a known Latino actor? Does this inclusion at all alter the effects, both large and small, that have been documented by social scientists? These are the questions facing Latina/o Media Studies scholars today. Hopefully these are the questions that this book has given you some tools to answer.

The field of Latina/o Media Studies is coming into its own. Accordingly, it is dynamic and complex. We have explored it from a Media Studies perspective. We explored what counts as Latina/o-produced media. In the process of figuring out what that meant, we found out that there is a growing amount of Latina/o-produced media. However, we also found out that it is very difficult to determine how, if, and when media are produced by Latina/os. Latina/os may have been present at the conceptualization of the medium, at the production of it in the organization such as the newspaper, radio or television station, Hollywood studio, website office, gaming production workship, or any other place where the process of producing media was located. Latina/os may have owned some of the production facilities and may have invested the capital necessary to pay the workers and maintain the technology necessary to produce that form of media. Latina/os may have started that particular media organization only to have become so successful that they were bought and incorporated into a media conglomerate whose impetus is profit rather than Latina/o cultural pride. Still, these were difficult matters to ascertain as much of mainstream media content does not carry a label that says "produced wholly or partly by Latina/os." As well, we pursued the theoretical element that the involvement of Latina/os in the production of media does not, by itself, mean that the media will have (recognizable) Latina/o themes. Is it fair to demand Latina/o themes from Latina/o producers? Who is to say what is a Latina/o theme? There are many gaps to be filled but, in relation to even a decade ago, we have an exponentially greater range of knowledge on the relationship between Media Studies and Latina/o Studies. As a demographic group, Latina/os have been demonstrated both to be large enough and to have sufficient disposable income for mainstream media to begin to take notice. As a cultural group, Latina/os are heterogeneous, creative, and dynamic. The fact is that, over 500 hundred years after the "discovery" of the Americas – and thus the creation of a category of people who would much later become known as Latina/os – Latina/os are still alive, thriving, and in no immediate danger of disappearing. The contact zone, to use Mary Louise Pratt's terminology, has expanded over the territory of the United States. The spread of the contact zone is not an entirely linear process, and bumps and slides along the way promise to make some happy and others despair, or at least object. The ripples from that contact zone have been felt globally. This is certainly the case in Latina/o Media Studies.

In Latina/o Media Studies we have to keep in mind that Latina/os interact with the larger society, make up part of the larger society, and change that larger society as they are changed by it. Neither the host culture nor Latina/os remain unchanged. To cite but one little piece of evidence that signals this hybridity, salsa is a more popular condiment than ketchup in the USA. Thus both Latina/os produce media and others contribute to the production of Latina/o media. The former's participation in media production includes mainstream and Latina/o media as well as English-, Spanish-, and Spanglish-language media. Latina/os are represented in media on their own and in relation to other members of their culture. As Mastro et al. (2008) remind us, we have to study the relationality between Latina/os and whites but also in terms of intra-Latino group relations as well as intra-ethnic group relations. Our comparison cannot always be in relation to whiteness. Latina/os interpret media, and they are interpreted by other members of the culture who consume media. Media have effects on Latina/os and also affect how others think about and treat Latina/os. Latina/os do not exist in a universe of their own, especially in relation to mainstream media. This has to be taken into account, although it certainly complicates research.

This book has focused on the mainstream for it remains the component of media that has the greatest circulation in the USA and abroad. It is the most easily accessible type of media. It is the type of media to which a broad range of people have easy and mostly free access. It presents the scholar with a number of challenges because the mainstream is both careless about the heterogeneity of Latinidad and much more vigilant about not alienating its white audience. The resulting form of media and representation has produced a light and sometimes nearly unrecognizable Latinidad. This Latinidad eludes those who try to count or measure the very explicit instances of Latinidad according to previous narratives. This book in large part argues against that position. Rather, it suggests that Latinidad is included in the media but often in such a light form that one almost has to have Latina/o radar to discern it.

Based on decades of research, this book has noted a number of findings and trends of study. First, it has noted that there has been a Latina/o Media Studies scholarship for at least four decades. In literature, film, and popular music studies, we find older research on which Latina/o Media scholars build. However, by 2009, Latina/o Media Studies has become a field of its own. The field is interdisciplinary and vibrant, but nonetheless coheres around issues of media and Latina/os. Elsewhere I have written about the need to read this scholarship (Valdivia, 2008), but it bears and deserves a bit of repetition. To wit, everybody thinks themselves a media scholar. This is well and good for members of the audience who develop their preferences and critical skills as common sense interpretive techniques. However, scholars really need to read Media Studies scholarship before they proceed to make unfounded and, most of the time, largely outdated, implicit theoretical connections. This applies as much to established disciplines such as History, Anthropology, Literature, Education, Sociology, Political Science, and Psychology as it does to Latina/o Studies. We teach our students that a literature review is the most important component of a research project. Just as I would not dare to engage in a historical approach without reading history, I wish that other scholars would not engage in a Media Studies project without engaging the literature in this field. Given the nearly irresistible temptation to engage in Media Studies within Latina/o Studies,[1] I encourage those scholars to read the material in this and other books on Latina/o Media Studies and follow up on the references that apply to their particular study. Keyword searches on Google Scholar should help as well. A literature review is a crucial starting point for research, yet many who venture into Latina/o Media Studies skip that critical step. Latina/o Media Studies is a field. It is not an inferential offshoot of the fields mentioned above. Scholars within Latina/o Media Studies have been pursuing issues of production, content and representation, audience and interpretation, and effects based on many decades of previously conducted research. Take Latina/o Media Studies seriously if you plan to work within it.

One other finding that forms a coherent thread throughout the middle four chapters has been the tendency within Media Studies, as with nearly all fields within the academy, to focus on dominant-culture populations. This has implications for Latina/o Studies, as it does for the study of any minority population. In the United States, the tendency following the whiteness era was to include African Americans in research, as a secondary pursuit. This is very consonant with media and popular culture wherein for a long time representations were nearly lily white, with an occasional and highly stereotypical black person added. Research and media reinforced this binary approach to the national imaginary. Scholars wrote books entitled *Blacks and White TV: African Americans in Television Since 1948* (MacDonald, 1992) because that was the representational terrain in the mainstream. News and popular culture represented the nation as if those were the only two ethnicities, without ambiguity about the fact that whites were superior to blacks. Latina/os unsettle this binary. In the mainstream, Latina/os provide a third space, albeit still a space of difference. In research they introduce the possibility of hybridity and thus lack of purity. Unsurprisingly, and in tension with hybridity as a concept, many take up that third space as a new site of purity, the Brown or Bronze race. Certainly this becomes a new shorthand for a media industry that relies on shortcuts to represent mediated images. Media rely on shortcuts for everyone. So the aim is not necessarily to rid the media of stereotypes. This would be nearly impossible. Rather, critical race scholars would like to see a broader range of types that do not serve as the racist backdrop of discrimination. Most working within Latina/o Studies trouble that homogeneity and remind us that there is diversity and radical relationality within Latinidad. Indeed, I see the major promise of Latina/o Studies as forcing us to face the inescapable hybridity in populations and culture at large, rather than locating it at the feet of particular groups. Neither whiteness nor blackness is pure. Latina/os come in white, brown, and black and in all other colors. That third space becomes *the* space. We are all part of the third space, and Latina/o Studies does not fail to remind us of this. The growing literature on being "brown" (see, e.g., forthcoming a special issue of the journal *Cultural Studies* entitled "Conjunctures of Brown," and Prashad, 2000) calls our attention to the muddled brown space in which not only Latina/os but also Indian, Native American and all First Nations or indigenous populations, and Middle Eastern and Mediterranean peoples all sign in as "brown." In Cultural and Critical Race Studies, troubling the concept of "brown" might go a long way to resolving some internal contradictions that have lingered for decades, in terms of diaspora, global flows, and mediascapes. In Media Studies, issues about representation, audience, and effects have to be sharpened and expanded to include the broader ethnic register and the impossibility of locating any given individual or group neatly within a constructed ethnic category.

Yet another coherent theme in this book, and one that would come up whether one chose to focus on the mainstream, as I did, or on alternative and community media, as many others do, is that, within mainstream media, there has been a nearly inexorable impetus toward concentration of media ownership. Alternative media are produced and circulated against the specter of the mainstream. As Benfield (forthcoming) notes, alternative producers are not a homogeneous group. Some seek to carve out an alternative space and remain in it. However, that is extremely difficult to do as everyone needs economic resources, even alternative media producers. It takes huge financial resources to produce mainstream media. At the very least, you need some technology and trained personnel that can take that technology and create something that others recognize as media. Moreover, Benfield adds that there is a significant portion of alternative or independent producers whose aim is to join the mainstream, and funding sources are more likely to favor precisely those with mainstream dreams. Benfield adds that government and corporate foundations tend to assume that alternative media producers want to eventually enter the mainstream.

More relevant to the central themes of this book is the tendency toward commodification. Commodifying Latinidad means that it is made for sale and purchase in the marketplace because it is believed it can turn a profit. Advertisers, who fund the commercial media, are a very conservative force. Their aim is to increase consumption and profits, not to foster activism. However, their conservative tendencies do not always yield desired effects. As well, advertisers might be more pragmatic than other forces in that their research will track the demographic growth of another niche market. Dávila (2001) has documented that the profit margin, a rational construct, has to be considered in relation to prejudice, an implicit and irrational attitude that refuses the cognition or acknowledgment of the presence and economic power of a new ethnic category. Commercial support of Latina/o media means also that the potential politics are toned down. A weekly or even a bimonthly produced by a group of women in Los Angeles is likely to be much more explicitly political than something like *Latina* magazine. Moreover, specificity is lost. If we return to that hypothetical Los Angeles bimonthly, chances are its content will be geographically and ethnically rooted to the everyday lived experience of Mexican Americans and Salvadoreños in a particular neighborhood rather than to the pan-Latina approach of *Latina*. While many fear a flattening of difference, recent research (Martínez, 2008) suggests that, even within the pan-Latinidad of *Latina*, there is a great effort made to represent a broad range of discrete and nation-specific women. The fear of homogenization is partly borne out, but the findings are not uniformly disheartening.

Linked to commodification is the conglomerate absorption of Latina/o media. As demonstrated by research in every one of the preceding chapters, while Latina/o media may have started at the margins, as they showed not only their staying power but also their mettle as a potential source of profit, big media took notice. Media industries can invest in or purchase outright an entire Latina/o media enterprise, whether this be a Latina/o radio station in the Southwest, a radio station in the new Latina/o South (the Southeast), or signing up crossover stars such as Shakira or Jennifer Lopez. Once under the bigger umbrella of the major media industry, Latina/o media transition or cross over, willingly or not, into a space of mainstream commodification where the main impetus becomes rendering a profit in the marketplace on as broad a platform of media and other products as possible. Synergy and convergence as global marketing strategies force the particular media product to co-exist with the other media holdings and marketing strategies of the conglomerate. In this universe, issues of ethnic pride often take a back seat, if not disappear altogether, in relation to the bottom line. Cultural difference, since that may be the element that makes a particular media property distinct from others, does not disappear, but rather morphs into a syncretic rather than a hybrid mode. As Levine (2001) proposes, the former is manageable and commodifiable while the latter is unsettled and thus difficult to market. The specificity that may have been sought becomes very difficult to maintain. The ethnic respect that may have been strived for might become muted. What Latina/o Media scholars have found is that commodification lightens ethnic approaches and indeed trumps these in favor of a homogeneous Latinidad that is deemed less challenging to the mainstream audience – read, "dominant culture" – while more likely to appeal to a broader range of Latina/os, and eventually to a global audience. While research about the global deployment of US-produced Latinidad remains to be conducted, the production of Latinidad is guided with a global marketing strategy in mind. We must not forget that today's media conglomerate thinks with a global audience in mind and that Latina/o media are not outside of that equation. Thus we can think of *Dora the Explorer* as a poster child of this strategy. Conceived in the United States as a vehicle to infuse dominant-culture children's vocabulary with a smattering of Spanish, she becomes a hit across ethnicities in the

United States and is globally marketed. She is ambiguous and light enough to avoid "turning off" anybody's sensitivity, and she turns into a brand, selling products across a range of categories from media, to food, clothing, and home decorations. While she teaches Spanish to English-dominant children in the USA, she teaches English to Hebrew-dominant children in Israel. She becomes a global language pedagogue, and she spawns another show, *Go, Diego, Go!* Next in line is *Teen Dora*. This is the fantasy projection of a global media conglomerate. *Dora* fulfills the fantasy.

Audiences, especially Latina/o audiences, might not be all that enthusiastic about *Dora*. They might think of how they would like her to be drawn a little differently, maybe lighter or darker, maybe shorter or taller, etc. They might want her to be rooted in a family, with particular traditions that show a culture and a history. They might want her to speak more Spanish. They might want her to speak a particular kind of Spanish. While some might prefer her to stay with Spanglish, others might wish for a Puerto Rican Spanish and yet others might want a more Castilian Spanish. Still other Latina/os might want her to stay within English as they fear that the residual Spanish contributes to the stereotype of the eternal foreigner who cannot learn English. Similarly English-only proponents might see her as yet another example of the debacle of common Anglo-Saxon culture. While she is really not directly within reach of these wishes as she is drawn and developed within a media industry – not in a Latina/o community nor in the English-only community – her producers exist within a culture wherein these "special interests," though differently empowered, nevertheless must be taken into account. Accordingly, we cannot say she is an unmitigatedly negative experience. She represents the inclusion of Latinidad in the mainstream. She is problematic to be sure, but she also represents acknowledgment of the importance of learning Spanish. Spanish is not going away. She also represents a form of acceptance. Not enough research has been conducted to explore what she means to children, and if this is in any way related to ethnicity or racial tolerance. However, she is an ethnic Latina child in a universe that was until quite recently mostly white with a tint of blackness, and she is a girl in the mostly boys' universe of animation.

While we might continue to speculate about Dora, I brought her up as an example of the perils of commodification, but also of the opportunities that she opens up. Without *Dora*, we might not have *Maya & Miguel*. *Dora* herself is the result of massive amounts of research and convincing of, in this case, television executives that representing Latinidad would not be a major disaster and that it could actually turn a profit. *Dora* is the cartoon equivalent of the embodied Latinas discussed in the "spectacular Latinas" section of chapter, 2 "Textual/

content analysis." The Latinas that are so prevalent in today's media must walk that tightrope somewhere between agency and structure. Some of them are able to assert more agency as they gain more power after demonstrating bankability. Stars, and brands, such as Jennifer Lopez and Salma Hayek not only are able to make demands in terms of their characters but also have crossed over into production and directing. They have, in addition, become sought after as spokespersons for a broad range of products from couture designs, to automobiles, make-up, and perfume. In turn their intervention generates a new type of media, focused on Latinidad, using big-name talent, and distributed in the mainstream. This cannot be discounted as it is certainly a gain in representational presence and political clout in media industries. After all it takes power to demand and assert inclusion. Above and beyond inclusion, it takes even greater power to have some form of agency over the terms of that inclusion.

As well, as much of the research suggested, spectacular Latinas both reiterate and disrupt dominant narratives of ethnicity and Latinidad. They disrupt that national imaginary of binary purity. They disrupt stereotypes and both the tropical and the traditional Mexican narratives. They seek not only to assert a presence but also to infuse a new texture into the fabric of media. Granted, they operate within an industry where the structure, in terms of ways of doing things, is quite strong, but they mine that small room for change. We do not know whether, or how, the many individual communicators working within media industries attempt to mine that wiggle room for a more diverse content and more democratic practices of production. "The Homicide Report" is but one example of one such successful intervention. It bears remembering that both *Dora* and "The Homicide Report" were initially conceived by non-Latina/os with a vision that did not necessarily include the empowerment of Latina/os. On the other hand, Ventanarosa Productions, the company that Salma Hayek started, set out explicitly to hire Latina/os and produce Latina/o-themed media. Both interventions resulted in foregrounding Latina/os and their reality and culture.

I am not engaging in a hallucinogenic celebration of the arrival of that hybrid utopian space wherein difference is acknowledged and celebrated, with respect paid to specificity and without a dominant force policing that difference. This is not the case. Latinidad exists in relation to a more powerful dominant mainstream culture that still sees itself as white and Anglo-Saxon. Moreover, in many locations Latinidad is still seen as a challenge to the previously dominant concept of "minority" and the easier binary proposition of black and white. The inclusion of heterogeneous Latinidad and the infusion of mixed race as a pervasive element in populations will further complicate the previously facile manner of envisioning popular culture and media.

Effects of particular types of content that represent Latina/os in stereotypical ways are being documented by scholars. These effects largely promise to increase fear of Latina/os. We have no research on the effects of the inclusion of Latina/os such as John Leguizamo in *ER*. Given the demand for operationalization and inter-coder reliability within effects studies, it appears that these are largely destined to include obviously Latina/o characters as the subtle ones cannot be either operationalized or equally well recognized by a broad range of coders. Other types of effects, in terms of the kinds of messages that Latina/o youth are getting, suggest that the space for positive intervention is being largely occupied by commodified messages about alcohol, cigarettes, and sex. One element scholars might want to explore is whether commodification messages can be harnessed toward issues such as safe sex, not smoking, healthy nutrition, exercise, and positive self-esteem. The large amounts of economic resources earmarked for health education in the stimulus package proposed by President Barack Obama should partly be used for health campaigns, deployed through the media, that serve to encourage a healthier lifestyle among Latina/os.

Another major gap in the research, considering its prominence in the mainstream, is the digital gaming industry. Nakamura (2007) reminds us that the scope of this industry now rivals that of most other media, pornography included. As well, the production of this medium comes from a different global location – the East – from most other media. Nonetheless, we still witness Latina/o representation in many of the most popular games. Basic research on representation, as well as more complex studies on issues of audience and effect, must be carried out in this latest "new medium"

The inclusion of case studies on "The Homicide Report" and Jennifer Lopez suggested to readers research avenues to be followed by a Latina/o Media Studies approach when applied to two different areas of mainstream media: an internet news blog of a major metropolitan-area newspaper and a celebrity branded spectacular female Latina. By using these diverging types of media content, I hope the reader can see how Latina/o Media Studies is a useful tool for the analysis and understanding of all types of media. Neither the Report nor Jennifer Lopez could have been as widely circulated prior to the current Latina/o boom in which the presence and economic power of Latinidad are widely acknowledged. In fact this book is also a result of that boom, as scholarship forms part of culture and thus is a representation of the attention that Latina/os and Latinidad are currently receiving. Latina/o Media Studies is now part of the field of communications, and as such it will continue to provide knowledge on ethnicity and media, a central component of the contemporary situation.

Notes

Introduction

1 Old media were once "new." That is why I put the word in quotes. Presently new media will be old media when they are replaced by a new wave of technological innovation.

2 One might argue whether this effort to reach out to Latina/os is genuine or merely strategic. However, what is undeniable is that Latina/os have become a crucial component of a successful national political campaign.

3 Proposition 187, also known as the "Save our State" proposition, was put on the ballot in California in 1994 and passed with a 59 percent of the vote. The major impetus behind this measure, later declared unconstitutional, was to deny access to health care, education, and other social services to undocumented immigrants.

4 I say "most often" because, once a category is generated, it is impossible to police its uses. Thus, both media and government use Latina/o a bit differently from the way it is defined by Latina/o Studies scholars.

5 Thus the refrain within Latina/o Studies: "we did not cross the border, the border crossed us."

6 As with the other two groups, immigrants have not limited themselves to only one area. Less studied has been Cuban migration to New Orleans. The latter explains the location of the Cuban Studies Institute at Tulane University.

7 Most of the other racial groups have differential growth rates for different regions of the country.

8 This included Puerto Rico (Pew Hispanic Center Statistical Portrait of Hispanics in the United States, 2006 [Table 1]).

9 Charo is actually a Spanish actress whose trademark comment is "cuchi cuchi" and who always appears in flamboyantly small outfits and speaks in nearly unrecognizable Spanish-accented English. She performs the classic role of a buffoon.

10 I am indebted to Christina Ceisel for her groundbreaking research on the topic of crossover in general and Juanes in particular.

11 *Casta* paintings were used primarily by the Spanish, but also by the Portuguese, in the seventeenth and eighteenth centuries, to illustrate and document the hybrid permutations arising from population mixtures in the colonies.

12 For example, Chapter 5 relies primarily on chapters in Clara Rodriguez's *Latin Looks* (1997) with very few other sources. Without denying the superior quality of that collection, the fact is that a book dated 2006 had eight more years' worth of scholarship to rely on.

1 Production

1 Quinceañeras are coming-of-age celebrations for girls when they turn 15. They are sometimes lavishly celebrated by peoples of Mexican origin and other Central Americans.
2 The other three would be the theme of the three following chapters: content/text, audience/reception, and effects.
3 Telenovelas are a phenomenally successful serial form of television produced in Latin America. Akin to soap operas, new telenovelas are broadcast in prime time and often dominate the ratings.
4 I thank Dafna Lemish of Tel Aviv University in Israel for conversations about Dora around the world.
5 This part of the data was not disaggregated according to race and ethnicity.
6 In a decidedly unscientific approach, I counted a total of 55 interns in this year's photo, 12 of whom were male – a rough ratio of 1:5 males to females. See photo on www.aaaa-maip.org/, retrieved April 17, 2008.
7 Workers after the 9–5 workday usually perform a follow-up and maintenance role rather than a creative role, plus they seldom have as much creative agency.
8 Certainly in dictatorships there is often a ministry or some such body called something like "The Office of Information," where there is a workforce dedicated to enforcing media rules.
9 This last one is sometimes substituted for "anti ideologies" though many hold that anti-communism is still a powerful ideology in a capitalist world.
10 Nor in any area of the contemporary global economy, but here I limit myself to issues of media industries.
11 Until 1940 NBC operated two radio networks, NBC Blue and NBC Red. After a Department of Justice judgment that owning both was a form of monopoly, the Blue network became ABC.
12 I am indebted for all my knowledge about reggaeton to the meticulous research carried out and yet to be published by Michelle Rivera.
13 I owe Rhiannon Bettivia thanks for pointing this blog out to me.

2 Textual/content analysis

1 Lest this read like one of those universalizing and ahistorical statements, Latina/os have been in the American Continent for roughly five centuries.
2 The classic example is the dehumanization of Jews during the Hitler years when they were represented as infectious and disease-carrying vermin, a move that partly laid the groundwork for the holocaust that followed.
3 Any visitor to this great city will immediately notice the abundance of green VW Beetle/Bug taxis – something that was used in the backdrop for a 2003 Super Bowl ad about Latina/os.
4 This study had 95% inter-coder reliability. It had two coders.
5 The black-and-white binary under-represents the diversity both among whites and among blacks. So this reductive strategy really is far more exclusionary than it seems.
6 Matt Garcia has commented that *Traffic* actually updates *Birth of a Nation* and recasts the villains as Latina/os. Personal conversation.
7 I mention her nationality to remind us that Latina characters are often played by Spanish actresses.
8 Another one of those Spanish actresses who get to play Latinas.

9 This is not peculiar to the United States, though the virulence of some of the policies may be. For instance, the contemporary global economy fuels many flows of migration today (2008), such as the one in Spain about which economists are nearly unanimous in agreeing that immigrants are needed to keep the nation productive and solvent, yet popular sentiment is beginning to turn against them.

10 Different waters have different colors. Note, for example, the dark navy blue color of Greek island waters, or the slightly grey color of US East Coast waters – both of these in representations in popular culture, but most notably in tourist literature.

11 I thank Michelle Rivera for information about this site from her ongoing research projects on reggaeton.

12 I am indebted to Robert Mejia for a presentation, as well as continued communication, on this topic.

3 Audience and reception

1 My own mother learned to speak English watching *Sesame Street*.

2 I use "almost" in case there is one that I have not found. I know of none prior to Rojas (2004).

4 Effects and cognition

1 "Beats" refers to the assignment a reporter is given, such as the crime beat, the city hall beat, the youth beat, etc.

Conclusion

1 I say this after I chaired a search committee for a Latina/o historian. Of course, all those interviewed took history very seriously. Yet almost inevitably, all but one ended up at a point where they were not only studying the media and popular culture, but also looking at the contemporary moment – something rather contradictory for a historian. In sum, most were trying to speak about contemporary media issues and nearly none had conducted any reading in Media Studies. This meant that they often deployed implicitly theories that have been largely discounted in the field of Media Studies as unproductive or just plain wrong.

References

Alaniz, M. (1998). Alcohol availability and targeted advertising in racial/ethnic communities. *Alcohol Health and Research World*, 22:4, 286–9.

Alaniz, M. and Wilkes, C. (1995). Reinterpreting Latino culture in the commodity form: the case of alcohol advertising in the Mexican American community. *Hispanic Journal of Behavioral Sciences*, 17, 431–51.

Alcalay, R., Alvarado, M., Balcazar, H., Newman, E. and Huerta, E. (1999). Salud para su corazón: a community-based Latino cardiovascular disease prevention and outreach model. *Journal of Community Health*, 24:5, 359–79.

Allison, A. (2006). *Millennial Monsters: Japanese Toys and the Global Imagination.* Berkeley: University of California Press.

Amaya, H. (2007a). Performing acculturation: rewriting the Latina/o immigrant self. *Text and Performance Quarterly*, 27:3, 194–212.

(2007b). Dying American or the violence of citizenship: Latinos in Iraq. *Latino Studies*, 5, 3–24. doi: 10.1057/palgrave.1st.8600240.

Aparicio, F. (1998). Whose Spanish? Whose language? Whose power?: Testifying to differential bilingualism. *Indiana Journal of Hispanic Literatures*, Spring, 5–25.

Aparicio, F. and Chávez-Silverman, S. (eds.) (1997). *Tropicalizations: Transcultural Representations of Latinidad.* Hanover, NH: University Press of New England.

Aparicio, F. R. (2003). Jennifer as Selena: rethinking Latinidad in media and popular culture. *Latino Studies*, 1, 90–105.

ASNE (American Society of Newspaper Editors) (2008). Newsrooms shrink: minority percentage increases slightly, April 13. www.asne.org/files/08Census.pdf. Retrieved April 16, 2008.

Báez, J. M. (2007). Towards a Latinidad feminista: the multiplicities of Latinidad and feminism in contemporary cinema. *Journal of Popular Communication*, 5:2, 109–28.

(2008). Mexican (American) women talk back: audience responses to Latinidad in U.S. advertising. In A. N. Valdivia (ed.), *Latina/o Communication Studies Today* (pp. 257–82). New York: Peter Lang.

Banet-Weiser, S. (2003). Elián González and "The purpose of America": nation, family, and the child citizen. *American Quarterly*, 55:2, 149–78.

Banks, M. C. (2005). White beauty: a content analysis of the portrayals of minorities in teen beauty magazines. Master's thesis. Brigham Young University.

Bargh, J. A., Chen, M. and Burrows L. (1996). Automaticity of social behavior: direct effects on trait construct and stereotype activation in action. *Journal of Personality and Social Psychology*, 71:2, 230–44.

Barrera, M. (2002). Hottentot 2000: Jennifer Lopez and her butt. In K. M. Phillips and B. Reay (eds.), *Sexualities in History: A Reader* (pp. 407–17). New York: Routledge.

Bejarano, C. L. (2005). *Que onda? Urban Youth Culture and Border Identity*. Tucson: University of Arizona Press.

Beltrán, M. (2002). The Hollywood Latina body as site of social struggle: media constructions of stardom and Jennifer Lopez's "cross-over butt." *The Quarterly Review of Film and Video*, 19:1, 71–86.

(2004). Más macha: the new Latina action hero. In Y. Tasker (ed.), *Action and Adventure Cinema* (pp. 186–200). London: Routledge.

(2005). Dolores Del Rio, the first "Latino invasion," and Hollywood's transition to sound. *Aztlán: A Journal of Chicano Studies*, 30:1, 55–86.

(2008). Mixed race in Latinowood: Latino stardom and ethnic ambiguity in the era of dark angels. In M. Beltrán and C. Fojas (eds.), *Mixed Race Hollywood: Multiraciality in Film and Media Culture* (pp. 248–68). New York: NYU Press.

Benfield, M. D. (forthcoming). Identifying the "Latino" (and Latina!) in "Latino independent media." In M. Garcia and A. N. Valdivia (eds.) *Geographies of Latinidad*. Durham, NC: Duke University Press.

Bobo, J. (1995). *Black Women as Cultural Readers*. New York: Columbia University Press.

Brodie, M., Kjellson, N., Hoff, T. and Parker, M. (1999). Perceptions of Latinos, African Americans, and Whites on media as a health information source. *Howard Journal of Communications*, 10:3, 147–67.

Cabán, P. (2003). Moving from the margins to where? Three decades of Latina/o Studies. *Latina/o Studies*, 1:1, 5–35.

Cacho, L. M. (2007). "You just don't know how much he meant": deviancy, death, and devaluation. *Latino Studies*, 5:1, 182–208.

Carey, J. (1989). *Communication as Culture: Essays in Media and Society*. Boston: Unwin Hyman.

Casas, M. C. and Dixon, T. L. (2003). The impact of stereotypical and counter-stereotypical news on viewer perception of Blacks and Latinos: an exploratory study. In A. N. Valdivia (ed.), *A Companion to Media Studies* (pp. 480–92). Malden, MA: Blackwell.

Casillas, D. I. (2005a). Latin Grammys. In S. Oboler and D. Gonzalez (eds.), *Encyclopedia of Latinas and Latinos in the United States* (Vol. 2, pp. 477–8). New York: Oxford University Press.

(2005b). Radio, Spanish-language. In S. Oboler and D. Gonzalez (eds.), *Encyclopedia of Latinas and Latinos in the United States* (Vol. 3, pp. 548–52). New York: Oxford University Press.

(2007). A morning dose of Latino masculinity: U.S. Spanish-language radio and the politics of gender. In A. N. Valdivia (ed.), *Latina/o Communication Studies Today* (pp. 161–85). New York: Peter Lang.

Castañeda, L. (2001). Bilingual defectors. *American Journalism Review*, 23:4, 44.

Castañeda Paredes, M. (2001). The reorganization of Spanish-language media marketing in the United States. In Vincent Mosco and Dan Schiller (eds.), *Continental Order? Integrating North America for Cybercapitalism* (pp. 120–35). Lanham, MD: Rowman and Littlefield.

(2003). The transformation of Spanish-language radio in the United States. *Journal of Radio Studies*, 10:1, 5–16.

Cepeda, M. E. (2000). Mucho loco for Ricky Martin; or the politics of chronology, crossover, and language within the Latin(o) music "boom." *Popular Music and Society*, 24:3, 55–72.

(2001). "Columbus effects": the politics of crossover and chronology within the Latin(o) music "Boom." *Discourse*, 23:1, 242–67.

(2003a). Mucho loco for Ricky Martin, or: the politics of chronology, crossover and language within the Latin(o) music "Boom." In M. T. Carroll and H. Berger (eds.), *Global Pop, Local Talk* (pp. 113–29). Jackson: University of Mississippi Press.

(2003b). Shakira as the idealized, transnational citizen: a case study of Colombianidad in transition. *Latino Studies*, 1, 211–32.

(2008). Survival aesthetics: U.S. Latinas and the negotiation of popular media. In A. N. Valdivia (ed.), *Latina/o Communication Studies Today* (pp. 237–56). New York: Peter Lang.

Chavez, L. R. (2001). *Covering Immigration: Popular Images and the Politics of the Nation*. Berkeley: University of California Press.

Children NOW (2003). *Fall Colors: Prime Time Diversity Report 2003*. Oakland: Children NOW.

Chomsky, N. and Herman, R. (1988). *Manufacturing Consent: The Political Economy of the Mass Media*. New York: Pantheon Books.

Citron, M. (1988). Women's film production: going mainstream. In E. D. Pribram (ed.), *Female Spectators: Looking at Film and Television* (pp. 1–32). New York: Verso.

Covert, J. J. and Dixon, T. L. (2008). A changing view: representation and effects of the portrayal of women of color in mainstream women's magazines. *Communication Research*, 35:2, 232–56.

Dávila, A. (2001). *Latinos, Inc.: The Marketing and Making of a People*. Berkeley and Los Angeles: University of California Press.

(2002). Talking back: Spanish media and U.S. Latinidad. In M. Habell-Pallán and M. Romero (eds.), *Latino/a Popular Culture*. New York and London: New York University Press.

Del Río, E. (2006). The Latina/o problematic: categories and questions in media communication research. In C. Beck (ed.), *Communication Yearbook 30* (pp. 387–429). Mahwah, NJ: Lawrence Erlbaum Associates.

DeSipio, L. (1998). *Talking Back to Television: Latinos Discuss how Television Portrays Them and the Quality of Programming Options*. Claremont, CA: The Tomás Rivera Policy Institute.

Diries, Gail and Humez, Jean M, (2002). *Race, Class, and Gender in Media: A Text Reader* (2nd edn.) Thousand Oaks, CA: Sage.

Dixon, T. L., Azocar, C. and Casas, M. (2003). The portrayal of race and crime on television network news. *Journal of Broadcasting & Electronic Media*, 47:4, 498–523.

Dixon, T. L. and Linz, D. (2000a). Television news, prejudicial pretrial publicity, and the depiction of race. *Journal of Broadcasting & Electronic Media*, 46, 112–36.

(2000b). Overrepresentation and underrepresentation of African Americans and Latinos as lawbreakers on television news. *Journal of Communication*, 50:2, 131–54.

(2000c). Race and the misrepresentation of victimization on local television news. *Communication Research*, 27, 547–73.

Dubrofsky, R. (2006). *The Bachelor*: whiteness in the harem. *Critical Studies in Media Communication*, 23:1, 39–56.

Durham, A. and Báez, J. M. (2007). A tail of two women: exploring the contours of difference in popular culture. In S. Springgay and D. Freedman (eds.), *Curriculum and the Cultural Body* (pp. 131–45). New York: Peter Lang.

Ericksen, C. A. (1981). Hispanic Americans and the press. *Journal of Intergroup Relations*, 9:1, 3–16.

Escobedo, E. (2007). The Pachuca panic: sexual and cultural battlegrounds in World War II Los Angeles. *The Western Historical Quarterly*, 38:2, 133–56.

Faber, R., O'Guinn, T. and Meyer, T. (1987). Televised portrayals of Hispanics: a comparison of ethnic perceptions. *International Journal of Intercultural Relations*, 11:2, 155–69.

Farhi, P. and Williams, K. (2006). Spanish-language radio's big voice: stations act as community center and tutor to bridge gaps between homeland, United States. *Washington Post*. July 3, p. D1.

Feagans, B. (2006). Latinos urge day of protest over bill. The *Atlanta Journal-Constitution*. March 24, p. 10A.

Fernandez, R. A. and Jensen, R. J. (1995). Reies Lopez Tijerina's "The Land Grant Question": creating history through metaphors. *Howard Journal of Communications*, 6, 129–45.

Fernandez, S., Hickman, N., Klonoff, E., et al. (2005). Cigarette advertising in magazines for Latinas, white women, and men, 1998–2002: a preliminary investigation. *Journal of Community Health*, 30:2, 141–51.

Fiol-Matta, L. (1999/2002). Pop Latinidad: Puerto Ricans in the Latin explosion. *Centro Journal*, 14:1.

Flores, J. (2000). *From Bomba to Hip-Hop*. New York: Columbia University Press.

Fregoso, R. L. (1995). Homegirls, cholas, and pachucas in cinema: taking over the public sphere. *California History*, 74:3, 316–27.

(2007). Lupe Vélez: Queen of the B's. In M. Mendible (ed.), *From Bananas to Buttocks: The Latina Body in Popular Film and Culture*. Austin: University of Texas Press.

Garcia, M. (2001). *A World of Its Own: Race, Labor and Citrus in the Making of Greater Los Angeles, 1900–1970*. Chapel Hill: University of North Carolina Press.

García Canclini, N. (2001). *Consumers and Citizens: Globalization and Multicultural Conflicts*. Minneapolis: University of Minnesota Press.

Georgiou, M. (2007). Transnational crossroads for media and diaspora: three challenges for research. In O. G. Bailey, M. Georgious and R. Harindranath (eds.), *Transnational Lives and the Media* (pp. 34–57). New York: Palgrave Macmillan.

Gerbner, G. (1993). *Woman and Minorities on Television: A Study in Casting and Fate*. Philadelphia: Annenberg School of Communication, University of Pennsylvania.

Goffman, E. (1976). *Gender Advertisements*. New York: Harper & Row.

Goldman, D. E. (2004). Virtual islands: the reterritorialization of Puerto Rican spatiality in cyberspace. *Hispanic Review*, 72:3, 375–400.

González, D. (2007). Aquí, allá y en todas partes: las audiencias juveniles en la frontera norte. In Guillermo Orozco (ed.), *Un mundo de visiones. Interacciones de las audiencias en múltiples escenarios mediáticos y virtuales* (pp. 117–31). Mexico, DF: Instituto Latinoamericano de Comunicación y Educación (ILCE).

(2008). Watching over the border. A case study of the Mexico–U.S. Television and youth audience. In A. Valdivia (ed.), *Latina/o Communication Studies Today* (pp. 219–36). New York: Peter Lang.

Goodman, J. R. (2002). Flabless is fabulous: how Latina and Anglo women read and incorporate the excessively thin body ideal into everyday experience. *Journalism and Mass Communication Quarterly*, 79:3, 712–27.

Greenberg, B. and Baptista-Fernandez, P. (1980). Hispanic-Americans – The new minority on television. In B. Greenberg (ed.), *Life on Television: Content Analyses of U.S. TV Drama* (pp. 3–12). Norwood, NJ: Ablex Publishing.

Greenberg, B., Burgoon, M., Burgoon, J. and Korzenny, F. (1983). *Mexican Americans and the Mass Media*. Norwood, NJ: Ablex Publishing.

Gutiérrez, F. (1998). Through Anglo eyes. Chicanos as portrayed in the news media. ERIC #: ED159693. eric.ed.gov.

Hacker, A. (2000). The case against kids. *New York Review of Books*, November 30, pp. 22–7.

Hall, S. (1980). Encoding/decoding. In S. Hall, D. Hobson, A. Lowe and P. Willis (eds.), *Culture, Media, Language* (pp. 128–38). London: Hutchinson.

Halter, M. (2000). *Shopping for Identity: The Marketing of Ethnicity*. New York: Schocken Books.

Harewood, S. J. and Valdivia, A. N. (2005). Exploring Dora: re-embodied Latinidad on the Web. In S. R. Mazzarella (ed.), *Girl Wide Web: Girls, the Internet, and the Negotiation of Identity* (pp. 85–103). New York: Peter Lang.

Jahlly, S. and Lewis, J. (1992). *Enlightened Racism: "The Cosby Show," Audiences and the Myth of the American Dream*. Boulder, CO: Westview Press.

Jenrette, J., McIntosh, S. and Winterberger, S. (1999). "Carlotta!" Changing images of Hispanic-American women in daytime soap operas. *Journal of Popular Culture*, 33:2, 37–48.

Johnson, M. A. (2000). How ethnic are U.S. ethnic media: the case of Latina magazines. *Mass Communication & Society*, 3:2 & 3, 229–48.

(2003). Constructing a new model of ethnic media. In A. N. Valdivia (ed.), *A Companion to Media Studies* (pp. 272–92). Malden, MA: Blackwell.

Journalism.org (2004). The state of the news media, 2004: an annual report on American journalism. www.stateofthenewsmedia.org/2004/narrative_ethnicalternative_spanishpress.asp?media=9. Retrieved April 18, 2008.

Katerí Hernandez, T. (2002). The Buena Vista Social Club: the racial politics of nostalgia. In M. Habell-Pallán and M. Romero (eds.), *Latino/a Popular Culture* (pp. 61–72). New York and London: New York University Press.

(2003). "Too black to be Latino/a": blackness and blacks as foreigners in Latino Studies. *Latino Studies*, 1:1, 152–9.

Larson, S. G. (2006). *Media & Minorities: The Politics of Race in News and Entertainment*. New York: Rowman & Littlefield.

Lashley, K. S. (1951). The problem of serial order in behavior. In L. A. Jeffress (ed.), *Cerebral Mechanisms in Behavior: The Hixon Symposium* (pp. 112–36). New York: Wiley.

Leonard, D. J. (2003). "Live in your world, play in ours": race, video games, and consuming the other. *SIMILE; Studies in Media & Information Literacy Education*, 3:4, 1–9.

(2006). Not a hater, just keepin' it real: the importance of race- and gender-based game studies. *Games and Culture*, 1:1, 83–8.

Levine, E. (2001). Constructing a market, constructing an ethnicity: U.S. Spanish language media and the formation of a Latina/o identity. *Studies in Latin American Popular Culture*, 20, 33–50.

Limón, J. E. (1973). Stereotyping and Chicano resistance: an historical dimension. *Aztlán: A Journal of Chicano Studies*, 4:2, 257–70.

Lipsitz, G. (1998). *The Possessive Investment in Whiteness: How White People Benefit from Identity Politics*. Philadelphia: Temple University Press.

López, A. M. (1992). Are all Latins from Manhattan? Hollywood, ethnography, and cultural colonialism. In L. D. Friedman (ed.), *Unspeakable Images:*

Ethnicity and the American Cinema (pp. 404–24). Urbana: University of Illinois Press.

(1998). From Hollywood and back: Dolores Del Rio, a trans(national) star. *Studies in Latin American Popular Culture*, 17, 5–32.

MacDonald, F. (1992). *Blacks and White TV: African Americans in Television since 1948*. Chicago: Nelson-Hall Publishers.

Magnet, S. (2006). Playing at colonization: interpreting imaginary landscapes in the video game *Tropico*. *Journal of Communication Inquiry*, 30:2, 142–62.

Martín-Rodriguez, Manuel M. (2000). Hyenas in the pride lands: Latinas/os and immigration in Disney's *The Lion King*. *Aztlán: A Journal of Chicano Studies*, 25:1, 47–66.

Martinez, K. Z. (2004). *Latina* magazine and the invocation of a panethnic family: Latino identity as it is informed by celebrities and Papis Chulos. *The Communication Review*, 7:2, 155–74.

(2008). Real women and their curves. Letters to the Editor and a magazine's celebration of the "Latina Body." In A. N. Valdivia (ed.), *Latina/o Communication Studies Today* (pp. 137–60). New York: Peter Lang.

Mastro, D. E. (2003). A social identity approach to understanding the impact of television messages. *Communication Monographs*, 70:2, 98–113.

Mastro, D. E. and Atkin, C. (2002). Exposure to alcohol billboards and beliefs and attitudes toward drinking among Mexican American high school students. *Howard Journal of Communications*, 13:2, 129–51.

Mastro, D. E., Behm-Morawitz, E. and Kopacz, M. A. (2008). Exposure to television portrayals of Latinos: the implications of aversive racism and social identity theory. *Human Communication Research*, 34:1, 1–27.

Mastro, D. E., Behm-Morawitz, E. and Ortiz, M. (2007). The cultivation of social perceptions of Latinos: a mental models approach. *Media Psychology*, 9:2, 347–65.

Mastro, D. E. and Greenberg, B. S. (2000). The portrayal of racial minorities on prime time television. *Journal of Broadcasting & Electronic Media*, 44:4, 690–703.

Mastro, D. E. and Ortiz, M. (2008). A content analysis of social groups in prime-time Spanish-language television. *Journal of Broadcasting & Electronic Media*, 52:1, 101–19.

Mastro, D. E. and Robinson, A. L. (2000). Cops and crooks: images of minorities on primetime television. *Journal of Criminal Justice*, 28:5, 385–96.

Mastro, D. E. and Stern, S. R. (2003). Representations of race in television commercials: a content analysis of prime-time advertising. *Journal of Broadcasting & Electronic Media*, 47:4, 638–47.

Mayer, V. (2001). From segmented to fragmented: Latino media in San Antonio, Texas. *Journalism & Mass Communication Quarterly*, 78:2, 291-306.

(2003a). Living telenovelas / telenovelizing life: Mexican American girls' identities and transnational novelas. *Journal of Communication*, September, 479–95.

(2003b). *Producing Dreams, Consuming Youth: Mexican Americans and Mass Media*. Brunswick, NJ: Rutgers University Press.

(2004). Please pass the pan: retheorizing the map of panlatinidad in communication research. *Communication Review*, 7:3, 113–24.

McLean, A. (2004). *Being Rita Hayworth: Labor, Identity, and Hollywood Stardom*. Brunswick, NJ: Rutgers University Press.

McQuail, D. (1997). *Audience Analysis*. Newbury Park: SAGE.

(2005). *McQuail's Mass Communication Theory*. London: SAGE.

Melican, D. B. and Dixon, T. L. (2008). News on the Net: credibility, selective exposure, and racial prejudice. *Communication Research*, 35:2, 151–68.

Mendible, M. (2007). Introduction. Embodying Latinidad: an overview. In M. Mendible (ed.), *From Bananas to Buttocks: The Latina Body in Popular Film and Culture* (pp. 1–28). Austin: University of Texas Press.

Merskin, D. (2007). Three faces of Eva: perpetuation of the hot-latina stereotype in *Desperate Housewives*. *Howard Journal of Communication*, 18:2, 133–51.

(2008). Picturing activism: a visual rhetorical analysis of broadcast coverage of *A Day Without an Immigrant*. Presented to the International Association of Communication, Montreal, Canada.

Molina Guzmán, I. (2005). Gendering Latinidad through the Elián news discourse about Cuban women. *Latino Studies*, 3, 179–204.

(2006). Mediating Frida: negotiating discourses of Latina/o authenticity in global media representations of ethnic identity. *Critical Studies in Media Communication*, 23:3, 232–51.

(2007a). Salma Hayek's Frida: transnational Latina bodies in popular culture. In Myra Mendible (ed.), *From Bananas to Buttocks: The Latina in Popular Film and Culture* (pp. 117–28). Austin: University of Texas Press.

(2007b). Marisleysis: discourses of disorderly bodies in the Elián story. In Myra Mendible (ed.), *From Bananas to Buttocks: The Latina in Popular Film and Culture* (pp. 219–42). Austin: University of Texas Press.

(2008). Policing the Latina/o other: Latinidad in prime-time news coverage of the Elián González story. In A. N. Valdivia (ed.), *Latina/o Communication Studies Today* (pp. 115–36). New York: Peter Lang.

(2010). *Dangerous Curves: Latina Bodies in the Media*. New York: New York University Press.

Molina Guzmán, I. and Valdivia, A. N. (2004). Brain, brow or bootie: iconic Latinas in contemporary popular culture. *The Communication Review*, 7:2, 205–21.

Mukherjee, R. (2006). *The Racial Order of Things: Cultural Imaginaries of the Post Soul Era*. Minneapolis: University of Minnesota Press.

Nakamura, L. (2002). *Cybertypes: Race, Ethnicity, and Identity on the Internet*. New York: Routledge.

(2007). *Digitizing Race: Visual Cultures of the Internet*. Minneapolis: University of Minnesota Press.

(2009a). Don't hate the player, hate the game: the racialization of labor in World of Warcraft. *Critical Studies in Media Communication*, 26:2, 117–28.

(2009b) The socioalgorithmics of race: sorting it out in jihad worlds. Afterword for S. Magnet and K. Gates (eds.), *New Media and Surveillance*. New York: Routledge.

National Association of Hispanic Journalists (2008). NAHJ disturbed by figures that mask decline in newsroom diversity, April 14. www.nahj.org/nahjnews/articles/2008/April/ASNE.shtml. Retrieved April 16, 2008.

National Council of La Raza, Center for Media and Public Affairs (1996). *Don't Blink: Hispanics in Television Entertainment*. Washington, DC: Author.

Navarrete, L. and Kanasaki, C. (1994). *Out of the Picture: Hispanics in the Media*. Washington, DC: National Council of La Raza, Center for Media and Public Affairs.

Negrón-Muntaner, F. (1997). Jennifer's butt. *Aztlán: A Journal of Chicano Studies*, 22:2, 182–95.

(2004). *Boricua Pop: Puerto Ricans and the Latinization of American Culture*. New York: New York University Press.

Olivarez, A. (1998). Studying representations of U.S. Latino culture. (Constructing [mis]representations.) *Journal of Communication Inquiry*, 22:4, 426–37.

Oliver, M. B. (1994). Portrayals of crime, race and aggression in "reality-based" police shows: a content analysis. *Journal of Broadcasting & Electronic Media*, 38:2, 179–92.

(2003). Race and crime in the media: research from a media effects perspective. In A. N. Valdivia (ed.), *A Companion to Media Studies* (pp. 421–36). Malden, MA: Blackwell.

Ono, K. and Sloop, J. M. (2002). *Shifting Borders: Rhetoric, Immigration, and California's Proposition 187*. Philadelphia, PA: Temple University Press.

Padín, J. A. (2005). The normative mulattoes: the press, Latinos, and the racial climate on the moving immigration frontier. *Sociological Perspectives*, 48:1, 49–75.

Paredez, D. (2002). Remembering Selena, re-membering Latinidad. *Theatre Journal*, 54, 63–84.

Pew Internet & American Life Project (2001). March 2001 Longitudinal Data Set. http://pewinternet.org/Shared-Content/Data-Sets/2001/March-2001-Longitudinal-Data-Set.aspx. Retrieved October 22, 2009.

Poindexter, P. M., Smith, L. and Heider, D. (2003). Race and ethnicity in local television news: framing, story assignments, and source selections. *Journal of Electronic Broadcasting & Media*. 47:4, 524–36.

Press, A. L. (1991). *Women Watching Television: Gender, Class, and Generation in the American Television Experience*. Philadelphia: University of Pennsylvania Press.

Quiñones Rivera, M. (2006). From *trigueñita* to Afro-Puerto Rican: intersections of the racialized, gendered, and sexualized body in Puerto Rico and the U.S. mainland. *Meridians: Feminism, Race, Transnationalism*, 7:1, 162–82.

Ramirez-Berg, C. (2002). *Latino Images in Film: Stereotypes, Subversion, and Resistance*. Austin: University of Texas Press.

Reyes, X. A. and Ríos, D. I. (2003). Imaging teachers: in fact and in the mass media. *Journal of Latinos & Education*, 2:1, 3–11.

Ricle Mayorga, P. (2001). Ethnic media and identity construction: content analysis of the visual portrayals of women in Latina and Glamour magazines. Master's thesis, Georgia State University.

Rinderle, S. (2005). The Mexican diaspora: a critical examination of signifiers. *Journal of Communication Inquiry*, 29:4, 294–316.

Ríos, D. I. (2000). Latina/o experiences with mediated communication. In A. González, M. Houston, and V. Chen (eds.), *Our Voices: Essays in Culture, Ethnicity, and Communication* (3rd edn., pp. 105–12). Los Angeles: Roxbury.

(2003). U.S. Latino audiences of "telenovelas." *Journal of Latinos and Education*, 2:1, 59–65.

Ríos, D. I. and Gaines, S. O. (1998). Latino media use for cultural maintenance. *Journalism and Mass Communication Quarterly*, 75:4, 746–6.

Rivadeneyra, R. (2005). From Ally McBeal to Sábado Gigante: contributions of television viewing to the gender role attitudes of Latino adolescents. *Journal of Adolescent Research*, 20:4, 453–75.

(2006). Do you see what I see? Latino adolescents' perceptions of the images on television. *Journal of Adolescent Research*, 21:4, 393–414.

Rivadeneyra, R., Ward, L. and Gordon, M. (2007). Distorted reflections: media exposure and Latino adolescents' conceptions of self. *Media Psychology*, 9:2, 261–90.

Rivera, R. Z. (2003). *New York Ricans from the Hip Hop Zone*. New York: Palgrave Macmillan.

Rodriguez, A. (1999). *Making Latino News: Race, Language, Class*. Thousand Oaks, CA: SAGE.

Rodríguez, C. (1997). Visual retrospective: Latinos film stars. In C. E. Rodríguez, *Latin Look Images of Latinas and Latinos in the U.S. Media* (pp. 84–4), Boulder, CO: Westview.

—— (2001). *Fissures in the Mediascape: An International Study of Citizen's Media*. Cresskill, NJ: Hampton Press.

—— (2008). Film viewing in Latino communities, 1896–1934: Puerto Rico as a microcosm. In M. Mendible (ed.), *From Bananas to Buttocks: The Latina Body in Popular Film and Culture* (pp. 31–50). Austin: University of Texas Press.

Rojas, V. (2004). The gender of Latinidad: Latinas speak about Hispanic television. *The Communication Review*, 7:2, 125–53.

Rojas, V., Roychowdhury, D., Okur, O., Straubhaar, J. and Ortiz, Y. (2000). *Beyond Access: Cultural Capital and the Roots of the Digital Divide*. www.utexas.edu/research/tipi/Beyond_Access.pdf.

Rubin, L. R., Mako, L. F. and Becker, A. E. (2004). "Whatever feels good in my soul": body ethics and aesthetics among African American and Latina women. *Culture, Medicine, and Psychiatry*, 27:1, 49–75.

Ruiz, M. V. (2002). Border narratives, HIV/AIDS, and Latina/o health in the United States: a cultural analysis. *Feminist Media Studies*, 2:1, 81–96.

Santa Ana, O. (2002). *Brown Tide Rising: Metaphors of Latinos in Contemporary American Public Discourse*. Austin: University of Texas Press.

Scharrer, E. (2002). Third-person perception and television violence: the role of out-group stereotyping in perceptions of susceptibility to effects. *Communication Research*, 29:6, 681–704.

Schooler, D. (2008). Real women have curves: a longitudinal investigation of TV and the body image development of Latina adolescents. *Journal of Adolescent Research*, 23:2, 132–53.

Seggar, John F. (1977). Television's portrayal of minorities and women 1971–1975. *Journal of Broadcasting*, 21, 435–46.

Shohat, E. and Stam, R. (1994). *Unthinking Eurocentrism: Multiculturalism and the Media*. London and New York: Routledge.

Singhal, A., Obregon, R. and Rogers, E. M. (1995). Reconstructing the story of *Simplemente Maria*, the most popular telenovela in Latin America of all time. *International Communication Gazette*, 54:1, 1–15.

Smythe, D. (1977). Communications: blindspot of Western Marxism. *Canadian Journal of Political and Society Theory*, 1:3, 1–28.

Sniderman, P. M. and Piazza, T. (1993). *The Scar of Race*. Boston, MA: Harvard University Press.

Social Science Research Council (2007). Grantee profile: study explores radio as a mobilization tool in Latino communities. http://mediaresearchhub.ssrc.org/news/grantee-profile-study-explores-radio-as-a-mobilization-tool-in-latino-communities. Retrieved October 19, 2007.

Subervi, F. (ed.) (2008). *The Mass Media and Latino Politics*. New York: Routledge.

Subervi, F. and Eusebio, H. (2005). Latino media: a cultural connection. In E. del Valle (ed.), *Hispanic Marketing and Public Relations: Understanding and Targeting America's Largest Minority* (pp. 29–46). Boca Raton, FL: Poyeen Publishers.

Subervi-Vélez, F. (1994). Mass communication and Hispanics. In F. Padilla (ed.), *Handbook of Hispanic Cultures in the United States: Sociology* (pp. 304–57). Houston, TX: Arte Público Press.

Subervi-Vélez, F. A. (1986). The mass media and ethnic assimilation and pluralism: a review and research proposal with special focus on Hispanics. *Communication Research*, 13, 71–96.

Tapia, R. (2005). Impregnating images: visions of race, sex, and citizenship in California's teen pregnancy prevention campaigns. *Feminist Media Studies*, 5:1, 7–22.

Top editor sharpens focus on Latino news coverage (2008). ASU News, February 7. http://asunews.asu.edu/20080206_rodriguez. Retrieved April 16, 2008.

Tuchman, G. (1972). Objectivity as strategic ritual: an examination of newsmen's notions of objectivity. *American Journal of Sociology*, 77, 660–79.

(1978). *Making News: A Study in the Construction of Reality*. New York: The Free Press.

Tuchman, G., Daniels, A. K. and Benet, J. (eds.) (1978). *Hearth and Home: Images of Women in the Mass Media*. New York: Oxford University Press.

Valdivia, A. N. (1998). Stereotype or transgression? Rosie Perez in Hollywood film. *The Sociological Quarterly*, 39:3, 393–408.

(2000). *A Latina in the Land of Hollywood and Other Essays on Media Culture*. Tucson: University of Arizona Press.

(2004). Latinas as radical hybrid: transnationally gendered traces in mainstream media. *Global Media Journal*, 4:7. http://lass.calumet.purdue.edu/cca/gmj/sp04/gmj-sp04-valdivia.htm.

(2007). Is Penélope to J-Lo as culture is to nature? Eurocentric approaches to "Latin" beauties. In M. Mendible (ed.), *Bananas to Buttocks: The Latina Body in Popular Culture* (pp. 129–48). Austin: University of Texas Press.

(ed.) (2008). *Latina/o Communication Studies Today*. New York: Peter Lang.

Vargas, D. R. (2002). Bidi bidi bom bom: Selena and Tejano music in the making of Tejas. In M. Habell-Pallán and M. Romero (eds.), *Latino/a Popular Culture* (pp. 117–26). New York: New York University Press.

Vargas, L. (2008a). Media practices and gendered identities among transnational Latina teens. In A. N. Valdivia (ed.), *Latina/o Communication Studies Today* (pp. 187–218). New York: Peter Lang.

(2008b). Ambiguous loss and the media practices of transnational Latina teens. *Popular Communication*, 6:1, 37–52.

Vuong, A. (2001). Latino internet population is growing in the U.S, but website area struggling. *The Denver Post*, July 26. www.hispanicbusiness.com//news/newsbyid.asp?NS=1&idx=4960&cat1=news. Retrieved April 16, 2008.

Weill, S. and Castañeda, L. (2004). "Empathetic rejectionism" and inter-ethnic agenda-setting: coverage of Latinos by the Black Press in the American south. *Journalism Studies*, 5:4, 537–50.

Weintraub Austin, E., Pinkleton, B. E. and Fujioka, Y. (2000). The role of interpretation processes and parental discussion in the media's effects on adolescents' use of alcohol. *Pediatrics.*,105:2, 343–50.

Wible, S. (2004). Media advocates, latino citizens and niche cable: the limits of "no limits" TV. *Cultural Studies*, 18:1, 34–66.

Williams, R. (1974/1992). *Television: Technology and Cultural Form*. London: Fontana.

Wilson, C. C., III and Gutiérrez, F. (1985). *Minorities and the Media: Diversity and the End of Mass Communication*. Beverly Hills, CA: SAGE.

Winge, T. (2008). Undressing and dressing Loli: a search for the identity of the Japanese Lolita. In F. Lunning (ed.), *Mechademia*, vol. III: *Limits of the Human* (pp. 47–64). Minneapolis: University of Minnesota Press.

Index